HISTORY

OF

WEST POINT,

HISTORY

OF

WEST POINT,

AND ITS

MILITARY IMPORTANCE DURING THE AMERICAN REVOLUTION:

AND THE

ORIGIN AND PROGRESS

OF THE

UNITED STATES MILITARY ACADEMY.

BY

CAPTAIN EDWARD C. BOYNTON, A. M.,

ADJUTANT OF THE MILITARY ACADEMY.

BOOKS FOR LIBRARIES PRESS

FREEPORT, NEW YORK

First Published 1863
Reprinted 1970

STANDARD BOOK NUMBER:
8369-5458-0

LIBRARY OF CONGRESS CATALOG CARD NUMBER:
71-126233

PRINTED IN THE UNITED STATES OF AMERICA

"I give it as my fixed opinion, that but for our graduated Cadets, the war between the United States and Mexico might, and probably would, have lasted some four or five years, with, in its first half, more defeats than victories falling to our share; whereas, in less than two campaigns we conquered a great country and a peace, without the loss of a single battle or skirmish."—MISC. DOC. SENATE, 2D SESSION, XXXVI. CONG., 176, 1861.

WINFIELD SCOTT.

PREFACE.

THIS History of West Point is designed to supply a want which all interested in the antecedents of the Post, or in the origin and progress of the United States Military Academy, have long desired to see supplied.

Emanating from the Custodian of the records of the Academy, who has been an instructor for many years in the Institution, and for many years in one of our prominent literary Colleges, the statements put forth are believed to be correct, and the comparisons instituted cannot be regarded as purely speculative.

If errors are found to exist, it is hoped, nevertheless, that a nucleus of truth has been established, which invites amendment and improvement.

No claim to literary merit or originality is asserted. The labors of Ruttenber on the "Obstructions of the Hudson," and of Sargeant on the "Life of André," have been freely used, with the consent of the authors or publishers. To these may be added extracts from the North American and Quarterly Reviews; and the whole, having been subjected to revision by competent authorities at the Academy, is, with their approbation, respectfully submitted.

To the Rev. ROSWELL PARK, D. D., Chancellor of Racine College, Wisconsin, and pioneer author of a Sketch

of West Point; Mr. GEORGE H. MOORE, Librarian of the
New York Historical Society; Mr. H. B. DAWSON;
Lieutenant ELDERKIN, U. S. A., and Cadets LYDECKER and
PETRIKIN, of the Military Academy, the author is indebted
for courteous assistance in the preparation of the volume.

ADJUTANT'S OFFICE,
WEST POINT, N. Y., *September 30th*, 1863.

LIST OF AUTHORITIES.

In the preparation of this History the following works have been freely consulted, and from some of them copious extracts have been taken :

AUTHENTIC NARRATIVE OF THE CAPTURE OF ANDRE. By Joshua Hett Smith.
AMERICAN STATE PAPERS,—Military Affairs.
AMERICAN ARCHIVES.
AMERICAN QUARTERLY REVIEW. Vol. XXII.
AMERICAN HISTORICAL MAGAZINE, Notes and Queries, &c., of America.
BATTLES OF THE UNITED STATES, BY SEA AND LAND. By H. B. Dawson.
CORRESPONDENCE OF THE AMERICAN REVOLUTION, being Letters of Eminent Men to George Washington. By J. Sparks.
HISTORY OF WESTCHESTER COUNTY. By R. Bolton.
HISTORY OF ORANGE COUNTY. By S. W. Eager.
HISTORY OF PUTNAM COUNTY. By W. J. Blake.
LIFE OF BENEDICT ARNOLD : Library of American Biography. By J. Sparks.
LIFE OF MAJOR JOHN ANDRE. By W. Sargeant.
MANUSCRIPTS OF MAJOR GEORGE FLEMING. Library of the U. S. Military Academy.
MANUSCRIPTS OF MAJOR-GENERAL GATES : Library of the New York Historical Society.
MANUSCRIPTS OF COLONEL LAMB : Library of the New York Historical Society.
MEMOIRS OF MAJOR-GENERAL HEATH. By Himself.
MEMOIRS OF COLONEL BENJAMIN TALLMADGE. By Himself.
MEMOIRS OF THE LIFE AND TIMES OF GENERAL JOHN LAMB. By I. Q. Leake.
MILITARY JOURNAL DURING THE AMERICAN REVOLUTIONARY WAR. By James Thatcher.

NORTH AMERICAN REVIEW. LVII. 1843.

OBSTRUCTIONS OF THE HUDSON RIVER. By E. M. Ruttenber. [Munsell's Hist. Series. No. V.]

OFFICIAL RECORDS at the United States Military Academy.

PICTORIAL FIELD-BOOK OF THE REVOLUTION. By B. J. Lossing.

REGISTER OF THE OFFICERS AND GRADUATES of the U. S. Military Academy. By Capt. G. W. Cullum.

REPORTS OF THE BOARDS OF VISITORS at the U. S. Military Academy.

REPORT MIL. COMMITTEE: House of Representatives, No. 466.

REVOLUTIONARY ORDERS OF GENERAL WASHINGTON. By H. Whiting.

WRITINGS OF GEORGE WASHINGTON. By J. Sparks.

CONTENTS.

CHAPTER I.

CHAPTER II.

CHAPTER III.

CHAPTER XV.

CHAPTER XVI.

APPENDIX.

xvi CONTENTS.

LIST OF ILLUSTRATIONS.

LIST OF ILLUSTRATIONS.

PART I.

MILITARY IMPORTANCE OF WEST POINT

DURING THE

AMERICAN REVOLUTION.

HISTORY OF WEST POINT.

CHAPTER I.

EARLY GRANTS OF THE LANDS AT WEST POINT.—TITLE ACQUIRED BY
THE UNITED STATES BY PURCHASE.—COMMISSIONERS SETTLE THE
BOUNDARIES.—FURTHER PURCHASE BY THE UNITED STATES.—
JURISDICTION CEDED BY THE STATE OF NEW YORK.—EARLY IM-
PORTANCE OF THE CONTROL OF THE HUDSON DURING THE REVO-
LUTION.—RESOLUTIONS OF THE CONTINENTAL CONGRESS, MAY 25,
1775.—APPOINTMENT OF COMMITTEE BY THE PROVINCIAL CON-
GRESS, AND RESOLUTIONS OF THE LATTER, AUGUST 18, 1775.

THE United States tract at West Point includes
2,105 acres of land, the title to which was secured by
purchase, as herein described.

West Point proper was originally granted to Captain
John Evans; but, having been vacated by him, it was
afterwards reassumed and held by the English Crown.

On May 17, 1723, by Royal Letters-Patent, a tract,
including the northern portion of the Point, and embracing 1,463 acres of land, was granted to Charles Congreve, upon the condition that, within three years, he or
his heirs or assigns should settle and cultivate at least
three acres for every fifty acres of land described in the
grant. The first settlement at West Point may therefore date from this period. On March 25, 1747, another portion of the Evans grant, adjoining the southwest corner of the Congreve patent, and embracing 332

acres of land, was patented to John Moore, on like condition of settlement within three years.

The patent of Congreve having been purchased in later
years by Moore, was conveyed by will, together with the
Moore patent, to his son, Stephen Moore, merchant, of
Caswell County, N. C.

It appears that a petition was presented to Congress
by the latter, praying that the United States would purchase West Point, which had already been so long occupied for public purposes. On this petition General Hamilton, then Secretary of the Treasury, made a favorable
report, June 10, 1790.

He quoted the opinion of General Knox, the Secretary
of War, as set forth by him in a report to Congress,
dated July 31, 1786, that West Point is of the most decisive importance to the defence of the Hudson River, for
the following reasons :

First. " The distance across the river is only about
fourteen hundred feet, a less distance by far than at any
other part.

Second. The peculiar bend, or turn of the river, forming almost a re-entering angle.

Third. The high banks on both sides of the river,
favorable for the construction of formidable batteries.

Fourth. The demonstrated practicability of fixing
across the river a chain or chains, at a spot where vessels in turning the Point invariably lose their rapidity,
and, of course, their force, by which a chain at any
other part of the river would be liable to be broken."

These considerations, together with the difficulty [at
that time] of taking West Point by siege ; its being within a single night's sail of New York, and its importance

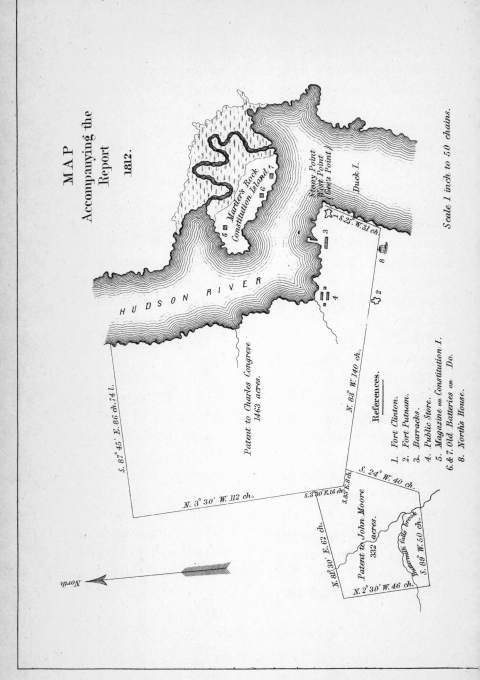

MAP
Accompanying the
Report
1812.

Scale 1 inch to 50 chains.

HUDSON RIVER

Marther's Rock
Constitution Island.
5
6

Stony Point
West Point
(Gee's Point)

Duck I.

S. 25° W. 31 ch.

3

8

2

4

N. 83° W. 140 ch.

Patent to Charles Congreve
1463 acres.

S. 87° 45′ E. 86 ch. 74 l.

References.

1. Fort Clinton.
2. Fort Putnam.
3. Barracks.
4. Public Store.
5. Magazine on Constitution I.
6. & 7. Old Batteries on Do.
8. North's House.

North

N. 3° 30′ W. 112 ch.

S. 3° 30′ E. 16 ch.

S. 89° E. 8 ch.

S. 24° W. 40 ch.

N. 81° 30′ E. 62 ch.

Patent to John Moore
332 acres.

Buttermilk falls brook.

S. 89° W. 50 ch.

N. 2° 30′ W. 46 ch.

in preserving communications between the Eastern and Middle States, induced General Hamilton to recommend its purchase by the United States, as a permanent military post.* Accordingly, both the patents held by Stephen Moore were deeded to the United States, on the payment of the sum of $11,085, September 10, 1790, in compliance with the act of Congress of July 5, of the same year.

A controversy having arisen in relation to the boundary of the public lands in after years, a commission was appointed by the Hon. Secretary of War, under an act approved January 22, 1811, to ascertain and settle the exterior lines of the Government property at West Point. This commission surveyed the tract, and submitted a report with map, dated January 22, 1812, establishing the boundary.

Which report was accepted and approved by act of Congress, dated January 5, 1813.

The tract adjoining Congreve's patent, immediately on the south, was one of the six tracts originally granted to Gabriel and William Ludlow, October 18, 1731, under the same condition of early settlement in the three years before referred to.

It was successively owned and afterwards occupied by Richard Williams, of Cornwall, N. Y., and Robert Armstrong, of Sussex County, N. J., by whom it was deeded to Benjamin Rose, December 1, 1785; by Rose to John Dunlap, of Ulster County, N. Y., September 6, 1788, and by Dunlap to Thomas North, of Cornwall, November 22, 1794. North also purchased a tract lying south of the

---

* Am. State Papers—Claims—19.

one under consideration, from Isaiah Smith, June 3, 1796, and on the 28th December, 1819, he deeded both tracts to Oliver Gridley, of Bergen County, N. J.

On the 13th of May, 1824, Gridley deeded them to the United States for the sum of $10,000, in accordance with the act of Congress, approved March 10, of the same year.

Vexatious claims having in later years arisen between the Government and citizens who resided on the lands, application was made to the legislature of the State of New York, to transfer to the United States a portion of the territory in question.

Accordingly, on March 2, 1826, an act passed the Senate and Assembly, ceding jurisdiction over the tract here described : * Beginning at the mouth of a small brook or creek, northwest of the present Engineer Barracks, and the Powder Magazine ; thence up said creek to its intersection with the road leading west to the Cemetery ; thence easterly along the northern brow of the bank bounding the road, to its intersection with the road near the west gate leading to Fort Putnam ; thence due south until the line intersects a line beginning thirty-one chains south of Gee's Point, and running westerly, seven chains south of the east piazza of the Academic Building.

The number of acres of land is not known precisely.

All was ceded that was deemed desirable or necessary.

The State reserved the right to execute any process, civil or criminal, wherein the real or personal property of the United States was not affected.

Taxes have never been claimed by the State authori-

* Official Records, U. S. M. A.

ties but once (in 1828), and then only the road-tax was demanded; but, in consideration of the liberal repairs habitually made by the Government, it was relinquished.*

A portion of the Moore patent having been offered for sale by the State of New York, for the payment of quit-rents, was purchased by William S. Watkins in 1828, and sold by him, in 1833, to Timothy Mahoney. A suit for trespass having been instituted against the latter, and the illegality and impossibility of his holding the land having been made manifest, in 1839, Mahoney determined to avoid trouble by giving a quit-claim to the United States.

When the Moore and Congreve patents were purchased by the United States, Hugh McClellan, a Revolutionary soldier, occupied a small house on the patent first named; and in consequence of distinguished services, the soldier was permitted by General Knox, then Secretary of War, to remain in occupancy and cultivate a garden. McClellan accordingly lived and died on the spot undisturbed, leaving a widow and daughter. The latter, having married, remained on the premises to aid and assist her aged mother. After the lapse of a few years, her husband claimed the whole of Moore's patent as the property of his wife, on the plea that, under the laws of the State of New York, McClellan had acquired a title to the land by years of undisputed possession, and that his own wife was the only lawful heiress.

A suit for ejectment was instituted, and a judgment, rendered in 1839, decided in favor of the United States.

A third suit for trespass, brought against Andrew

* Pub. Doc., 1848.

Swim, for the recovery of a portion of the Ludlow patent, which had also been sold for the payment of quit-rents, resulted in the removal and ejectment of the trespasser, in 1840.*

The annoyances caused by these parties led to a new survey of the boundaries of the public lands in April, 1839, and the lines as then established have remained unchanged to the present day.

The intervals between the granting of the patents and the transfer of the titles, before described, down to the period at which the American Revolution commenced, are blanks in historical literature.

No traditions even of early settlers are extant, and the probabilities are, that beyond a settlement made to secure a title or grant, West Point—being in a region of primary stratified rocks, heavily covered with *drift* deposits, and without a suitable soil for cultivation—remained a mere wood-land tract, possessing no higher value than attaches to similar adjoining points in the Highlands, which have remained unsettled and uncultivated to the present day.

Even after hostilities commenced, its importance as a key to the passage of the Hudson remained, for a period of nearly three years, practically of no interest to the Provincial or Continental authorities.

† The student of American history is familiar with the fact, that to obtain control of the navigation of the Hudson River, was a favorite project with the British Government, during the whole progress of the War of Independence.

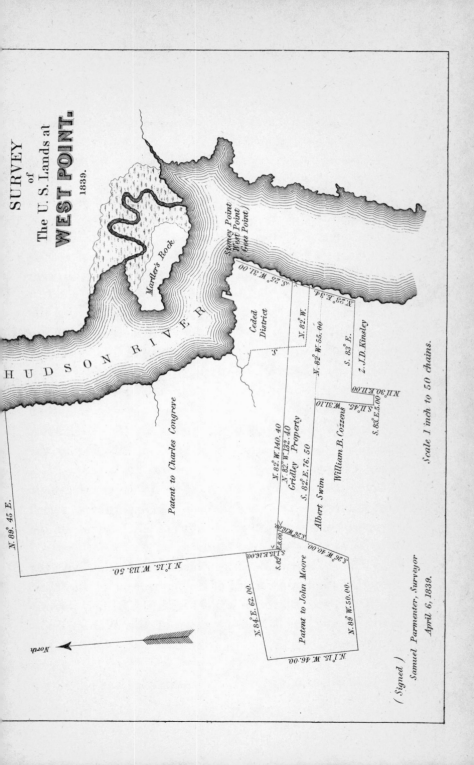

SURVEY
of
The U. S. Lands at
WEST POINT.
1839.

HUDSON RIVER

Marlier's Rock

Stoney Point
Kast Point
West Point

Ceded District

Patent to Charles Congreve

N. 89°. 45. E.

N. 15. W. 113. 50.

N. 84°. E. 62. 00.

Patent to John Moore

N. 89° W. 50. 00.

N. 15. W. 46. 00.

S. 36°. W. 40. 00.

S. 115. E. 16. 00.

S. 82° E. 8. 00.

S. 28° W. 60. 00.

N. 82°. W. 140. 40

N. 82°. W. 132. 40

Gridley Property

S. 82° E. 76. 50

Albert Swin

N. 82. W. 31. 00

N. 82° W. 55. 00

William B. Cozzens

S. 83° E.

S. 11.45. W.

S. 83 E. 5. 00

N. 11. 30. E. 11. 00

S. 83°. E.

Z. J. D. Kinsley

N. 33. E. 34.

N. 82°. W.

S. 25. W. 31. 00

North

Scale 1 inch to 50 chains.

(Signed)
Samuel Parmenter, Surveyor
April 6, 1839.

In order to a proper understanding of the reasons on which this project was based, we should examine with some attention the topography of the river, not simply as limited to the section of country through which its waters flow, but taking a broader view, and regarding its connection with those more remote and wide-spread regions, that find through it their most direct and natural channel to the seaboard.

Even at the present day, when the skilled enterprise of a numerous and commercial people has linked the interior to the coast, by many and various artificial channels, the great thoroughfare of the State of New York holds a pre-eminent position, mainly due to its unrivalled natural advantages. But these advantages were of paramount importance, both before and during the Revolutionary struggle, when the canoe of the Indian, or the bateau of the *voyageur*, furnished the most convenient and speedy transportation, for purposes either of commerce or of war. Then, to the north, at the head of boat navigation, the Hudson was connected by an easy portage with Lakes George and Champlain, and through them with the St. Lawrence, the great river of the Canadas; whilst, towards the west, its principal affluent, the Mohawk, gave easy access, scarcely interrupted by a few short portages, to the basin of the great lakes, and to the magnificent river system of the Mississippi.

Thus established by nature as the main artery, connecting a vast network of interior water communications with the Atlantic, and draining the resources of almost half a continent, the Hudson occupied a position of the highest strategic importance.

The British Government had been taught this fact in

the course of the long struggle between England and France, then but recently terminated.　They knew that by the possession of the Hudson they could separate the eastern part of the Province of New York and the Provinces of New England from the remainder of the Confederacy, and thus, by cutting off communication between these points, speedily reduce the patriots to subjection. Hence, in a letter dated London, July 31st, 1775, conveying to the colonists the plan of operations decided upon by the British Government, it is said that their design is: "to get possession of New York and Albany; to fill both of these cities with very strong garrisons; to declare all rebels who do not join the King's forces; to command the Hudson and East rivers with a number of small men-of-war, and cutters, stationed in different parts of it, so as to cut off all communication by water between New York and the Provinces to the northward of it, and between New York and Albany, except for the King's service; and to prevent also all communication between the city of New York and the Provinces of New Jersey, Pennsylvania, and those to the southward of them.　By these means," continues the letter, "the Administration and their friends fancy that they shall soon either starve out or retake the garrisons of Crown Point and Ticonderoga, and open and maintain a safe intercourse and correspondence between Quebec, Albany, and New York, and thereby afford the fairest opportunity to their soldiery and the Canadians, in conjunction with the Indians, to be procured by G. J.,* to make continual irruptions into New Hampshire, Massachusetts, and Connecticut, and so

---

* Col. Guy Johnson, a son-in-law of Sir William Johnson, Superintendent of Indian affairs of the Province of New York.

distract and divide the Provincial forces as to render it easy for the British Army at Boston to defeat them, break the spirits of the Massachusetts people, depopulate their country, and compel an absolute subjection to Great Britain."*

But the colonists were equally familiar with the importance of maintaining possession of the river. In a report submitted by the Provincial Congress of New York to the Continental Congress, early in 1775, the subject is thus treated: "If the enemy persist in their plan of subjugating these States to the yoke of Great Britain, they must, in proportion to their knowledge of the country, be more and more convinced of the necessity of their becoming masters of the Hudson river, which will give them the entire command of the water communication with the Indian nations, effectually prevent all intercourse between the eastern and southern Confederates, divide our strength, and enfeeble every effort for our common preservation and security. That this was their original plan, and that General Carlton and General Howe flattered themselves with the delusive hope of uniting their forces at Albany, every intelligence confirms, and it appears to the Committee that they will not give up this grand object until they shall finally relinquish the project of enslaving America."†

With this brief explanation of the natural causes which gave to the Hudson river its importance in the struggle for Independence, and of the plans adopted by the British Government to secure its control, we come to consider some of the means employed by the colonists to defeat

---

* Jour. of the Prov. Cong. of N. Y., 172.   † Jour. Prov. Cong. N. Y., 723.

the efforts of the English.   The general operations of the Continental forces are amply detailed in our histories. Still, there are many facts of interest which have not been recorded, especially in regard to the Fortifications in the Highlands, and the character of the obstruction to the navigation of the river.   To supply details in reference to these subjects, will constitute an interesting section in this history.

The plan of operations adopted by the British Government, while aiming at general results, immediately involved the Province of New York; and hence the Congress of that Province took early steps to prevent its consummation.   Prior to the reception of the letter of July 31st, already quoted, the Provincial Congress had taken action upon the subject of fortifying the Highlands and obstructing the navigation of the river, and had invited the prompt action of the Continental Congress.

On the 25*th May*, 1775, the latter body communicated to the former a series of resolutions in reference to the defence of New York, one of which is as follows:

" *Resolved*, That a post be taken in the Highlands, on each side of the Hudson river, and batteries erected; and that experienced persons be immediately sent to examine said river, in order to discover where it will be most advisable and proper to obstruct the navigation."*

This Resolution received the action of the Provincial Congress at its session held *May* 30*th*, 1775, when the following order was passed :

" *Ordered*, That Col. Clinton and Mr. Tappan be a Committee (and that they take to their assistance such persons as they shall think necessary) to go to the High-

* Jour. Prov. Cong., 16.

lands and view the banks of the Hudson River there; and report to this Congress the most proper place for erecting one or more fortifications, and likewise an estimate of the expense of erecting the same."*

This Committee made a report on the 13*th of June*, 1775, in which they suggested the erection of what were afterwards known as Forts *Constitution*, *Clinton*, and *Montgomery*. In their report they also say:

"Your Committee begs leave to observe, that they are informed that by means of four or five Booms, chained together on one side of the river, ready to be drawn across, the passage can be closed up to prevent any vessel passing or repassing."†

On the 18*th of August*, 1775, the Provincial Congress passed the following resolution:

"Resolved and ordered, That the Fortifications formerly ordered by the Continental Congress [May 25, 1775], and reported by a Committee of this Congress, as proper to be built on the banks of Hudson's River, in the Highlands, be immediately erected. Mr. Walton dissents. And that Mr. Isaac Sears, Mr. John Berrien, Colonel Edward Flemming, Mr. Anthony Rutgers, and Mr. Christopher Miller, be Commissioners to manage the erecting and finishing the fortifications. That any three or more of them be empowered to act, manage, and direct the building and finishing thereof."

* Jour. Prov. Cong., 20.   † Ibid., 41.

MARTELAER'S ROCK (CONSTITUTION ISLAND).

CHAPTER II.

THE Hudson River, in passing the upper Highlands,
flows south through the gorge between abrupt and lofty
mountains for a distance of nearly eight miles; the channel then changes east about one-fourth of a mile, and,
thence changing, again pursues its southerly direction.
Projecting half way across the river, and forming the
left bank opposite West Point on the north, between the
two right angles made by the channel, is an island; its

west and northwestern sides are formed of bold and inaccessible precipices, while on the east is a large flag meadow, partially drained by ditches recently cut through it. This island, nowhere more than one hundred and thirty-four feet high, is probably two miles in circumference, and half a mile in width from north to south. It is covered with timber of an inferior description, and uncultivated, except on its southern and eastern edges.

The marsh meadow on the east, separated now from the island by the Hudson River Railroad, contains about three hundred acres, and the island probably two hundred and fifty.

Previous to, and at the commencement of the Revolution, this island was known as *Martelaer's Rock Island*, and otherwise as *Martler's Rock*, or *Martyr's Cliff*. The name is derived from a French family named *Martelaire*, who resided upon, or in its vicinity, about the year 1720. After the erection of the fortification known as *Fort Constitution*, the island received, and has retained to the present day, the name of *Constitution Island*.*

" The Commissioners appointed by the Provincial Congress, accompanied by an escort of twenty-four men and Col. *Bernard Romans*,† as an engineer, arrived at the

---

* Hist. Putnam Co.

† *Bernard Romans* was born in Holland, but early in life removed to England, where he studied the profession of an engineer, and was employed as such by the British Government in America some time before the Revolution. Subsequently he was employed as a botanist, under the auspices of the same government; and while in New York, engaged in the publication of a Natural History of Florida, he was offered a position as military engineer by the New York Committee of Safety. In this capacity he submitted to Congress, on the 18th September, 1775, plans for fortifications to be erected in the Highlands opposite to West Point (Am. Archives, III.). Colonel Romans remained in service (Captain Pennsylvania Artillery, Feb. 8, 1776) until near the close of the war, when he was captured at sea by the British, *en route* from New Haven or New London to Charleston, S. C. He is reported to have died about 1783.

island on the 29th of August, 1775, and immediately commenced the erection of the first of the ' Fortifications in the Highlands.' "

The "Fortifications in the Highlands" embraced not only the works to be erected on Constitution Island, but those also on Fort Hill, directly east of " Garrison's Station," known as the North and South Redoubts [the latter afterwards called Middle Redoubt]; one on Sugar-loaf Mountain, and the two Forts, Montgomery and Clinton, on the north and south sides of Pooplopen's Kill.

The New York Committee of Safety, to whom had been intrusted the management of public affairs during the recess of the Provincial Congress, transmitted to the Continental Congress, on the 19th of September, the plans, estimates, and report, prepared by Colonel Romans, of the works then in process of construction at Martelaer's Rock Island.

From the accompanying report it appears that Colonel Romans proposed to erect five block-houses; barracks, eighty by twenty feet; store-houses and guard-room, sixty by twenty feet; five batteries, mounting sixty-one guns and twenty swivels; a fort with bastions, and a curtain two hundred feet in length; a magazine,—and the whole was estimated at £4,645 4s. 4d.

On the same day the Committee forwarded the plans of Mr. Romans to Congress, the following note was addressed to Colonel Beverly Robinson, with a view to the purchase of the island, of which he was reputed to be the owner :

"IN COMMITTEE OF SAFETY,
"NEW YORK, Sept. 19th, 1775.

" SIR:—By order of the Continental Congress, founded

on the necessities of the present times, the Provincial Congress of this Colony has undertaken to erect a fortification on your land, opposite to the West Point, in the Highlands. As the Provincial Congress by no means intend to invade private property, this Committee, in their recess, have thought proper to request you to put a reasonable price upon the whole point of dry land, or island, called Martelaer's Rock Island; which price, if they approve of it, they are ready to pay you for it.

" We are, Sir, your humble servants.

" To BEVERLY ROBINSON, Esq., at his seat in the Highlands."

" IN PROVINCIAL CONGRESS, NEW YORK, 6th October, 1775.

" A letter from Beverly Robinson, Esq., was read and filed, and is in the following words, to wit:

" HIGHLANDS, October 2d, 1775.

" SIR :—Your letter of the nineteenth of September I received a few days ago, in answer to which I must inform you that the point of land on which the fort is erecting does not belong to me, but is the property of Mrs. Ogilvie and her children. Was it mine, the public should be extremely welcome to it. The building a fort there can be no disadvantage to the small quantity of arable land on the island. I have only a proportion of the meadow land, that lays on the east side of the island.

" I am, Sir, your most humble servant,
" BEV. ROBINSON.

" To JOHN HARING, Esq.,
" Chairman of the Committee of Safety, at New York."

In the mean time the Commissioners, Bedlow, Grenell, and Bayard, writing from Fort Constitution, Sept. 25, 1775, strongly urged upon the Committee of Safety, that Romans's plan was not sufficient, and being but a temporary expedient, the ruin of the Province would be insured if the position were permitted to fall into the possession of the enemy.

To these objections the Committee replied, that upon the re-assembling of the Provincial Congress, the subject would be laid before them.

As might have been anticipated, the Commissioners and Romans soon became involved in an unpleasant controversy; the former claiming, as superintendents, the right to approve or reject his plans, and to direct the mode of operations, while they openly declared the expense to be greater than the Province could tolerate. Romans as emphatically informed the Commissioners that they had simply to furnish men and money, and while by virtue of his appointment he would build the works, they must reserve their condemnation or approval until the Fortification was completed.

The Continental Congress, while debating Romans's plans early in October, passed a resolution of inquiry as to the propriety of constructing a battery at *"Moore's house"* [situated in what is now known as Washington's Valley], and at a point on the west side of the river, above Verplanck's [now Caldwell's Landing].

To this inquiry the Commissioners replied on the 16th of October, noting the progress of the works on the island, and declaring that a battery at "Moore's house" would be entirely useless. The point above Verplanck's they pronounced too easy of access, but at Pooplopen's Kill, opposite Anthony's Nose, they earnestly recommended that defences be erected. This is the earliest mention made of the position afterwards known as Fort Montgomery.

The Provincial Congress, on the 3d of November, having ordered three companies to proceed to, and constitute the garrison at Martelaer's Rock, it was *"Resolved"* on the

8th, by the Continental Congress, " That a Commander, with the rank of *Colonel*, be appointed to take command of the Fortifications or Fortresses in the Highlands on Hudson's River." On the same day this body further appointed Robert R. Livingston, Robert Treat Paine, and J. Langdon a Committee, to "take an accurate view of the state of our Fortifications on Hudson's River, and to report as soon as it can be conveniently done."

This Committee reported to John Hancock, the President of Congress, on the 23d of November, "That the Fortress at Martelaer's Rock was in charge of Messrs. Grenell, Bedlow, and Lanman, Commissioners appointed by the Provincial Congress to superintend the work, which was carried on by Mr. Romans, agreeably to his plans presented to Congress. We must own," continues the report, "that we found the Fort in a less defensible situation than we had reason to expect. It does not command the reach to the southward, nor can it injure a vessel turning the West Point; and after she has got around, a small breeze, or even the tide, will enable a ship to pass the curtain in a few minutes.

" The Fortress is unfortunately commanded by all the grounds about it; but the most obvious defect is, that the grounds on the West Point are higher than the Fortress, behind which an enemy might land without the least danger. In order to render the position impassable, it seems necessary that this place should be occupied, and batteries thrown up on the shore opposite, where they may be erected with little expense, as the earth is said to be pretty free from stone, &c."*

* Am. Arch., IV., III., 1657.

This is the first official recommendation to occupy West Point, and establish batteries on the east side of the river, near Garrison's, on record [Nov. 23, 1775].

From Fort Constitution, December 7, the Commissioners again reported to the Provincial Congress, that " the point at Pooplopen's Kill is the best by far for any defensive works in the Highlands, and that a battery there would command the river up and down, the length of point-blank shot."

The controversy with Colonel Romans at this time had attained such proportions, and was accompanied with such exhibitions of warmth, that Messrs. Nicoll, Palmer, and Drake were directed by the Provincial Congress to repair to the Highlands, and there endeavor to adjust the difference between the parties.

Mr. Palmer, on the part of this Committee, reported on the 14th of December, that Romans " must either have mistaken the charge committed to him, or else he has assumed powers with which he was not intrusted." The report reiterated the opinion before given, that the works did not sweep the river southward; and to effect this a barbette battery on the Gravel Hill, on the southeast shore of the island, to mount eight eighteen-pound guns, was recommended. [The Hudson River Railroad now skirts the Gravel Hill.] The Committee were earnest in the opinion that the works on the island were insufficient, and strong in their recommendation to plant a work at Pooplopen's Kill, which would mount sixteen or eighteen guns, and " sweep the river to the point of the Dunderberg, a distance of three miles, and up the river quite as far."*

* Am. Arch., IV., IV., 421.

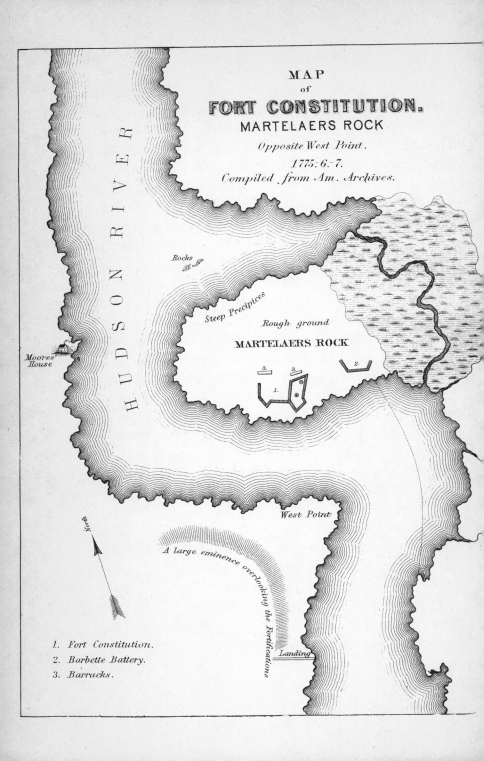

MAP
of
FORT CONSTITUTION.
MARTELAERS ROCK
Opposite West Point.
1775. 6.- 7.
Compiled from Am. Archives.

HUDSON RIVER

Rocks

Steep Precipices

Rough ground

MARTELAERS ROCK

Moores House

North

West Point

A large eminence overlooking the Fortifications

Landing

1. *Fort Constitution.*
2. *Barbette Battery.*
3. *Barracks.*

This report having been favorably received by the Provincial, and transmitted to the Continental Congress, the latter body, on the 5th January, 1776, "*Resolved*, That no further Fortifications ought to be erected at Martelaer's Rock on the Hudson River, and that a point of land at Pooplopen's Kill, on said river, ought to be effectually fortified without delay."* On the 15th of February following, notwithstanding the foregoing resolution, Congress authorized the erection of the barbette battery on the Gravel Hill before mentioned, to mount eighteen heavy guns. And further *Resolved*, "That a redoubt be erected on the eminence on the east side of the river opposite the West Point, to mount thirty guns," urging at the same time the early completion of works at Pooplopen's Kill. In the mean time, and in compliance with the resolution of Congress, the Committee of Safety appointed, on January 16th, Colonel *Isaac Nicoll* to the command of the Fortifications in the Highlands; and Mr. Romans having been superseded by Col. Smith, Engineer, ordered up by General Lee, the barbette battery on the island was laid out by him—so wrote the Commissioners, Feb. 29th—"much to our satisfaction."†

On the 20th of March, Benjamin Franklin, Samuel Chase, and Charles Carroll of Carrolton, were appointed by the Continental Congress, Commissioners to visit Canada, and invite the co-operation of the people of that Province in the struggle for freedom.

While *en route* to their destination, they arrived "off Constitution Fort, April 5th," and going ashore, "from curiosity," they reported the state of the Fort as follows:

---

* Am. Arch., IV., IV., 1033.   † Am. Arch., IV., V., 326.

The garrison consisted of three companies of minute-men, whose combined strength was 124 men. "On the south bastion, thirteen six-pounders and one nine-pounder were mounted; the east bastion mounted seven nine-pounders and one six-pounder. The block-house contained eight double fortified four-pound guns, mounted; and that the fortifications ordered by Congress on the 15th of February, and laid out by Engineer Smith, remain wholly neglected."

At this time the head-quarters of the army were in New York. On the 4th of May, Washington directed Lieut.-Col. Livingston, of Col. James Clinton's regiment, to repair to the Highlands and relieve Col. Nicoll of the command, to which he was but temporarily assigned. The latter, however, refused to be superseded, and remained until discharged by the Provincial Congress, on the 8th of June. Col. James Clinton followed Livingston, and, arriving on the 20th of May, reported to head-quarters that he had discharged all the Commissioners except two, which he would retain until an Engineer was sent to him.

On the 21st of May, Washington wrote Gen. Putnam, then in the city and under his command :—" I have great reason to think that the Fortifications in the Highlands are in a bad situation, and the garrison, on account of arms, worse.

" I would have you send Brigadier *Lord Stirling*, with Col. *Putnam*, and Col. *Knox* (if he can be spared), to see and report such alterations as may be judged necessary for putting them into a fit and proper position for defence."*

* Am. Arch., IV., VI., 534.

Putnam reported, on the 27th of May, that Lord Stirling, Col. Putnam, and Captain Sargeant left on this mission the day before.

The report of this Board is given at length, because the works, and the grounds adjacent thereto, were then surveyed for the first time by officers possessing military experience, and whose opinions were valuable and powerful in deciding the after operations on the points in question.

*Lord Stirling to General Washington.**

"JUNE 1, 1776.

"SIR :—Agreeable to your request, I left New York on Sunday last, in order to view the fortifications on the Hudson's River in the Highlands. I took with me Colonel [Rufus] Putnam, Chief Engineer, and Captain Sargeant, of the Artillery. The winds were so adverse that we did not reach Fort Montgomery until Wednesday evening; but, with the help of our boat, we employed our time in visiting several other parts of the river that appeared proper for fortifying. At the mouth, or south end of the Highlands, about four miles below Fort Montgomery, there is a post [Stoney Point] which to me appears well worth possessing on many accounts; should the enemy be in possession of it, we should be cut off from our best communication with the whole country below the Highlands, eastward as well as westward. There is a very remarkable spot of ground [Verplanck's Point], easily fortified, which commands the passage of the river as well as either of the other posts; it also

* Am. Arch., IV., VI.,672.

commands the mouth and landing of Peek's Kill, from which there is an excellent road into Connecticut, which is only twenty miles off; on the opposite side is an excellent road into New Jersey and Pennsylvania. In the passage from this place to Fort Montgomery is a large island, which would be very useful to the enemy in their approaches to that place.

"Fort Montgomery is situated on the west bank of the river, which is there about half a mile broad, and the bank one hundred feet high; on the opposite shore is a point of land called Anthony's Nose, which is many hundred feet high, very steep, and inaccessible to any thing but goats, or men very expert in climbing. A body of riflemen placed here would be of very great use in annoying an enemy, as the decks of every vessel that passes must lie open to them.

"The works begun and designed at Fort Montgomery are open lines, and all lie on the north side of a small creek called Pooplopen's Kill, on the south side of which is a point of land which projects more into the river, commands all the principal works, and is within two and three hundred yards of them. On the top of this point is a level spot of ground, of near an acre, commanded by nothing but the high, inaccessible mountains, at about twelve hundred yards distance; this spot, I think, should by all means be fortified, as well for the annoyance of the enemy in their approach up the river, as for the protection of the works at Fort Montgomery. Indeed, this appears to me the most proper place I have seen on the river to be made the grand post; and, in my opinion, should be a regular strong work, capable of resisting every kind of attack, and of containing a grand magazine

of all kinds of warlike stores.   The whole would then
command the passage of the river with so formidable a
cross fire as would deter any attempt to approach with
shipping.   Those works built are all faced with fascines,
and filled in with strong, good loam; but as they are
liable to take fire, the Commissioners who have the care
and direction of the works, propose to roughcast the
faces of the embrasures with a strong mortar made of
quicklime and sharp sand, of which there is plenty at
hand.   I advised them to try the experiment on part of
the work as soon as possible.   As these open lines are
entirely defenceless on the land side, it will be very
proper to erect a small redoubt on the hill, in the rear of
them.

" Fort Constitution is about six miles above Fort Montgomery, on an island near the east side of the river, and
near the north end of the Highlands, which on the west
and south sides is bounded by the river, and on the
north and east sides by low marsh and small creeks running through it.   The works here consist of four open
lines or batteries, fronting the river; the two easternmost command the approach up the river very well; the
next, or middle line, commands the approach from West
Point upwards; the westernmost battery is a straight
line, constructed by Mr. Romans, at a very great expense; it has fifteen embrasures, which face the river at
a right angle, and can only annoy a ship in going past;
the embrasures are within twelve feet of each other; the
merlons on the outside are but about two feet in the face,
and about seven feet deep, made of square timber covered with plank, and look very neat; he also built a
log-house or tower on the highest cliff, near the water,

mounted with eight cannon (four-pounders) pointed out
of the garret windows, and looks very picturesque.
Upon the whole, Mr. Romans has displayed his genius
at a very great expense, and to very little public advantage. The works, in their present open condition and
scattered situation, are defenceless; nor is there one
good place on the island on which a redoubt may be
erected that will command the whole; however, I have
marked in the plan (No. 3) those heights which are most
commanding; yet every work on the island is commanded by the hill on the West Point, on the opposite
side of the river, within five hundred yards, where there
is a level piece of land of near fifty acres in extent. A
redoubt on this West Point is absolutely necessary, not
only for the preservation of Fort Constitution, but for its
own importance on many accounts. One also is necessary at the west end of the island, to command the approach that way, and to prevent a landing at the north
side of the island. An easy communication by land, as
well as by water, may be made with Fort Montgomery
from the West Point.

" The garrison of Fort Constitution consists of two companies of Colonel James Clinton's regiment, and Captain
Wisner's company of minute-men, in all about one hundred and sixty, rank and file. The garrison at Fort
Montgomery consists of three companies of the same
regiment, amounting to about two hundred men, rank and
file. The field-officer of the regiment is Lieutenant-
Colonel Livingston; but the command of the whole of
both garrisons is still in the hands of Colonel Nicoll, who,
it seems, last fall raised a regiment of minute-men for
the purpose of garrisoning Fort Constitution, which regi-

ment is all dismissed except Captain Wisner's Company of about forty privates. Lieutenant-Colonel Livingston has very prudently avoided any dispute with Col. Nicoll about the command, rather referring the matter to your Excellency's determination. The whole of the troops at both these posts are miserably armed, as will appear by the return (No. 4). Lieutenant-Colonel Livingston informs me he has lately received about forty fire-locks, all in very bad order, from the Committees of Dutchess County, and expects several hundred more in a few days in the same condition. I have therefore directed the black-smith's shop at Fort Constitution to be enlarged, so that it will at the same time serve for an armory. A black-smith's shop and armory of the like kind, I have directed at Fort Montgomery, and the artificers in those branches in Clinton's Regiment to be employed in them.

*   *   *   *   *   *   *   *

"The direction of the works at both these forts is in the hands of Commissioners appointed by the Provincial Congress of New York. Two Commissioners, with four carpenters, two blacksmiths and seven attendants, are at Fort Constitution; two Commissioners, one clerk, fifteen carpenters, and four masons, are at Fort Montgomery; the pay of these amounts to at least eight hundred dollars per month, besides their provisions, &c. One good engineer, with artificers from the army, might, I think, do the whole business as well.

*   *   *   *   *   *   *   *

"The artillery and ordnance stores, at these posts, appear by Captain Sargent's reports herewith (No. 6). The cannon in general are, to all appearance, excellent of their kind, excepting two nine and three six-pounders,

3

which are dubious. There are also, I am informed, six cannon, six-pounders, four of them good and two dubious, at New Windsor, a place about six miles above Fort Constitution; they had better be brought down to Fort Montgomery.

"Considering the different directions all these matters are under, I have avoided giving any determinate orders about them, but it is highly necessary that explicit orders should soon issue.

"I am your Excellency's most humble servant,

(Signed)   " Stirling.

"To his Excellency, General Washington."

No. 4.

RETURN OF THE PRESENT STATE OF THE GARRISON AT FORT CONSTITUTION, MAY 29, 1776, LIEUTENANT-COLONEL LIVINGSTON.

NAMES OF THE CAPTAINS.	Captains.	Subalterns.	Sergeants.	Corporals.	Drummers and Fifers.	Privates.	Sick and Lame.	Absent by Leave.	On Command.	Deserted.	Guns fit for Use.	Guns not fit.	Cartridge-Boxes.	Bayonets.	Tomahawks.	Guns Wanting.	Bayonets Wanting.	Tomahawks Wanting.	Axes Wanting.	Pails Wanting.	Cartridge-Boxes Wanting.
Captain William Jackson's Company	1	*3	4	4	2	73	17	1	8		4	31	86	1		82	82	82			
Captain John Wisner's Company of Minute-Men	1	3	4	4	2	42	10				31			3							
Increase Childs' Company	1	3	4	1	1	37					6		3			41	41	41			41
Total at Fort Constitution	3	9	12	9	5	152	27	1	8		41	31	89	4		123	123	123			41

* Lieutenant Ellsworth gone to Albany, with a guard of six men, with powder.

I do hereby certify the above to be a true return.

(Signed)   ISAAC NICOLL,

Commissary of Stores.

No. 5.

COMMISSIONERS, SUPERINTENDENTS, MECHANICS, ETC., AT THE
WORKS CARRYING ON AT FORT CONSTITUTION.

Two Commissioners,—William Bedlow and Jonathan
Lawrence.

One Clerk of the Check,—Jonathan Lawrence, Jr.

One Steward,—Adolph Delgrove.

Mechanics at work:—4 Carpenters, 2 Blacksmiths,
1 Overseer, 1 Cook for the Commissioners, 1 Cook for
the Artificers, 1 Waiter on the Commissioners, 1 Seaman
in care of the barge.

The Sloop Liberty, Henry Palmer, in the service of
Fort Constitution and Fort Montgomery: Master and
two hands.

(Signed)   WILLIAM BEDLOW.

FORT CONSTITUTION, *May* 31, 1776.

RETURN OF PERSONS EMPLOYED AT FORT CONSTITUTION.

	Per Month.		
2 Commissioners, pay 10s. per day each	£30	0	0
2 Waiters, 53s. 4d. - - - - -	5	6	8
4 Carpenters, at 6s. per day each - - -	36	0	0
1 Overseer, 80s. per month - - -	4	0	0
1 Clerk, at 100s. - - - - -	5	0	0
1 Steward, at 100s. - - - - -	5	0	0
1 Cook, at 53s. 4d. - - - - -	2	13	4
1 Hired man, at 53s. 4d. - - - -	2	13	4
1 Blacksmith, at 6s. per day - - -	9	0	0
1 Blacksmith - - - - - -	4	10	0
	£104	3	4

FORT CONSTITUTION, *May* 31, 1776.

No. 6.

A REPORT OF ORDNANCE AND ORDNANCE STORES, WITH ALL THE IMPLEMENTS FOR THE SERVICE OF THE ARTILLERY, AT FORT CONSTITUTION, May 30, 1776.

	1	2¼	3	4	6	9	12
Number of Cannon.	2	4	5	17	84	15	
Size—Pounders.	1	2¼	3	4	6	9	12
Metal.	do.	do.	do.	do.	do.	do.	Iron
Carriages, Garrison.					12	16	14
Carriages, name unknown.						2	
Sponges with Rammers.					8	16	19
Ladles with Worms.					6	7	4
Cartridges, filled.					16	26	21
Cartridges, empty.				64	1,217	752	1,470
Cartridge-cases.					12	12	12
Round-shot.				86	654	900	1,010
Double-headed Shot.					12	314	
Chain-shot.						12	
Star-shot.						7	
Grape-shot.				11	22	19	31
Canister-shot.					8		
Empty Canisters.					100		
Wads.					108	108	108
Cannon Covers.						2	
Formers.					2	4	
Copper Measures.					1	1	1
Aprons.					3	10	8
Pompions.					10	6	8
Priming-Wires.							6
Powder-horns.							20
Linstocks.							62
Handspikes.							80
Budge-barrels.							8
Lanthorns.							6
Six-ounce Shot, Lead—pounds.							493
Cartridge-paper, in reams.							10½
Junk, for Wads—pounds.							300
Sheet Lead.							144
Hand-grenades.							86
Slow-matches.							319
Powder—77 qr. Casks and 1¼ bls.							1925 lbs
Small Gin, with its Apparatus.							1

To the Right Hon. WILLIAM EARL OF STIRLING, *Brigadier-General.*

(Signed) WINTHROP SARGENT, *Captain-Lieutenant of Artillery.*

The views contained in Lord Stirling's report were transmitted by Washington, on June 10th, to the officers in charge at Fort Constitution, and the desire expressed to have them adopted with as little delay as possible. In acknowledging their receipt, Colonel Livingston called attention to the omission in the copy of the importance " of throwing up a work on a point called West Point, directly opposite to us, which would be easy of access to our enemies should they pass or take Fort Montgomery. If," said this efficient officer, " I could obtain your Excellency's approbation, a work should be immediately thrown up on this place."

At this time, while Lieutenant-Colonel Livingston held the immediate charge of Fort Constitution, the whole command in the Highlands was exercised by Colonel James Clinton, who was more particularly interested in the construction of the works at Pooplopen's Kill, and which, as early as the 14th of May, had been commenced under Messrs. Palmer and Livingston, Commissioners under the Provincial Congress.*

* Am. Arch., IV., V., 1414.

CHAPTER III.

APPOINTMENT OF A SECRET COMMITTEE FOR OBSTRUCTING THE CHAN-
NEL OF THE HUDSON.—THEIR ACTION AND LETTER TO WASHING-
TON.—ASSIGNMENT OF GENERAL GEO. CLINTON TO COMMAND IN
THE HIGHLANDS.—GENERAL CLINTON AND OTHER OFFICERS EX-
AMINE THE WORKS AND REPORT UPON THE NECESSITY OF A BOOM
AND CHAIN AT FORT MONTGOMERY.—MAJOR-GENERAL PUTNAM AP-
POINTED TO COMMAND.—ADVANCE OF SIR HENRY CLINTON UP THE
HUDSON TO CO-OPERATE WITH GENERAL BURGOYNE.—ASSAULT
AND CAPTURE OF FORTS MONTGOMERY AND CLINTON.

THE suggestions of the Committee of *June* 13*th*, 1775
(p. 14), in regard to *obstructing the navigation* of the
river, do not, however, appear to have been acted upon,
further than to order the survey mentioned, until the
subsequent year (1776) ; when, on the 16th of July, a
few days after the Declaration of Independence, the Provincial Convention* again took up the matter, and appointed a *Secret Committee* to take the whole subject in
charge, as will be seen by the following resolutions :

" *Resolved, unanimously*, That a Secret Committee be appointed to devise and carry into execution such measures
as to them shall appear most effectual for *obstructing the
channel* of the Hudson River, or annoying the enemy's
ships in their passage up said river ; and that this Convention pledge themselves for defraying the charges incident thereto.

" *Resolved*, That Mr. Jay, Mr. Robert Yates, Major C.
Tappan, Mr. Robert R. Livingston, and Mr. Paulding, be
said Committee."

* The title of the Legislature of the State was changed on the 10th July, 1776,
from Congress to Convention.

The proceedings of this Secret Committee, appointed 16th July, 1776, have been recently discovered by Mr. James C. Bolton, among the papers of his grandfather, General James Clinton. Besides these minutes, Mr. Bolton has found maps of the Chain at Fort Montgomery, showing the manner in which it was fastened and floated, and the character of the Booms placed in front of it. These long-hidden and valuable documents receive additional illustration from a relic of the original obstruction at West Point, which was raised from the river's bed by Bishop's derrick, in 1855. Collating and combining this mass of new and important materials, with that to be derived from the proceedings of the Provincial Convention, and from other previously known sources, we find that—

There were four points at which it was sought to obstruct the navigation of the river, by means, either singly or combined, of *fire-ships*, *booms* and *chains*, and *chevaux-de-frise*. The *first* point was at Fort Washington, the *second* at Fort Montgomery, the *third* at Pollopel's Island, and the *fourth* at West Point. The fire-ships and obstructions at Fort Washington were constructed in the summer of 1776; the obstructions at Fort Montgomery and Pollopel's Island, in the autumn of 1776 and springs of 1777 and 1778; and those at West Point in 1778.

The Secret Committee, on the 17th of July, addressed a letter to the Commander-in-chief, soliciting his advice as to a plan for the defences of Hudson's River, which, they alleged, had been unfortunately too long neglected. To this Washington replied on the 21st, detailing his order to Lord Stirling, and stating that while he had repeatedly urged on Colonel Clinton to spare no pains to put them

on the best possible footing, he had reason to suppose
they were in tolerable order to receive the enemy. On
the same day Lieutenant Machin was despatched by him
to Colonel Clinton, as the Engineer of the works in the
Highlands. He was described as "an ingenious man,
who was a proper person, and one who had given great
satisfaction as an engineer."

As early as the 15th of July, at the request of the
Commander-in-chief, General George Clinton had been
appointed by the Provincial Congress to command the
newly raised levies, and this officer was now actively co-
operating with his brother in obstructing the river at
Pollopel's Island, and expediting the erection of Forts
Clinton and Montgomery, at Pooplopen's Kill.

The garrison at Fort Constitution, weakened by detachments to prosecute the latter operations,* was, on
the 1st of December, strengthened by the addition of
two regiments, which, under the command of General
George Clinton, were to furnish working parties to aid in
obstructing the channel of the Hudson at Pollopel's
Island;† this General being, in addition, specially instructed on the 10th of December, by the New York
Committee of Safety, in relation to the necessity of securing the passes in the Highlands, and on "no account
to place himself beyond the power to regain them."‡

The spring of 1777 approached, and the task of
strengthening the defences in the Highlands still continued. On the 25th of March, Congress appointed
George Clinton a brigadier-general, thus transferring
him from the Provincial rank before held by him, to the

* Am. Arch., V. III., 1040.   † Am. Arch., V. III., 348.
‡ Am. Arch. V., III., 1157.

Continental Service; and although, upon the adoption of the State Constitution, he was chosen Governor in July, he nevertheless continued cordially co-operating in the work before mentioned.

On the 7th of May, from head-quarters at Morristown, N. J., Washington wrote Brigadier-General McDougall, who had succeeded Brigadier-General Heath in the command of the New England troops at Peekskill* and vicinity, that the imperfect state of the fortifications at Fort Montgomery gave him great uneasiness, and that a concurrence of circumstances indicated a movement of the enemy up the North River.

General McDougall was directed, in connection with General George Clinton, to employ every measure to put the works in a condition to resist a sudden attack, or detain the enemy until re-enforcements could arrive.†

In compliance with these instructions, Generals McDougall, Knox, Greene, George Clinton, and Wayne, proceeded to examine the works already erected; and on the "17th of May, these officers submitted a joint report to the Commander-in-chief, in which they recommended the obstruction of the river at Fort Montgomery by stretching a boom or chain across, in front of which should be one or two cables, to break the force of a vessel before it should strike the chain; that two Continental ships then on the spot, and two row-galleys, should be manned and stationed just above the obstruction, in such

---

* The command of the department in the Highlands and vicinity, including Forts Constitution, Montgomery, and Independence, the passes, and the Division of Connecticut and Massachusetts troops, had been assigned to Brigadier-General *Heath*, 12th November, 1776—head-quarters at Peekskill.—[Heath's Memoirs, 85.]

† Writings of Washington, Sparks, IV., 409.

a manner as to fire upon the enemy's ships in front when they approached." They also added: "We are very confident, if the obstructions of the river can be rendered effectual, the enemy will not attempt to operate by land, the passes through the Highlands are so exceedingly difficult."*

Unfortunately, this latter course, by penetrating overland, through the defiles in the mountains, was the very one adopted, and so successfully carried out by the enemy.

At this time the command of the forces in and near the Highlands had assumed such proportions as to require a Major-General for its head, and accordingly Major-General Putnam was directed to relieve General McDougall early in the month of May.

On the 1st of July, from head-quarters at Middlebrook, Washington wrote Putnam : * * * "It appears almost certain to me that General Howe and General Burgoyne design, if possible, to unite their attacks and form a junction of their two armies, * * * and I am persuaded, if General Howe is going up the river, he will make a rapid and vigorous push to gain the Highland passes."†

These indications of an active movement on the part of the enemy were continued throughout the summer, and served to prepare the way for more decisive results in the autumn of 1777.

"The advance of General Burgoyne from the North towards Albany had been checked, and his army was suffering from want of provisions, while at the same time

---

* Sparks's Writings of Washington, IV., 416.   † Id., IV., 476.

General Howe, with the main body of the army under his command, was struggling with General Washington for the possession of Philadelphia. For the purpose of diverting the attention of the American forces, to secure the passes in the Highlands, and, if possible, to withdraw a portion of General Gates's army from its careful attention to General Burgoyne, General Sir Henry Clinton, then in command in the city of New York, organized an expedition for the capture of the forts in the Highlands, and for such other movements in that direction as the circumstances might warrant."*

In addition to the works already mentioned, redoubts had been thrown up by the troops encamped around Peekskill, at Verplanck's Point. and on the southern base of Anthony's Nose.

" Early in October the British General embarked his forces, ostensibly for a southern expedition, and awaited a favorable wind for the execution of his real design.

"The opportunities were propitious, and a powerful naval armament, with about four thousand troops on board, suddenly menaced Putnam's position and landed at Verplanck's Point, the garrison at which retreated on the approach of the fleet. Putnam was caught by the device ; and, believing the defences on the east side of the river to be the object of the British General, obstinately refused the entreaties of officers more sagacious than himself, to send adequate succors to the posts opposite. Nor after the main body of the British had on the next day crossed over to Stony Point, and were on their march to Forts Clinton and Montgomery, and even after

* Battles of the U. S., I., 332.—Dawson.

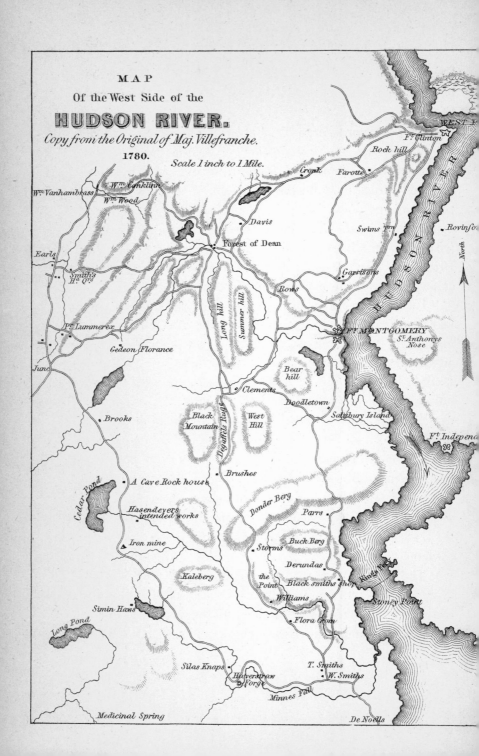

MAP

Of the West Side of the

HUDSON RIVER.

Copy from the Original of Maj. Villefranche.

1780.

Scale 1 inch to 1 Mile.

Wm Vanhambrass
Wm Conklin
Wm Wood

Cronk
Farotte

Fᵗ Clinton
Rock hill

Davis

Swims Pᵗ
Rovins

Earls

Forest of Dean

Smith's Hᵈ Qᵣˢ

Garrisons

North

Pᵗ Lummerex

Rows

Gedeon Florance

Long hill
Summer hill

Fᵗ MONTGOMERY
Sᵗ Anthonys Nose

Junc

Bear hill

Clements

Doodletown

Brooks

Black Mountain house
West Hill

Salisbury Island

Fᵗ Independa

Degattels Ridge

A Cave Rock house

Brushes

Hasendeyers intended works

Donder Berg

Parrs

Iron mine

Buck Berg

Storms

Kaleberg

Derundas

the Point
Black smiths shop

Kings Ferry

Williams

Stony Point

Simin Haws

Flora Gom

Long Pond

Silas Knaps

T. Smiths
W. Smiths

Haverstraw Forge

Minnes Fall

Medicinal Spring

De Noells

Cedar Pond

HUDSON RIVER

WEST

the firing was heard at the forts above him, could he be persuaded to send forces to the relief of the beleaguered posts."

"But Governor George Clinton was not so easily blinded. As soon as he heard that the fleet was on the river, he adjourned the Legislature, then in session at Kingston, and collecting such militia as could be assembled, proceeded to the point to which he had before been assigned by Congress. He had scarcely time to throw himself with four hundred followers into the works, when the British, having deceived Putnam, landed at Stony Point at daybreak on the morning of the 6th of October."*

" Five hundred regulars and four hundred loyal Americans under Colonel Beverly Robinson, the whole commanded by Lieutenant-Colonel Campbell, moved as an advanced guard around the Dunderberg to the base of Bear Mountain, followed by General Vaughn with twelve hundred men. Lieutenant-Colonel Campbell was directed to make the *détour* of Bear Mountain seven miles around to the west, and *débouche* in rear of Fort Montgomery; while General Vaughn was to proceed eastward between the two mountains, accompanied by Sir Henry Clinton, and assail Fort Clinton on its south flank and rear. The rear-guard, under Ex-Governor General Tryon, was left in the valley, at the point of separation of the two columns.

" The former body reached the vicinity of Fort Clinton at about 5 P. M., and receiving a scornful refusal from the garrison to surrender, commenced the assault at about the same moment the first column under Campbell at-

---

* Life and Times of Colonel Lamb, 174.—Leake.

tacked Fort Montgomery, aided by the vessels of war which had moved up the river to participate in the conflict."*

The garrisons, for the most part composed of untrained militia, and wholly inadequate to man the extensive lines, resisted and repeatedly repulsed with great vigor the attack of superior numbers, and not until darkness closed around were the six hundred brave defenders overpowered.

Part of the garrisons were made prisoners, but both commanders escaped: Governor George Clinton by a boat across the river, while General James Clinton, the commander of the fort bearing his name, forced his passage to the rear.

A sloop of ten guns, the frigate Montgomery, and two row-galleys, stationed near for the defence of the boom and chain, were burned to prevent their capture by the enemy. The frigate Congress, ordered up the river on the 5th, ran on the flats near Fort Constitution, and shared the same fate.

Lighted by the flames of the burning vessels, the fugitives dispersed through the mountains, and pursuing their flight over the plain at West Point, found a resting-spot with General James Clinton, at New Windsor.

"The garrison at Fort Constitution, reduced to a mere guard under Captain Gershom Mott, who had there assumed command on the 9th of August, and now completely at the mercy of an enemy's battery if planted at West Point, awaited a summons to surrender, borne under a white flag, on the morning of the 7th. Captain

---

* Sir H. Clinton's Despatch.

Mott fired on the flag, and that night abandoned the island, after burning the barracks and leaving his guns unspiked, with a portion of his stores unconsumed.

" On the morning of the 8th, two thousand men under General Tryon proceeded on the fleet from Fort Montgomery up the river, and landing on the east side, completed the demolition of the 'Fortifications in the Highlands.' "*

Thus was effected, in the brief time of two days, the destruction of works and stores which had cost the country not less than a quarter of a million of dollars, no portion of which had been appropriated to the erection of a single battery at West Point, so often urged as "the key to the passage in the Highlands."

A portion of the British force, left as a garrison at Fort Clinton, commenced its reconstruction under the name of Fort Vaughn, while another party made an expedition to "Continental Village," on the east side of the river, and about four miles distant.

At this point a large amount of supplies, and barracks for fifteen hundred men, were destroyed without molestation.

The capture of the army under General Burgoyne having been ascertained, the whole expedition abandoned the Highlands, after twenty days' occupation, and returned to New York.

* Life and Times of Colonel Lamb, 185. Idem, MSS. N. Y. Hist. Col.

CHAPTER IV.

RENEWED EFFORTS TO OBSTRUCT THE HUDSON.—SELECTION OF WEST
POINT AS A SUITABLE PLACE.—LETTERS OF WASHINGTON TO PUT-
NAM AND CLINTON UPON THE SUBJECT.—APPOINTMENT OF A COM-
MITTEE BY THE NEW YORK PROVINCIAL CONVENTION TO CONFER
WITH PUTNAM.—REPORT OF THE COMMITTEE, IN WHICH THEY RECOM-
MEND THE FORTIFICATION OF WEST POINT.—COMMENCEMENT OF
THE WORKS BY GENERAL PARSONS.—CONTRACT MADE BY COLONEL
HUGHES FOR THE GREAT CHAIN AT WEST POINT.—REPORT OF
GENERAL PUTNAM ON THE PROGRESS OF THE FORTIFICATIONS.—
REPORT OF GENERAL PARSONS ON THE SAME.—GENERAL McDOU-
GALL ORDERED TO RELIEVE GENERAL PUTNAM.—INSTRUCTIONS TO
GENERAL PARSONS RELATIVE TO THE CONSTRUCTION OF THE WORKS.

IMMEDIATELY after the return of Sir Henry Clinton's
expedition to New York, the necessity for a more thorough
fortification of the Highlands engaged the attention of
those to whom the defence of this most important point
had been intrusted.

On the 6th of November, Colonel Hughes wrote General
Gates from Fishkill: * * * "The General, Governor
Clinton, and General James [Clinton], an Engineer, and
your humble servant, were at the forts yesterday, viewing
the River, Bluffs, Points, &c., in order to erect some further obstructions, which are immediately set about. The
Boom will be near Fort Constitution, and a work on the
west shore to defend it."† * * From New Windsor,
on the 24th of November, General Clinton wrote General
Gates: "I know of no other method of obstructing the
passage of Hudson's River, but by Chevaux-de-frise,

† Gates, MSS. N. Y. Hist. Col.

Chains, and Booms, well defended by heavy artillery and strong works on the shore. The former is impracticable at any place lower down than where the present are, near this place; and even there, the river is rather too wide to admit of their being properly defended; they may, however, when completed, be a very considerable obstruction. This with a chain or boom, at a part of the river called the West Point, where it is quite narrow, and the wind, owing to the crookedness of the river, very uncertain, with proper works on the shore to defend it, and water-batteries on shore calculated to annoy shipping, would, in my opinion, perfectly obstruct the navigation." * * * "We have a boom, calculated for the narrow part of the river, well forward, but our works go on extremely slow indeed, for want of tools,"* &c. * * * This feeling of solicitude was not confined to the local commanders. The comparative ease with which the British expedition had passed the Highlands had awakened an apprehension of its early repetition in the mind of General Washington, who, in a letter dated December 2d, 1777, instructed General Putnam to consult with Governor Clinton, General Parsons, and the French engineer, Lieutenant-Colonel Radière, with a view to the erection of such "works and obstructions as may be necessary to defend and secure the river against any future attempts of the enemy."

The following is Washington's letter:

"HEAD-QUARTERS, 2d December, 1777.

"DEAR SIR:—The importance of the Hudson River in the present contest, and the necessity of defending it, are subjects which have been so frequently and fully

* Gates, MSS. N. Y. Hist. Col.

discussed, and are so well understood, that it is unnecessary to enlarge upon them. These facts at once appear, when it is considered that it runs through a whole State; that it is the only passage by which the enemy from New York, or any part of our coast, can ever hope to co-operate with an army from Canada; that the possession of it is indispensably essential to preserve the communication between the Eastern, Middle, and Southern States; and further, that upon its security, in a great measure, depend our chief supplies of flour for the subsistence of such forces as we may have occasion for, in the course of the war, either in the Eastern or Northern Departments, or in the country lying high up on the west side of it. These facts are familiar to all; they are familiar to you. I therefore request you, in the most urgent terms, to turn your most serious and active attention to this infinitely important object. Seize the present opportunity, and *employ your whole force and all the means in your power for erecting and completing, as far as it shall be possible, such works and obstructions as may be necessary to defend and secure the river* against any future attempts of the enemy. You will consult Governor Clinton, General Parsons, and the French engineer, Lieutenant-Colonel Radière, upon the occasion. By gaining the passage, you know the enemy have already laid waste and destroyed all the houses, mills and towns accessible to them. Unless proper measures are taken to prevent them, they will renew their ravages in the spring, or as soon as the season will admit, and perhaps Albany, the only town in the State of any importance remaining in our hands, may undergo a like fate, and a general havoc and devastation take place.

" To prevent these evils, therefore, I shall expect that you will exert every nerve, and *employ your whole force in future, while and whenever it is practicable, in constructing and forwarding the proper works and means of defence.* The troops must not be kept out on command, and acting in detachments to cover the country below, which is a consideration infinitely less important and interesting.

" I am, dear Sir," &c.

In a letter to Governor Clinton of the same date, General Washington expressed much solicitude on the subject. Governor Clinton, in reply, assured the Commander-in-chief of his hearty concurrence in any effort that might be agreed upon ; and he gave several important hints respecting the construction of new works on the river, and especially recommended that a "strong fortress should be erected at West Point opposite to Fort Constitution."*

On the same date, Washington also addressed a letter to Major-General Gates, directing him, " with a certain part of the Northern army, and the assistance of the militia of New York and the Eastern States, to attempt the recovery of the posts upon the North River from the enemy, and to put them, if recovered, in the best posture of defence." But General Gates was appointed, at about the same time, President of the Board of War, and did not act in the matter. Washington also addressed a letter to Governor Clinton, requesting him " to take the chief direction of superintendence of this business." Governor Clinton replied, that he would co-operate with any one charged with the chief direction

* Sparks's Writings of Washington, V., 178

of the works, but in consideration of his other duties must decline the appointment.

The matter thus remained under the direction of General Putnam, who, early in January, 1778, brought the subject before the Provincial Convention of New York, as appears from the following proceedings :—

"THURSDAY, *Jan.* 8, 1778.

" Application being made by Major-General Putnam, Commanding Officer of the Middle Department, that this Convention would appoint a committee to confer with him relative to the necessary works to be constructed for the defences of the passes in the Highlands—

"*Resolved,* That the General's request be complied with, and that Mr. Scott, Mr. Pawling, Mr. Wisner, Mr. Snyder, Mr. Killian Van Rensselaer, Mr. Drake, Mr. Hathorn, and Mr. Hoffman, be a committee for that purpose."*

"FRIDAY, *January* 9, 1778.

" General Scott, from the Committee appointed yesterday evening, to confer with General Putnam and General James Clinton, the Lieutenant-Colonel of Engineers, and other military officers, relative to the necessary works to be constructed for the passes in the Highlands, and the place or places where the same ought to be erected, reported that they had conferred with the said Generals and other officers; that on such conference there was a disagreement in sentiment between those gentlemen (arising from certain different facts alleged), as to the place where such works ought to be erected; and, therefore, that it was the opinion of the said Committee and the military gentlemen, that this Convention appoint Commissioners to view the several passes on Hudson

* Jour. Prov. Conv., 1113.

River, *with the Generals and other officers,* and advise in fixing the places where such fortifications should be erected.

"*Resolved,* That John Sloss Hobart, Esq., one of the Justices of the Supreme Court, the Hon. Robert R. Livingston, Chancellor of this State, Mr. Platt, Mr. Wisner, and Colonel Hathorn, be, and hereby are, appointed Commissioners for the purpose above mentioned, and proceed in that business with all possible despatch."*

The result of the conference of these two Committees, after devoting three days in examining the ground at and near West Point, will be found in the following report :   *   *   *   *   *   *   *   *   *

" WEDNESDAY, *January 14th,* 1778.

"Your Committee, who were sent to ascertain the place for fixing a chain and erecting fortifications for obstructing the navigation of the Hudson River, beg leave to report, That they have carefully viewed the ground on which Fort ·Clinton lately stood, and its environs, and find that the ground is so intersected with long, deep hollows, that the enemy might approach without any annoyance from the garrison within the Fort, to within a few yards of the walls, unless a redoubt should be raised to clear the hollows next the Fort, which must be built at such distance from the Fort that it could not be supported from thence in case of an assault, so that the enemy might make themselves masters of the redoubt the first dark night after their landing, which would be a good work, ready to their hand, for annoying

* Jour. Prov. Conv., 1113.

5

the Fort and facilitating their operations against it; and, together with the eminences and broken grounds within a short distance of the Fort, would render it impossible for the garrison to resist a general assault for many hours together. Another objection that appeared to the Committee was the want of earth on the spot, which would reduce the engineer to the necessity of erecting his works entirely of timber, which must be brought to Pooploop's Kill in rafts, and from thence drawn up a steep and difficult road to the top of the hill. The rafts cannot be made till the water is warm enough for men to work in it, by which it is probable that a Fort cannot be erected before the ships of the enemy will come up the river. Beside, at this place, the chain must be laid across the river, so that it will receive the whole force of the ships coming with all the strength of tide and wind on a line of three or four miles. Add to these, if the enemy should be able to possess themselves of the passes in the mountains through which they marched to the attacks of Forts Montgomery and Clinton, it would be extremely difficult, if not impossible, for the militia of the country to raise the siege.

" Upon viewing the country at and about West Point, the Committee found that there were several places at which the enemy might land and proceed immediately to some high grounds that would command a Fort erected at West Point, at the distance of six or ·seven hundred yards, from which they might carry on their approaches through a light gravelly soil, so that it would be impossible for the Fort to stand a long siege. But to balance this disadvantage in this place, there is plenty of earth. The timber may be brought to the spot by good roads from the high grounds at the distance of one to three miles. Three hundred feet less of chain will be requisite at this place than at Fort Clinton. It will be laid across in a place where vessels going up the river most usually lose their headway.* Water-batteries may be built on both sides of the river for protecting the chain and annoying the ships coming up the river, which will be completely commanded from the walls of the Fort. There are so many passes across the mountains to this place, that it will be almost impossible for the enemy to prevent the militia from coming to the relief of the garrison.

"From these considerations, the Committee are led to conclude that the most proper place to obstruct the navigation of the river is at West Point; but are at the same time fully convinced that no obstructions on the banks of the river can effectually secure the country, unless a body of light troops, to consist of at least two thousand effective men, be constantly stationed in the mountains while the navigation of the river is practicable, to obstruct the enemy in their approach by land.

" Jno. Sloss Hobart,
" Henry Wisner,
" John Hathorn,
" Zeph. Platt.

" Poughkeepsie, *Jan. 14th*, 1778."†

Immediately following the reception of this report, on or about the 20th of January, the brigade of General

---

* Those who are acquainted with the place where the obstruction was fastened to the shore, will see the force of this description. A point of land here juts out into the stream abruptly, and compels vessels, sailing under even the most favorable breeze, to make such change in their course as will materially lessen their headway.

† Jour. Prov. Conv., 1117.

Parsons crossed over to the Point, and notwithstanding the severity of the winter, and a deep fall of snow on the ground, operations were commenced.

Without shelter, materials for building, or proper tools to labor with, a work was laid out on the northeast angle of the Plain, and a series of water-batteries commanded by it, were located on the eastern front by Lieutenant-Colonel Radière, Engineer, under the supervision of Major-General Putnam.

Radière, an impatient, petulant officer, planned the work at the outset, on a scale entirely too large. He required means altogether beyond the resources at command, and projected curtains, banquettes, and terre-pleins sufficient to enclose the greater portion of the north and east crest of the river's bank.[*]

Embarrassing as this display of science was, the work of construction progressed as rapidly as the difficulties first mentioned would permit, and zealous means were taken to carry out the recommendation of the Committee to obstruct the *navigation* of the river.

By direction of General Putnam, Hugh Hughes, Deputy Quartermaster-General, visited the Stirling Iron Works[†] of Noble, Townsend and Company on the 2d of February, and entered into a contract with the proprietors to construct a chain. This contract was as follows :—

"Articles of Agreement between Noble, Townsend and Company, proprietors of the Stirling Iron Works,

---

[*] Zodiac, Nov., 1835, 67.

[†] The Stirling Iron Works are still in operation. They are situated on the outlet of Stirling Pond, about five miles southwest of the Sloatsburgh Station, on the Erie Railway. They are owned by descendants of Peter Townsend, and have now been in operation about one hundred years.

in the State of New York, of the one part, and Hugh
Hughes, Deputy Quartermaster-General to the Army of
the United States, of the other part, witnesseth :—

"That the said Noble, Townsend and Company,
jointly and severally engage to have made and ready to
be delivered at their works to the said Hugh Hughes,
Deputy Quartermaster-General, or to the Deputy Quartermaster-General of the Middle Department for the
time being, on or before the first day of April next
ensuing the date hereof, or as much sooner as circumstances will admit, an iron chain of the following dimen-
sions and quality : that is, in length five hundred yards,
each link about two feet long, to be made of the best
Stirling iron, two inches and one-quarter square, or as
near thereto as possible, with a swivel to every hundred feet, and a clevis to every thousand feet, in the
same manner as those of the former chain.

"The said Noble, Townsend and Company also engage to have made and ready to be delivered at least
twelve tons of anchors of the aforesaid iron, and of such
sizes as the said Hugh Hughes or his successors in
office shall direct, in writing, as soon as the completion
of the chain will admit.

"In consideration of which the said Hugh Hughes,
in behalf of the United States, agrees to pay to the said
Noble, Townsend and Company, or their order, at the
rate of four hundred and forty pounds* for every ton
weight of chain and anchors delivered as before mentioned, unless the general regulations on trade, provisions, &c., which are now supposed to be framed by

---

* Continental money, probably.

deputies from the United States, shall be published and take effect before the expiration of four months from the date of this ; in which case the price is to be only £400 per ton for the said chain and anchors. The payment, if demanded, to be made in such proportion as the work shall be ready to be delivered, which shall be determined in ten days after requisition made by a number of competent judges, not less than three nor more than five, unconcerned with the proprietors, or the works, and, if condemned, to be completed at the expense of the said Company, who are also to repair, as aforesaid, all failures of their work, whenever happening, whether at the works or river, or in extending it across.

" The said Hugh Hughes also engages to procure of the Governor of this State, for the said Noble, Townsend and Company, an exemption for nine months from the date hereof, from military duty, for sixty artificers that are steadily employed at the said chain and anchors till completed. Agreeable to the said exemption, the said Company complying with the terms thereof. Providing also that the said Company give the said Hugh Hughes, or his successors in office, the refusal, by letter, of all the bar iron, anchors, &c., made at the said works in the said term of nine months, at the current price, unless what is necessary to exchange for clothing and other articles for the use of the works.

" It is also agreed, by the said parties, that if the teams of the said Company shall transport the said chain or anchors, or any part thereof, to any assigned post, they shall receive for such services the same pay as shall be given by the United States for the like ; the teams of the Company being exempted from impress by any of the Quartermaster-General's deputies during the space of nine months.

"Lastly, the said Company engage to use their utmost endeavors to keep seven fires at forging and ten at welding, if assisted with such hands as are necessary and can be spared from the army, in case of their not being able to procure others, the said Company making deduction for their labor.

"In witness whereof, the parties have interchangeably subscribed their names this second day of February, one thousand seven hundred and seventy-eight, and in the second year of American Independence.

"PETER TOWNSEND,

"In behalf of Noble & Company.

"HUGH HUGHES,*

"In behalf of United States.

"In presence of
  "P. TILLINGHAST."†

On the 13th of February, General Putnam wrote to the Commander-in-chief as follows :

"At my request the Legislature of this State have

---

* *Hugh Hughes* was of Welsh origin, born in 1727.   He resided in New Jersey in 1765, removing to New York the same or in the following year.

Closely identified with the Revolutionists in 1769, he was appointed in 1776, by the Provincial Convention, Commissary of Military Stores, and by Washington, Deputy Quartermaster-General of the forces.

Resigning in 1778, he was in 1780 urgently solicited by Colonel Pickering, then Quartermaster-General, to resume his former rank in the American Army, which invitation was accepted.   In this capacity he served throughout the war until 1784, at which time he was elected a member of the General Assembly from the city of New York.   The writings of Washington and General Greene furnish strong testimony to his spotless integrity and fitness for the faithful discharge of his duties.   He died at Tappan, March 15, 1802.

† Copy of original in Clinton Papers, State Library.

appointed a Committee to affix the places and manner of securing the river, and to afford some assistance in expediting the work. The state of affairs now at this post, you will observe, is as follows : the chain and necessary anchors are contracted for, to be completed by the first of April; and from the intelligence I have received, I have reason to believe they will be completed by that time. *Parts of the boom intended to have been used at Fort Montgomery*, sufficient for this place, are remaining. Some of the iron is exceedingly bad; this I hope to have replaced with good iron soon. The *chevaux-de-frise* will be completed by the time the river will admit of sinking them at (Pollopel's Island). The batteries near the water, and the Fort to cover them, are laid out. The latter is, within the walls, six hundred yards around, twenty-one feet base, fourteen feet high, the *talus* two inches to the foot. This, I fear, is too large to be completed by the time expected. Governor Clinton and the Committee have agreed to this plan; and nothing on my part shall be wanted to complete it in the best and most expeditious manner. Barracks and huts for about three hundred men are completed, and barracks for about the same number are nearly covered. A road* to the river has been made with great difficulty."

On the day following the date of this report, General Putnam left West Point for Connecticut, to attend to some private affairs, leaving the prosecution of the defences in charge of Brigadier-General Parsons, who re-

---

* This road, doubtless, was the one leading down to Gee's Point. "Villefranche's" Map shows a road to, and a dock at that place in 1780. The road is yet visible.

ported, on the 18th of February, "that almost every obstacle within the circle of possibility has happened to
retard their progress. Preparations [continues .this
officer] for completing them in April are now in a state
of forwardness, unless something unforeseen as yet
should prevent."

Again, from the "Camp at West Point, March 7,
1778," General Parsons communicated to Washington
the perplexities arising from the Acts of Congress relative to the direction of the works, and declared : " I
most ardently wish to aid Governor Clinton, or any other
gentleman appointed to superintend the work. At
present, no person has the direction. I have kept the
troops at work because I found them here when I took
the command. The weather has been such, since the
15th of February, as has greatly retarded the works—
about seven days of the time has been such that we
could do nothing.

" Lieutenant-Colonel Radière, finding it impossible to
complete the Fort and other defences intended at this
post, in such a manner as to render them effectual early
in the spring, and not choosing to hazard his reputation
on works erected on a different scale, calculated for a
short duration only, has desired leave to wait on Your
Excellency and Congress, which I have granted him."

On the 16th of March, General Parsons reported : " If
the chain is completed we shall be ready to stretch it over
the river next week. I hope to have two sides and one
bastion of the Fort in some state of defence in about a
fortnight; the other sides need very little to secure
them. We have the works going on as fast as could be
expected from our small number of men and total want

of money and materials provided.   I have several times
advanced my last shilling towards purchasing materials,
&c., and I believe this is the case with almost every
officer here."*

The absence of General Putnam still continued, and
the people of the Province, still regarding the works as
under his command, and greatly incensed at the course
he had pursued as Commander in the Highlands, refused
to render the necessary assistance while he remained
even nominally at the head of the Department; indeed,
the current of public opinion ran so strongly against
him, that on the 16th of March, Washington ordered
Major-General McDougall to repair to the Highlands,
and assume the chief command there, comprehending
" the Forts among the other objects of his trust."

Radière had left as early as the 11th of March, and,
visiting Congress, was relieved from duty by the appointment of Kosciuszko as the Engineer, who arrived at
the works on the 26th of March.   General McDougall
arrived on the 28th of the same month and assumed the
command.

Colonel Rufus Putnam† had early in the war been appointed an Engineer with the rank of Colonel, which
position he subsequently resigned to take the command
of a Massachusetts regiment, and with it he had shared

---

* Early Settlers of Ohio.—Hildreth.

† *Rufus Putnam* was born April 9, 1738, at Sutton, Massachusetts, and enlisted
as a soldier on 15th March, 1757, to serve in the French war.   After the outbreak
of the Revolution he joined a Massachusetts regiment, and at Boston, Roxbury,
&c., he displayed marked abilities as an Engineer.   On the 11th of August, 1776,
he was appointed by Congress an Engineer with the rank of Colonel.   Resigned
to take the command of the 5th Massachusetts Regiment, Dec. 8, 1776.   Brigadier-General January 8th, 1783.   Resigned February 15, 1793; died in May, 1824.
—[Hildreth's Early Settlers of Ohio.]

the triumph of Gates over Burgoyne. Early in March
he was ordered with his regiment to repair to West
Point, at which post he arrived at the same time with
General McDougall. As he had been a co-laborer with
Kosciuszko under General Gates at the North, his practical skill and experience rendered him a valuable assistant to advise in concert with the Engineer.

Operations were at once resumed, and pushed forward
with great vigor. " As the Fort then in progress was
designed to annoy the enemy's shipping, should they attempt to turn the Point and force the boom a little
higher up, no provision existed against a land attack in
its rear. A chain of Forts and redoubts was therefore
laid out on the high ground bordering the plain." [Forts
Wyllis, Webb, and Putnam.]

" The principal Fort was built by Putnam's own regiment, and was named by General McDougall, *Fort Putnam*. It stood on an elevated rocky eminence commanding both the plain and the Point. This rock sloped gradually to the plain on one side, while to the assailants
[in rear] it presented a mural front of fifty feet perpen-
dicular."*

Colonel Putnam joined the army at Peekskill in the
following June.

On the 11th of April, 1778, General McDougall issued
to General Parsons the following

" INSTRUCTIONS :

" The hill which Colonel Putnam is fortifying is the
most commanding and important of any that we can now

---

* Early Settlers of Ohio, 73.—Hildreth.

attend to. Although it is secure in the rear from esca-
lade, yet as it is practicable to annoy the garrison from
Snook Hill, the parapet in the rear should be made can-
non-proof against such as may be fired from Snook Hill.
The parapet should be raised as much as possible with
fascines and earth, to prevent the ill consequence of
splinters from the rocks. The easternmost face of this
work must be so constructed as to command the plain
on which Colonel Putnam's regiment is now encamped,
and annoy the enemy if he should force the works now
erecting by Colonel Meigs' and Colonel Wyllis' regiments, as well as to command the northernmost and highest part of the ground last mentioned, which commands
the plain in the rear of the principal works at West
Point. A temporary magazine should be built without
delay on Colonel Putnam's hill, and have ten days' provision, of salt meat and biscuit, for his regiment, deposited on the hill as soon as it arrives at West Point.
This store must not be broke in upon on any pretence,
till the enemy appears in force, and puts it out of Colonel Putnam's power to procure supplies from West Point.
The next principal ground to be occupied for the safety
of the Post, is the rising ground to the northward of the
Fort, near the northwest corner of the Long Barrack.
It will be necessary to erect a redoubt on this ground,
capable of containing one hundred and twenty men.
The west, north, and east faces should be proof against
battering cannon, and the south slightly palisaded to
guard against surprise. The westernmost face, flanked
by the fire of the Fort, must be ditched, and to mount
two pieces of cannon. The north face strongly abba-
tised. The parapet of the west face should be raised so

high, if practicable, as to cover the garrison from the fire that may be made against it from the ground on which Colonel Putnam is now encamped. This redoubt is so important, that it must be finished without delay. The chain to be fixed on the west side, in or near the Gap of the Snook, commanded by the fire from the east curtain of the work. The water-batteries now erected on the Point, to be completed as soon as possible, and two cannon placed in each, with the necessary shot and stores placed near them; if any of the cannon to be placed there require to be proved, it must be done before they are brought into the batteries. Such provisions as are on the Plain, to be removed into the Fort on the enemy's first appearing in force on the river, and no quantity left out at any time. Two small temporary magazines for ammunition to be made in the Fort for the present, to guard against rain; one also to be made for that of the cannon, in the batteries on the Point.

"It must be left to the discretion of the commanding officer at West Point, all circumstances considered, when to fire the alarm. In case of this event taking place in the present state of the works, the security of the Fort depends so much on the heights in the rear, on which the greatest force should be placed, that the commanding officer at West Point should take his quarters on the hill Colonel Putnam is now fortifying. Colonel Meigs's regiment, now at Robinson's farm, on hearing the alarm, will repair to West Point by the safest and securest passage. Six companies of his and Colonel Wyllis's regiment will take post in the works they are respectively erecting. The other two companies, with the invalids of the post and artificers, are to garrison the Fort,

under the orders of Major Grosvenor. Colonel Webb's
regiment is to take post in the works they are now making, and Colonel Sherburn's to defend the redoubt to
be erected near the northwest corner of the Long Barrack. Colonel Putnam's to take post on the hill which
they are now fortifying, and not to be ordered from
thence, but such detachments as he or the commanding
officer at the Post may judge necessary to secure the
avenues to his works. Should the enemy force the regiments of Colonels Wyllis, Meigs and Webb from their
works, it will be most advancive of the defence of the
hills, which command the Fort, that those corps retire
to defend to the last extremity, the avenues leading to
Colonel Putnam's redoubt, and the ground on which he
is now encamped, unless some manœuvre of the enemy
should induce the commanding officer of the post to detach some of those corps for the security of Putnam's
redoubt. If the ground on which the enemy intend to
land, or the route on which he advances to our works,
render it necessary to detach any corps to oppose him,
it must be taken from the works erecting by Colonel
Wyllis's, Meigs's or Colonel Webb's regiment, and not
from the Fort, or Putnam's redoubt, as in case of misfortune, the enemy's possessing the works first mentioned, will not be so fatal to the Post as his getting possession of the Fort, or Putnam's redoubt."

" P. S. The west face of the redoubt to be built near
the Long Barrack, to be eighteen feet [high], the north
and east faces fourteen feet; the stones to be kept a
much as possible from the upper part of the parapet of
the works."*

* Zodiac, Nov., 1835, 67.

Two days after the foregoing instructions were issued [13th], General McDougall wrote that "the Fort was so nearly enclosed as to resist a sudden attack of the enemy; but the heights near it were such that the Fort would not be tenable if the enemy should possess them. For this reason we are obliged to make some works on them.

"Mr. Kosciuszko is esteemed by those who have attended the works at West Point to have more practice than Colonel Radière,* and his manner of treating the people is more acceptable than that of the latter, which induced General Parsons and Governor Clinton to desire the former may be continued at West Point."†

On the 18th of April, Colonel Robert Troup wrote from Fishkill to General Gates, President of the Board of War, that the works at West Point were in a great state of forwardness; that Kosciuszko‡ was very much

---

* Colonel *Louis Deshaix de la Radière*, was one of four Engineers sent over from France by the Commissioners Franklin and Deane, and was employed by order of Congress. On the 8th of July, 1777, he was appointed Lieutenant-Colonel of Engineers, in accordance with a Treaty made in France, Feb. 13, 1777; promoted to the rank of Colonel, Nov. 17, 1777; retained at reorganization of the Army, January 1, 1779, and died in service, at New Windsor [in camp], on the 30th of October, 1779, in the 35th year of his age.*

† Writings of Washington, Sparks, V., 311.

‡ *Thaddeus Kosciuszko* was born in Lithuania, Poland, in 1756, and educated in the Military School at Warsaw. Under the auspices of Franklin, he came to America and was appointed an Aide to Washington. In October, 1776, he was appointed by Congress an Engineer, with the rank of Colonel. In this capacity he served as the Chief Engineer of the Northern Army against Burgoyne, and was subsequently assigned to the works in progress at West Point, where his reputation became greatly increased. He remained in service until the close of the War, receiving the thanks of Congress, and the grade of Brigadier-General by Brevet, Oct. 13, 1783. Returning to his native country in July, 1784, and becoming identified with the Polish Revolution, he there rose to the rank of Major-

* Phila. Packet, Nov. 9, 1779.

esteemed as an able engineer, and that the latter had
made many alterations in the works, which were univer-
sally approved.

The chain, he added, " will be put across the river
this week, and if the enemy let us alone two weeks
longer, we shall have reason to rejoice at their moving
this way."*

General under Poniatowski.   On the 10th of October, 1794, he was captured by
the Russians and confined at St. Petersburg.

After his liberation he visited the United States, in 1797, at which time Congress
presented him a grant of land.

He died in Switzerland, Oct. 16, 1817, and was buried at Warsaw, with almost
divine honors.—[Encyclopædia Americana.]

* Gates, MSS. N. Y. Hist. Col.

CHAPTER V.

PROGRESS OF OBSTRUCTING THE HUDSON.—RELIC OF THE BOOM AND
CHAIN.—LETTERS OF GENERAL GLOVER AND CAPTAIN MACHIN.—
DISPOSITION OF THE BOOM, CHAIN, ETC.—FORT ARNOLD.—DIS-
CREPANCIES IN THE NAME OF THE WORK.—ASSIGNMENT OF MAJOR-
GENERAL HEATH TO THE COMMAND.—HEAD-QUARTERS OF WASH-
INGTON ESTABLISHED AT WEST POINT.—WASHINGTON'S ORDERS.—
SEVERITY OF THE WINTER OF 1779–'80.—ASSIGNMENT OF GEN-
ERAL HOWE TO THE COMMAND OF THE POST.

THE obstructions to the navigation of the river had
suffered less from the delay before mentioned than the
Forts. Governor Clinton, in accordance with his promise to "render any assistance in his power," had
exercised considerable supervision over that branch of
the service; and had directed Captain Machin,* who had
been employed in completing the obstructions at Pollopel's Island, to take charge of the obstructions at West
Point also. The links of the Chain were brought from
the Stirling Iron Works to Captain Machin's Forges at
New Windsor, where they were joined together and
properly fastened to the logs which formed the support
of the Chain when completed.

From the Contract of Noble & Townsend, dated Feb.
2d, 1778, we are enabled to fix the time of the com-

---

* *Thomas Machin* was born in Staffordshire, England, 20th March, 1744. He
took up his residence in Boston, and, espousing the popular feeling of the time,
made one of the Tea-Party in 1773; was wounded at Bunker Hill, while acting as
Lieutenant of Artillery. He continued in service until the close of the War, having
attained the rank of Captain of Artillery, and died April 3d, 1816, at the age of
72.—[Sim's History of Schoharie County.]

6

mencement of the manufacture of the Chain. The letter of General Putnam, dated 13th February, same year, referring to "*Parts of the Boom intended to have been used at Fort Montgomery;*" the Plans accompanying the Proceedings of the Secret Committee, showing how the Chain and Boom were disposed at the latter place; the relic found in the river at West Point, in the summer of 1855; and the subjoined bill for the Boom at latter place, the last payment for which was made on the day the Chain was contracted for, demonstrate that the obstructions at West Point consisted of a Boom and a Chain, the former being *in front* of the latter.

The Relic here referred to consists of two logs, one of white wood and the other of white pine, about eighteen feet in length, and about fifteen inches in diameter, dressed in the centre in the form of an octagon, and rounded at the ends. These logs are united to each other by an iron band around each end, and two links of Chain of nearly two-inch bar iron, but which have evidently lost much of their original size from corrosion. This Boom extended the whole width of the river.

The Plan of its construction and disposition is represented by the accompanying engraving.

The strength of this Boom may be inferred from the bill of Noble & Townsend, which specifies 136 tons of iron wrought into booms, bolts, clips, chains, swivels, and bands, the very articles of which the relics are composed, and which were in part recovered. The following is the Bill for the Boom—that for the Chain has not been found.*

* A part of the chain at *Fort Montgomery*, near Pooplopen's Kill, was brought from Lake Champlain, having been designed to obstruct the River Sorel; the

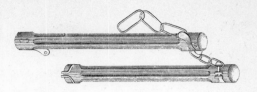

Portion of the Boom at West Point
During the Revolutionary War.

Arrangement of the great Boom and Chain at

West Point.

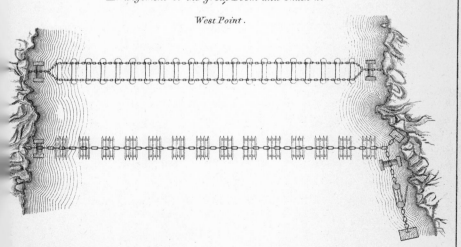

Quarter Master General, by Messieurs THOMAS MACHIN *and* JOHN NICOLL.

TO NOBLE & TOWNSEND, *Dr.*

1777.	No. Clips.	No. Chains.	No. Swivels.	No. Clevises.	No. Bolts.	No. Bands.	BY WHOM SENT.
Aug. 6..........	24		6		24		Daniel McCoun.
" 21..........	24		6		24		Francis Welding.
" "..........	20		5		20		Amos Mills.
" 23..........			3	6	6	6	Francis Welding.
Sept. 2..........	16	8			16		David Sutherland.
" 6..........	12	6			12		D. McCoun, as far as Thorn's.
" 17..........	12	8			12		Partrick Sutherland.
" 25..........	12	9			12	2	David Sutherland.
Oct. 2..........		9					Daniel McCoun.
Nov. 13..........	22		1	1	22		Solomon Curtis.
Still at Works		18			36		And one Lod was sent by the Clove that I have not got the number Clips, &c.
	142	58	21	7	184	8	

	£	s.	d.
To making 29,249 lbs. clips, chains, &c., at 1s. 3d.........	2,453	1	3

	Tons.	C.	Qrs.		£	s.	d.
The Wgt. is	17	10	1	of Boome Iron &c., at 140s.	2,453	1	3
June 19.	20	0	0	Bar Iron by my team, at 140s.	140	0	0
" 24.	30	0	14	do. do. at 140s.	210	17	6
" 26.	20	0	4	do. Col. Curlies, at 140s.	140	5	0
July 7.	20	0	0	do. our team, at 140s.	140	0	0
" "	8	0	14	do. Sam. Bruster, at 140s.	56	17	6
1778.							
Jan. 20.	10	0	14	do. by Mandeville, at 330s.	167	1	3
" 28.	10	1	14	do. do. do.	171	3	4
	Carting	78		of the Boome Bar Iron.......	12	16	0
					£5,945	3	1

			£	s.	d.
Augt.	By Cash paid Mr. Hawxhurst.....	£	500	0	0
Sept. 14.	By Cash................... ..		1,000	0	0
Nov. 14.	By Cash paid Nathaniel Satly		240	0	0
Feb. 2.	By Cash received by Col. Hughes...		4,027	0	0
			5,747		

	£	s.	d.
Ballance due.........................	£ 198	3	1

other part was made at Poughkeepsie, out of iron furnished from the Livingston Manor. [Am. Arch., V. III.] This chain was first stretched across the river in October, 1776. It broke by the action of accumulated water, and after repairing and adding new floats, it was finally placed in position in March, 1777, and remained until removed by the British at the capture of the Fort.—[Munsell's Hist. Series, No. V., 68.]

By the Bill of Captain Machin, which is also annexed,
it will be observed that he calls the Boom, *Chain Logs*,
and that they were taken to West Point on April 7th.
The Chain appears from the same Bill to have been
taken down on the 16th April, and stretched across the
river on the 30th.

The United States of America—To THOMAS MACHIN Dr. *for Travelling expenses and Money paid out in their service from January 1778 to Sept.
20 Agreeable to the Acount here under.*

				£	s.	d.
1778.	Jan.	1.	Exploring Hudsons River with 7 Men six days	6	10	0
"	do.	7.	Expences to Poughkeepse..................	1	10	6
"	do.	12.	Expences at Fish Kill four Days Detayned on the publick service......................	4	0	0
"	do.	16.	Expences on the Road to Chester to agree for the New Chain 3 Days	3	12	6
"	do.	20.	Expences Getting Timber for the Chain four Days...................................	4	0	0
"	do.	26.	Getting up Drift Timber...................	1	0	0
"	Feb'y	2.	Expences to New Burgh, New Malbrough and New Paltz 4 Days	4	4	6
"	do.	2.	For Ten Quire of Paper	2	10	0
"	do.	12.	Expences to New Paltz 3 Days, Hiring on Hand two Days	4	10	6
"	do.	17.	Expences to West Point	0	12	6
"	do.	24.	Expences when in persute of Deserters, for Myself and Men, at McDonelds	0	6	0
"	do.		at Capt. Smiths	4	8	0
"	do.		at Sidmans	5	10	0
"	do.		paid Onderdunk to Carry a Letter	1	12	0
"	March	5.	Getting the Logs to Drye for the Chain at New Paltz................................	3	10	0
"	do.	11.	Expences to Jews Creek, Plattor Kill and New Burgh, two days.......................	2	0	0
"	do.	14.	Expences to West Pt......................	0	12	0
"	do.	15.	Expences from West Pt.......	0	12	0
"	do.	16.	Expences to Fish Kill, Pough Keepse, New Paltz and New Malbrough, six Days	6	0	0
"	do.	24.	Expences to Fish Kill for Rigging	0	10	0
"	do.	26.	Expences Down the High Lands collecting Drift Timber	0	12	6
"	do.	29.	Expences to West Pt......................	0	8	0
"	April	7.	Expences *Getting Down the Chain Logs* with 40 Men, 4 Days	6	0	0

1778.

			£	s.	d.
"	April 12.	Expences to Chester	1	0	0
"	do. 16.	*Taking Down the Chain*	0	16	0
"	do. 19.	Expences to Jews Creek	0	10	0
"	do. 26.	Expences to Sterling	1	10	6
"	do. 30.	*While Getting the New Chain* across*	0	11	0
"	May 3.	Expences when Reascending the Lady Washington Galley at Kingston Creek, 20 Days.	9	10	6
"	June 1.	Expences to Peeks Kill	1	11	0
"	do. 4.	Expences to Pough Keepse	2	0	0
"	do. 6.	Expences to Fish Kill	0	12	0
"	do. 10.	Expences to Kingston	4	0	0
"	do. 19.	Expences to Peeks Kill with four men	2	0	0
"	do. 24.	Expences to Fish Kill with Ferrys	1	12	6
"	do. 29.	Expences to Pough Keepse and Ferrys	2	10	0
"	July 2.	Expences to Fish Kill	0	10	8
"	do. 10.	Expences to Pough Keepse and Ferrys with four men	8	16	0
"	do. 19.	Expences to Chester	1	0	6
"	do. 20.	Expences to Fish Kill	0	11	0
"	Augt. 1.	John Buchanons Bill for Travelling Expences.	5	1	0
"	do. 2.	William McBrides Bill for Travelling Expences in the service of the States	5	4	0
"		Joseph Holsteads Bill for Travelling Expences in the service of the States	3	6	4
"	do. 7.	Expences to Pough Keepse	2	0	0
"	do. 20.	Expences to Fish Kill	0	12	0
"	do.	Expences to Wit Plains	6	0	0
			£126	1	6

It will be observed that the Boom combined great strength with practicability. It was indeed the main obstruction, and placed below the Chain to receive the first shock of approaching vessels.

Contrary to the usual belief, the Boom must have been placed in position some time after the chain had been drawn across. The following letter confirms this opinion :—

* So called in the correspondence of the day, to distinguish it from the older chain at *Fort Montgomery.*

FORT ARNOLD, 2d *July*, 1778.

" Hon. Major-General GATES :—

"SIR :—These [enclosed] will inform your honor the
state of the garrison at this place, ' which is by no means
in a defensible condition, the works not near finished.'
Fort Putnam, ' on which the strength of the Post
depends, is far from being complete ; the Boom is not
yet come down, nor do I know when it will, or who to
apply to about it.'†   *   *   *   *   *   *

[Signed]   " JOHN GLOVER,

" *Brigadier-General.*"

The Chain designed to obstruct the river is fully described in the contract with Noble & Townsend, already
quoted, and its accuracy is confirmed by an examination of the portion yet remaining at West Point.

On the 20th of April, 1778, Captain Machin, the
Engineer, wrote General McDougall : " Lieutenant
Woodward, who I told you was at the Stirling Iron
Works inspecting the Chain, is now returned, and informs me that seventeen hundred feet of the great
Chain, which is more than equal to the breadth of the
river at the place last fixed upon, is now ready for use.
   *   *   *   The capson [capstan] and docks are
set up in the lower place ; the mud blocks are launched,
and only wait for good weather to carry them down.
   *   *   *   *   If the weather should be favorable, I am in hopes to take the Chain down *all fixed* in
about six days."‡   If the date of this letter has been
erroneously printed 20th, instead of 10th, the latter
will be found to agree with Captain Machin's bill.   The

chain was put together, " *all fixed*," at New Windsor, and floated down to West Point, and secured in its proper place in the latter part of April, 1778, as appears from the following extract from a letter from General Clinton to Captain Machin, dated Poughkeepsie, 3d of May, 1778 :—

" DEAR SIR :—I received your letter, and am happy to learn that the Chain is across the river, and that you had the good fortune to accomplish it so expeditiously and so much to your satisfaction."

The chain, as it appeared when placed in its position, is thus described by General Heath in his Memoirs :

" *November* 14*th*, 1780.—The great chain, which was laid across the Hudson at West Point, was taken up for the winter. It was done under the direction of Colonel Govion, Captain Buchanan, and Captain Nevers [Niven], with a strong detachment of the garrison, and with skill and dexterity. This chain was as long as the width of the river between West Point and Constitution Island, where it was fixed to great blocks on each side, and under the fire of batteries on both sides of the river. The links of this chain were probably 12 inches wide, and 18 inches long ; the iron about 2 inches square. This heavy chain was buoyed up by very large logs, of perhaps 16 or more feet long, a little pointed at the ends, to lessen their opposition to the force of the water on flood and ebb. The logs were placed at short distances from each other, the chain carried over them, and made fast to each by staples, to prevent their shifting ; and there were a number of anchors dropped at distances, with cables made fast to the chain, to give it a greater stability. The short bend of the river at this

place was much in favour of the chain's proving effectual; for a vessel coming up the river with the fairest
wind and strongest way must lose them on changing her
course to turn the Point; and before she could get
under any considerable way again, even if the wind was
fair, she would be on the chain, and at the same time
under a heavy shower of shot and shells."

"*April* 10*th*, 1781.—The great chain was hauled from
off the beach near the Red House at West Point, and
towed down to the blocks, in order to its being laid
across the river. About 280 men were ordered on this
duty."

"*April* 11*th*.—The chain was properly fixed with
great dexterity, and fortunately without any accident."

A great variety of traditions have been repeated, his-
torically, in reference to the obstructions at West Point,
and which may be fully explained when the precise
character of the latter is understood. For example, it
is said in the "Field-Book of the Revolution:" "Arnold
wrote a letter to André in a disguised hand and manner,
informing him that he had weakened the obstruction in
the river by ordering a link of the chain to be taken out
and carried to the smiths, under a pretence that it
needed repairs."

He assured his employer that the link would not be
returned to its place before the Forts should be in possession of the enemy.

A link could not have been thus displaced without removing that part of the obstruction altogether; but the
boom might easily have been weakened by taking out a
link from either side. Governor Clinton, it is further
said, walked across the river on the chain, and this

statement is repeated in the narratives of others as having been accomplished by them.

These traditions are easily reconciled by substituting the word Boom for that of the Chain. The Boom could readily be converted into a bridge, and it is not improbable that in its construction reference was had to this object, as it would afford facilities for the transport of troops from one side of the river to the other.

Another writer affirms that the Chain was removed every winter " by means of a large windlass," and that it made a " huge pile on the river-bank." It has also been represented that one end of the Chain and of the Boom being loosened from its fastenings, a windlass was employed to swing the whole around to the shore,—a process easily accomplished.

Those who have witnessed the movements of the immense fields of ice in December and March at West Point, ebbing and flowing with the tide, will perceive the impossibility of the Chain remaining attached by one end, floating as it would with the masses of ice; nor would securing both ends have prevented its destruction from the agency mentioned.

The first statement concerning its disposition is doubtless the correct one, and is sustained by the following, from "Heath's Memoirs:" "*April* 10.—The great Chain was hauled from off the beach near the Red House, at West Point, and towed down to the blocks, in order to its being laid across the river."

The Red House was situated in " Washington's Valley," where a safe anchorage on the flats, from the moving fields of ice, could be secured. The Chain and Boom were fastened when in position to cribbage-blocks, the remains of which are yet visible in the little cove just above the boat-house, on Constitution Island, and direct-

RELIC OF THE GREAT CHAIN, 1863.

ly across from the "Chain Battery," yet in existence, and near which the south end was secured. Sixteen links of the Chain yet remain united at West Point, including a swivel and clevis. Two of the largest links weigh respectively 130 and 129 pounds. Two of the smallest weigh 109 and 98 pounds, while the medium weight is 114 pounds. The whole Chain is said to have weighed 186 tons.*

A portion of the Chain [about thirty-four tons] was sold to the Cold Spring Foundry Association, and removed to New York many years ago, where it was worked up.

In removing the Boom finally, a portion of it became detached, and the logs, being water-soaked, sank to the bottom of the river, where, after being washed by the tide for eighty years, they have been in part recovered, and now serve the noble purpose of elucidating an

* Hist. Orange Co.—Eager.

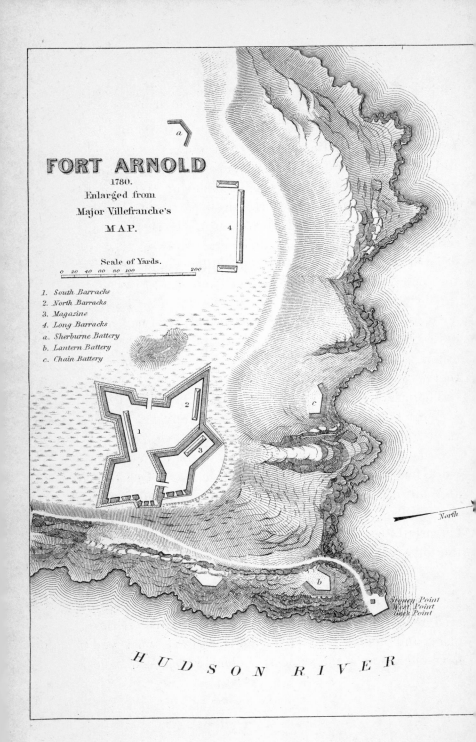

FORT ARNOLD
1780.
Enlarged from
Major Villefranche's
MAP.

Scale of Yards.
0 20 40 60 80 100   200

1. South Barracks
2. North Barracks
3. Magazine
4. Long Barracks
a. Sherburne Battery
b. Lantern Battery
c. Chain Battery

North

Stoney Point
West Point
Gees Point

H U D S O N   R I V E R

important point in the defensive operations at West Point, in the struggle for independence.

Returning to the fortifications at West Point, the work on which continued to progress under the general direction of General McDougall, superintended by Kosciuszko as engineer, until the assignment of General Gates to command the Northern department [Head-Quarters at Fishkill, and at Robinson's house], when, on the 22d of April, 1778, General McDougall was ordered to join the main army* at Valley Forge, leaving the command again under General Parsons.

The operations of the army in the Eastern department led this officer, at intervals, to the performance of duties in that quarter to which his brigade had been ordered ; but his nominal command was not changed thereby.

The principal work on the eastern angle of the Plain at West Point had, early in June, so far advanced as to receive its garrison, and was named *Fort Arnold.*†

Some discrepancy exists in regard to the name of this work, for Washington, while *en route* from Head-Quarters, at White Plains, to Fishkill, to examine the condition of the Highlands, first visited West Point, and to General Duportail, the Chief Engineer of the army, he addressed the following, dated,

"FORT CLINTON, WEST POINT, *Sept.* 19, 1778.

" SIR:—I have perused the memorial which you delivered relative to the defence of the North River at this place, and upon a view of it, highly approve what you have offered upon the subject. Colonel Kosciuszko, who

---

* Sparks, V., 333.　　　　† Gates, MSS. N. Y. Hist. Col.

was charged by Congress with the direction of the Forts and batteries, has already made such progress in the constructing of them as would render any alteration of them in the general plan a work of too much time, and the favorable testimony which you have given of Colonel Kosciuszko's abilities prevents any uneasiness on this head."*

Again, nine months later, he reported to Congress from the "Ringwood Furnace," the intention of the enemy to advance *viâ* Continental Village, and "gain, if possible, Nelson's Point opposite to *Fort Arnold*."†

Many other authorities conduce to the belief, now become general, that *Fort Arnold*, the original appellation, was continued until the defection of Arnold was made known, at which time every individual in the army seemed to vie with each other in the bitterness of their denunciations of him.

Then every memento of his existence was expunged from the garrison he had so basely undertaken to betray; and the name of *Fort Clinton* was bestowed in place of one unknown in history, save in the military correspondence and garrison orders of that day.

In response to the inquiries of the Commander-in-chief as to the disposition of the army for the winter, General Parsons urged, on the 17th of October, that six or seven thousand men be stationed at Fishkill, or near it; one thousand be posted as the garrison at West Point; three thousand near the Clove on the west side of the river; and the remainder, two thousand, in Connecticut.

---

* Writings of Washington, Sparks, VI., 67.
† Id., ibid., 269.

This arrangement was partially adopted; for in the assignment of the army to winter quarters in November, nine brigades were stationed on the west side of the Hudson, covering the lower part of New Jersey, and six on the east side of the river.

Three Massachusetts regiments were assigned, one to West Point, in addition to the garrison, and two to Fishkill and the Continental Village. The remaining three brigades were to cover the Sound in Connecticut, while the general Head-Quarters were located at Middlebrook.

The spring of 1779 brought no change in the disposition of affairs until the end of May, at which time Verplanck's and Stony Points were captured by the enemy, and directly afterwards the American army was concentrated in the Highlands.

General McDougall was again transferred to the command at West Point, on the 23d of June; the garrison at the time consisting of Larned's, Patterson's, and the Carolina Brigades; while at the same time, the command of the troops on the east side of the river was assigned to Major-General Heath.*

The main body of the army, under Major-General Putnam, was posted at Smith's Clove; Nixon's Brigade on Constitution Island; Parsons's, near the Robinson House, opposite West Point; and Huntington's, on the road above, leading to Fishkill.†

On the twenty-fifth of July, the Head-Quarters of the Commander-in-chief were transferred to West Point, and there remained until the twenty-eighth of November following.‡

* Heath's Memoirs, 205.   † Sparks, VI., 276, Writings of Washington.
‡ Heath's Memoirs, 224.

During the summer, the completion of the works around and above Fort Putnam was effected, there being no less than two thousand five hundred men on fatigue duty daily.*

It was at this period that the following General Orders, selected from the MS. Order Book of the General, were issued. Aside from the interest they impart to the locality, they portray in a strong manner the decision, patriotism, and religious character of Washington.†

[HEAD-QUARTERS, MOORE'S HOUSE],
"WEST POINT, *July* 4, 1779.

" This day being the anniversary of our glorious independence, will be commemorated by the firing of thirteen cannon from West Point, at one o'clock, P. M.

"THE COMMANDER-IN-CHIEF thinks proper to grant a general pardon to all prisoners in this Army under sentence of death. They are to be released from confinement accordingly."

[HEAD-QUARTERS, MOORE'S HOUSE],
"WEST POINT, *July* 10, 1779.

" At a Brigade General Court Martial, held by order of General Woodford, the 2d instant, Major Clark, President, *John Develin*, of the 8th Virg^a Regiment, was tried for ' Desertion in attempting to go to the enemy,' found guilty and sentenced to suffer death, two-thirds of the Court concurring therein. THE COMMANDER-IN-CHIEF confirms the sentence—but as it was previous to the pardon of the 4th instant, the prisoner is comprehended in the benefit of it."

---

* Sparks, VI., 304, Writings of Washington.
† The original MS. Order-Book, in Washington's own hand-writing, is in the possession of Professor WEIR, at the Military Academy.

[HEAD-QUARTERS, MOORE'S HOUSE],
"WEST POINT, *July* 16, 1779.

"THE COMMANDER-IN-CHIEF is happy to congratulate the Army on the success of our arms under Brigadier-General WAYNE, who, last night, with the Corps of light infantry, surprised and took the enemy's post at Stony Point with the whole garrison, cannon and stores, with very inconsiderable loss on our side. The General has not yet received the particulars of the affair; but he has the satisfaction to learn that the officers and men in general gloriously distinguished themselves in the attack. He requests the Brigadier and his whole Corps to accept his warmest thanks for the good conduct and signal bravery manifested upon the occasion."

[HEAD-QUARTERS, MOORE'S HOUSE],
"WEST POINT, *July* 18, 1779.

"At a General Court Martial held at Stony Point in the light infantry on the 17th inst., by order of Brigadier-General WAYNE, whereof Colonel MEIGS was President,

William Fitzgerald, of the 9th Penn[a] Regiment,
Isaac Wilson, of Colonel Bradford's,
John Williams, of the 4th Maryland,
Joseph Chace, of the 1st Connecticut, and
John Blackman, of Colonel BRADLEY'S—

were tried for 'Deserting to the enemy,' found guilty, and sentenced (two-thirds of the Court agreeing thereto) to suffer death. His Excellency the COMMANDER-IN-CHIEF confirms the sentences, and orders the above-mentioned criminals to be hanged this afternoon at 5 o'clock, in the flag bastion [at Stony Point]."

"HEAD-QUARTERS, MOORE'S HOUSE,
[WEST POINT,] *July* 29, 1779.

"Many and pointed orders have been issued against that unmeaning and abominable custom of swearing, notwithstanding which, with much regret, the General observes that it prevails, *if possible*, more than ever; his feelings are continually wounded by the oaths and imprecations of the soldiers whenever he is in hearing of them.

"The name of that Being from whose bountiful goodness we are permitted to exist and enjoy the comforts of life, is incessantly imprecated and profaned, in a manner as wanton as it is shocking. For the sake therefore of religion, decency, and order, the General hopes and trusts that officers of every rank will use their influence and authority to check a vice which is as unprofitable as it is wicked and shameful.

"If officers would make it an unavoidable rule to reprimand, and, if that does not do, punish soldiers for offences of this kind, it could not fail of having the desired effect."

To superintend the fatigue parties employed on the works, the following orders were issued :

[HEAD-QUARTERS, MOORE'S HOUSE],
"WEST POINT, *July* 30, 1779.

"Lieutenant Colonel HOWARD, with Lieutenant HUGO as his assistant, the redoubts assigned to General SMALLWOOD's brigade. Lieutenant Colonel WILLIAMS, with Captain GOSMER, Fort Putnam and Fort Webb. Colonel TUPPER, with Captain DREW, the works at the Point, in-

cluding Fort Clinton [Fort Arnold]. Captain HALL and
Captain TATUM, the works on Constitution Island.
Major TROOP, with Captain HOLMES, the works on the
east side of the river."

In the autumn of this year, the garrison consisted of
two Massachusetts brigades on the Point; the Connecticut line on the east side of the river, between Garrison's
and the Robinson House; and the North Carolina brigade on Constitution Island. The light infantry and
the Maryland line were encamped from Fort Montgomery northward, and Nixon's brigade occupied the
Continental Village.

In the assignment of the army to winter quarters, the
Massachusetts line were left to garrison West Point and
the Highlands, the command of which General Heath
assumed on the 28th of November.*

The winter of 1779 and 1780 was one of unexampled
severity at West Point. The troops, except those on
garrison duty, were cantonized in huts two miles back of
West Point, on the "public meadows," and at "Budd's,"
on the east side of the river. So intense was the cold,
that for a period of forty days, no water dripped from
the roofs which sheltered them.†

The snow was four feet deep on a level, requiring a
heavy force to be constantly engaged in keeping open
the communication with the six or seven redoubts built
and building. Twice during the winter the North
Redoubt barely escaped total destruction by fire. The
parapet, built of logs, covered with earth, and difficult
of access, burned nearly three days before the fire could

* Heath's Memoirs.   † Sim's Hist. Schoharie Co.
7

be extinguished. The South Barrack in Fort Arnold was entirely consumed, with a large quantity of stores; but the adjacent buildings were saved by the indefatigable labor of the garrison, and the personal efforts of General Patterson.*

On the 21st of February, General Heath obtained a leave of absence, and being shortly afterward appointed by the State of Massachusetts to superintend the recruiting service, the command at West Point was transferred, early in April, to General Robert Howe. Throughout the spring of 1780, the movements of the enemy so fully impressed the Commander-in-chief with their intention to assail West Point, that he directed Generals McDougall and Steuben to repair thither. The garrison was reinforced, and the army moved up to cover the entrance of the Highlands.

* Heath's Memoirs.

CHAPTER VI.

Major-General Arnold ordered to Relieve General Howe.—Disaffection of Arnold.—Disheartening Condition of the American Cause.—Advantages of West Point if Captured by the Enemy.—Sir Henry Clinton's Idea.—The Secret Correspondence with Arnold.—Appointment to meet John Anderson.—The "Robinson House," and its Original Proprietor.—The Meeting between Arnold and Anderson Thwarted.—A Flag of Truce from the Vulture, and its Purport.—Smith's House.—Joshua Hett Smith.—Meeting between Arnold and Anderson.—Attempt of Anderson to Return to New York by Land.—Cow-boys and Skinners.—Capture of Anderson.

On the 3d of August, Major-General Arnold was instructed from general head-quarters at Peekskill, to proceed to West Point and relieve General Robert Howe of the command of that Post, and its dependencies. In pursuance of this order, Arnold arrived on the 5th, and established his Head-Quarters at the "Robinson House."*

Real and imaginary grievances had already unsettled

* On the 8th of August, Arnold wrote Washington: "I wish your Excellency would be kind enough to order Mr. Erskine [Geographer to the Army] to send me a map of the Country from this place to New York, particularly on the east side of the river, which would be very useful to me." * * * * * "Major Villefranche has surveyed the works at West Point, and informs me that there is a vast deal to do to complete them." * * *—[Correspondence of the Revolution, III., 57.—Sparks.]

this officer's attachment to the cause of the Revolution, and later evidences have brought to light the fact, that he sought this command with a predetermination to abandon the cause, and betray his trust and associates into the hands of the enemy. "The moment was truly a favorable one. The English were weary of the continued strife, and really anxious for peace with America on any terms that might not involve Independence. The mess-rooms no more, as in Howe's days, echoed the toast of 'A glorious war, and a long one!' The Royal officers now pledged 'A speedy accommodation of our present unnatural disputes!' On the other hand, America too was tired of the war. A cloud of witnesses of the best authority, testify to the probability of a majority of our people being desirous of accommodating the quarrel, and of reuniting with England on conditions of strict union, if not of mediated dependence. The public chest was empty. The miserable bubble by which it had hitherto been recruited was on the verge of explosion, and the Continental paper-money, always really worthless, though long sustained by the force of laws and bayonets, was now rapidly approximating its ultimate value. The ranks were supplied with children, whose service for nine months was bought for $1,500 apiece. 'Hundreds even of the staff officers,' said Greene, in May, 1780, 'were ruined by the public charges they had been forced to incur, while every obstacle was opposed to a settlement of their accounts, lest their demands on government should become fixed.' 'However important our cause, or valuable the blessings of liberty,' he continues to Washington, 'it is utterly impossible to divest ourselves of our private feelings while we are contending for them.' ' It is obvious that the bulk of the people are weary of the war,' said Reed, in August. ' There never has been a stage of the war,' said Washington, ' in which the dissatisfaction has been so general and so alarming.' The army, ill-paid, ill-fed, ill-clad, avenged its sufferings and its wrongs by such means as lay in its power. Martial law was published to procure its supplies in States that had not a hostile ensign within their borders. Regiment after regiment rose in mutiny ; nor could the rope or the scourge check the devastation and desertion that marked the army's course. At this very period, despite the repeated sentences of courts-martial, and the general order for the officer of the day, on his individual authority, to flog any straggler within the limit of fifty lashes, we find in Washington's own words the most unwelcome evidences of the necessities of his followers, and their consequent marauds along the banks of the Hudson.

" Not until the end of August, was the pay due in the preceding March forthcoming. In September, Hamilton found the army a demoralized, undisciplined mob ; disliking the nation for its neglect, dreaded by the nation for its oppressions. Our chiefs, with mortification and regret, confessed the day impending, when, unless the war was carried on by foreign troops and foreign treasure, America must come to terms.

" ' Send us troops, ships, and money,' wrote Rochambeau to Vergennes, ' but do not depend upon these people, nor upon their means.' Yet it was known that the aid of France and Spain was merely sporadic ; and there was now reason to fear that, without some great stroke on our part, the former would soon abandon us as a profitless ally, and make her own peace with Britain.

"Congress too, rent by faction and intrigue, no longer commanded the entire confidence of the Whigs. Its relations with the States were not satisfactory, and with the army were decidedly bad. Jealousy on the one hand, aversion and distrust on the other, daily widened the unacknowledged breach. * * * The party hostile to the Chief—deep-rooted in New England, and pervading Jersey, Pennsylvania, and Virginia—which, from the beginning of the war to its end, dreaded lest the tyranny of a Commodus should lurk behind the wise virtues of a Pertinax, though foiled in a former effort to displace him, still retained power to hamper his movements and embarrass his designs. It was very evident that his removal would be the signal for the army's dissolution, and the inevitable subjection of the infant State; but it was yet feasible to limit his powers, deny his requirements, and in a hundred ways exhibit a distrust of his capacity or integrity that would have caused many soldiers to throw up the command."

"Much of this was known to the British, and the reduction of West Point had long been their hope; but to accomplish it without loss of life would indeed have been a triumph for Sir Henry Clinton, and a most brilliant conclusion to the campaign. Mr. Sparks has clearly mapped out the advantages he must have contemplated in this contingency. In the first place, the mere acquisition of a fortress so important, with all its dependencies, garrison, stores, magazines, vessels, &c., was an achievement of no secondary magnitude. The supplies gathered here by the Americans were very great, and, once lost, could not have been readily, if at all, restored. The works were esteemed our tower of salvation, an American Gibraltar, impregnable to an army 20,000 strong. Even though yet unfinished, they had cost three years' labor of the army, and $3,000,000, and were thought an unfailing and secure resort in the last extremity. But the ulterior consequences of its possession were of even greater importance. It would have enabled Sir Henry to have checked all trade between New England and the Central and Southern States. It was in Washington's eyes the bolt that locked this communication. The Eastern States, chiefly dependent for their breadstuffs on their sisters in the Union, were commercial rather than agricultural communities; and the power that at once commanded the seaboard and the Hudson might easily bring upon them all the horrors of famine.

" From Canada to Long Island Sound, a virtual barrier would have shut out New England from its supplies, as the wall of Antonine barred the free and rugged Caledonians from the Roman colonies and the south of Britain. But even these advantages were of less moment than those more immediate. The French, under D'Estaing, had already bickered with the Americans. It was hoped that similar ill-blood might arise in Rochambeau's camp, and be fanned into a flame. It was shrewdly and correctly suspected by Clinton, that the allies meditated a combined attack on New York. To execute this movement, with West Point strongly garrisoned by the British, would be impossible ; and nothing was more likely than that the French should have all their jealousies aroused by the defection of one of the most distinguished

American generals, and the surrender of the most important American citadel, on the very ground of repugnance to the alliance. Ignorant of the extent of the plot, it would be difficult for them to repose in confidence with an American army by their side, and a British before them and in their rear.' ' My idea,' said Sir Henry Clinton, ' of putting into execution this concerted plan with General Arnold with most efficacy, was to have deferred it till Mr. Washington, co-operating with the French, moved upon this place to invest it; and that the Rebel magazines should have been collected and formed in their several dépôts, particularly that at West Point. 'General Arnold surrendering himself, the forts, and garrisons at this instant, would have given every advantage that could have been desired. Mr. Washington must have instantly retired from King's bridge, and the French troops on Long Island would have been consequently left unsupported, and probably would have fallen into our hands.' "

A secret correspondence had been commenced as early as 1779, between John Anderson, who afterwards proved to be Major John André, the Adjutant-General of the British army, and Arnold, in which the latter wrote over the pseudonym of " *Gustavus*." The value of the information imparted in this way had, at an early day, attracted the attention of the British Commander, and led him to infer the character and rank of the writer.

The kind of information thus obtained was greatly enhanced in importance by the assignment of Arnold to the command at West Point; and that the correspondence was regular and rapid will be seen from the following letter, written five days after Arnold arrived at his station :

"*August 30th*, 1780.

"SIR:—On the 24th instant, I received a note from you without date, in answer to mine of the 7th of July; also a letter from your house of the 24th July, in answer to mine of the 15th, with a note from Mr. B—— of the 30th of July; with an extract of a letter from Mr. J. Osborn of the 24th. I have paid particular attention to the contents of the several letters: had they arrived earlier you should have had my answer sooner. A variety of circumstances has prevented my writing you before. I expect to do it very fully in a few days, and to procure you an interview with Mr. M——e, when you will be able to settle your commercial plan, I hope, agreeable to all parties. Mr. M——e assures me that he is still of opinion that his first proposal is by no means unreasonable, and makes no doubt when he has had a conference with you that you will close with it. He expects when you meet, that you will be fully authorized from your House; that the risks and profits of the copartnership may be fully and clearly understood.

"A speculation might at this time be easily made to some advantage with *ready money*, but there is not the quantity of goods *at market* which your partner seems to suppose, and the number of speculators below, I think, will be against your making an immediate purchase. I apprehend goods will be in greater plenty and much cheaper in the course of the season: both dry and wet are much wanted, and in demand at this juncture: Some quantities are expected in this part of the country soon. Mr. M——e flatters himself that in the course of ten days he will have the pleasure of seeing you: he re-

quests me to advise you, that he has ordered a draft on
you in favor of our mutual friend S——y for £300,
which you will charge on account of the *tobacco*.

"I am, in behalf of Mr. M——e & Co.,

"Your obedient, humble Servant,

"Gustavus."

"Mr. John Anderson, Merchant.

"To the Care of James Osborne—to be left at the Reverend Mr. Odell's,
New York."

"Translated from its commercial phraseology into
plain English, this letter teaches us that on the 7th of
July, Arnold had declared the probability of his obtaining the command of West Point, and the tour of inspection he had just made of its defences; and had written
on the 15th, when the project connected with the arrival
of the French may have been mentioned. The terms on
which he was to surrender were also doubtless named.
To these Anderson had replied in two notes; and if we
suppose B. stood for Beverly Robinson, and J. Osborn
for Sir H. Clinton, communications from these were
apparently conveyed. It may be easily gathered that
the present strength of the garrison, both in militia
and Continentals, was indicated, and that the feasi-
bility of a *coup de main*, and the danger of the troops at
Verplanck's retarding such an undertaking, were suggested.

"It will be observed, that Gustavus writes as agent for
Mr. M——e; elide the dash and we have Mr. Me—in
other words, *himself*."

"It became necessary at this instant" [says Sir
Henry Clinton], "that the secret correspondence under
feigned names, which had so long been carried on,

should be rendered into certainty, both as to the person being General Arnold, commanding at West Point, and that in the manner in which he was to surrender himself, the forts, and troops to me, it should be so conducted, under a concerted plan between us, as that the King's troops sent upon this expedition should be under no risk of surprise or counterplot; and I was determined not to make the attempt but under such particular security.

"I knew the ground on which the forts were placed, and the contiguous country, tolerably well, having been there in 1777; and I had received many hints respecting both from General Arnold. But it was certainly necessary that a meeting should be held with that officer for settling the whole plan. My reasons, as I have described them, will, I trust, prove the propriety of such a measure on my part. General Arnold had also his reasons, which must be so very obvious as to make it unnecessary for me to explain them.

"Many projects for a meeting were formed, and consequently several attempts made, in all of which General Arnold seemed extremely desirous that some person, who had my particular confidence, might be sent to him—some man, as he described it in writing, of *his own mensuration*.

"I had thought of a person under this important description, who would gladly have undertaken it, but that his peculiar situation at the time, from which I could not release him, prevented him from engaging in it. General Arnold finally insisted that the person sent to confer with him should be Adjutant-General Major André, who indeed had been the person on my

part, who managed and carried on the secret correspondence."*

On the 7th of September, Anderson wrote Colonel
Sheldon, the commander of an American cavalry outpost [page 135, Proceedings of the Board], that he
desired permission to meet a friend near his lines on
Sunday, the 11th, at 12 o'clock.

This letter was artfully designed to secure two objects; for presuming, as was the case, that the note
would be transmitted to the Commanding General, it informed Arnold that the writer sought an interview with
him, and afforded the former an opportunity to instruct
Colonel Sheldon to escort Anderson to head-quarters,
in case he should arrive within the American lines.

Arnold accordingly notified Sheldon that he expected
to meet a person at his quarters, with whom he could
open a regular "channel of intelligence;" to which Sheldon replied, pleading his inability to be present at the
meeting with the emissary, on account of ill health, and
advising Arnold to meet him at Dobb's Ferry at the
appointed time.

Arnold left the Robinson House in his barge on the
afternoon of the 10th, and reaching Haverstraw, passed
the night at the house of Joshua Hett Smith. On the
next morning, he proceeded in the barge down the river
twenty miles to Dobb's Ferry, where lay the Vulture,
which had brought up Anderson and Colonel Beverly
Robinson.

The "Robinson House" yet stands in the Highlands
on the east side of the Hudson, two miles below West

* Clinton to Lord G. Germain.—Sparks's Arnold, 168.

Point. Three buildings joined together, extending east
and west, and fronting north and south, constitute the
mansion. Nearest to the river is the farm-house, one
story high. Next east are the main buildings, each
two stories high. A neat piazza surrounds the eastern
structure on the north, east, and south sides, which

THE "ROBINSON HOUSE"—SOUTH FRONT.

extends also along the south side of the central building.

The house now belongs to Colonel Thomas B. Arden,
of the U. S. Volunteer Service, who, in making the
needful repairs, has in no way changed its original appearance, either inside or out. The same low ceiling,
with large bare beams overhead; the same panel-work
and polished tiles adorn the fireplace without a man-
tel; and the absence of all ornament, so characteristic of
progress in architecture, preserves complete the interest
which the stirring scenes of the Revolution have flung
around the Robinson House.

" Beverly Robinson was a gentleman of high standing. His father, speaker of the Virginia legislature, was an early friend of Washington, whose modesty and valor he complimented in language that is yet remembered. The son was married to a great heiress of the day, the daughter of Frederic Philipse, and with her acquired large estate on the Hudson. At his house Washington had met, and sought to win, the younger sister and co-heiress. His country-seat in the Highlands, surrounded by pleasant orchards and gardens, and environed by sublime scenery, was the head-quarters of the American generals, who, considering it public property, since its owner was in arms for the crown, were wont to use it as their own. It was now Arnold's, and sometimes Washington's Head-Quarters.

" Robinson's circumspect and cautious character was thought needful to check the buoyancy of his comrade, and he was likewise fully acquainted with the pending negotiations. Indeed, it was probably through him that Arnold's first overtures were made. But the large acquaintance and interests he had in the region, and his knowledge of the country, made his presence additionally desirable.

" The interview was to occur on the east side of the river, at Dobb's Ferry; but as Arnold drew near, one of those circumstances which the pious man calls providence, and the profane calls luck, prevented an encounter, that must in all human probability have resulted in the consummation of the plot. Some British gunboats were stationed at the place, which opened such a fire on the American barge that Arnold, though twice he strove hard to get on board, was put in deadly peril of his life and obliged to fall back. How this came to pass without Robinson's intervention we cannot imagine; for it is impossible but that an intimation from him would have caused the firing to cease. Or had he repaired, with Anderson and his flag, to meet the solitary barge that evidently belonged to an officer of rank, an interview might at once have been effected in the most plausible manner in the world. The circumstances of the case would have rendered it easy for Arnold to publicly say that he would, since they were thus thrown together, waive the prerogative of rank that otherwise might have induced him to refer the enemy's flag to an officer of an equal grade, and to grant an interview on shore. The condition of Robinson's estate was a ready pretext for even a private reception, and there was no obstacle to Anderson being of the party. In the hope of being thus followed, Arnold retired to an American post on the west shore, above the Ferry, where he remained till sundown, but no flag came. It is scarcely possible that the statement attributed to Rodney could have had an actual foundation here. At all events, he went back that night to West Point, and his coadjutor returned to New York. The failure of the meeting can only be accounted for by supposing that the English messengers were on the east bank of the Ferry when Arnold was fired at, and could not interfere in season. They could hardly have been on the Vulture, since its boat was lowered to pursue the American barge, which it did so far and so vigorously as to have nearly captured it."

To avoid suspicion, Arnold wrote on the same day, dating his letter " Dobb's Ferry," to the Commander-in-chief, informing him of his trip to that point for the purpose of establishing a beacon on the mountain, and a set of signals to give the alarm, in case the enemy came up the river.

On the 16th of September the Vulture again appeared up the river, with Colonel Robinson on board, and anchored off Teller's Point, in full view of King's Ferry, and about fifteen miles from Arnold's quarters. From this anchorage, on the 17th, under a flag of truce, and with the pretext of desiring to inquire about his property affairs, he thus managed to signify to Arnold his presence, and wish to renew negotiations with him.

On Monday, the 18th, Washington and his staff arrived at King's Ferry, and crossed the Hudson with Arnold in the ferry-barge, on his way to meet the French Commander at Hartford.

With the Vulture in full view, the object of her visit was discussed, during which Arnold exhibited the letter of Robinson, but only received the strong disapproval of his Commander upon the propriety of the proposed interview. The night was passed at Peekskill, and on Tuesday, the 19th, Arnold parted from Washington for the last time, and returned to the Robinson House, leaving the Chief to pursue his journey. The same day, Arnold replied to Robinson's note, and declined to hold further communication with him in relation to private affairs, declaring that all such ought to be referred to the civil, and not to the military authorities; but within the official letter were enclosed and sealed two notes, one for Colonel Robinson, and the other from *"Gustavus"* to John Anderson.

To Robinson he wrote that he would send a trusty person to the Vulture, or to Dobb's Ferry, with a boat and a flag of truce, on Wednesday night, the 20th. To Anderson he signified his wish to meet him, and that a person would be at Dobb's Ferry, on the east side of the river, on the night of the 20th, who would conduct him to a place where a meeting could be held in safety.

These letters were forwarded to New York, and on the morning of the 20th, Anderson left the city and arrived at Dobb's Ferry in the afternoon, where, instead of remaining, he proceeded on up to Teller's Point, and went on board the Vulture at 7 o'clock that evening. The night passed, and no person appeared.

On Thursday, the 21st, an excuse was found to send a flag to the shore, with a complaint signed by the captain of the vessel, but countersigned by John Anderson as his secretary, and by this expedient the presence of the latter in the vessel was made known to Arnold.

A ride of thirteen miles south from West Point, on the Hudson River Railroad, carries the traveller to Verplanck's Point, on the east side of the river. King's Ferry, the principal channel of communication between the Eastern and Southern States, crossed from this point to Stony Point, on the west side. Two and a half miles below Stony Point is yet to be seen a commodious two-story stone house, standing on an elevated position, and commanding an extensive view southward of Haverstraw Bay and Teller's Point. Joshua Hett Smith, the former occupant of this mansion, was a man of education and ample estate. Politically opposed to the Convention which adopted the Declaration of Independence, he was, with his family in general, classed among those who were not cordial in their attachment to the American cause.

8

He was hospitable and courteous in his demeanor; and as no stronger evidence existed of his disaffection than suspicion, his society, and his services in obtaining supplies, made him acceptable to General Howe, Arnold, and other American officers. To this man Arnold had recourse, to assist him in the fulfilment of the plan which thus far had so signally failed.

To what extent he was admitted into Arnold's confidence will never probably be known; but under the pretence that an agent from the enemy was to communicate valuable information to the American Commander, Arnold induced him to become the messenger before designated to proceed to Dobb's Ferry, on the night of the 20th September. Why he failed in his mission at that time does not appear; but having determined to select Smith's house for the interview, should concealment become necessary, Smith's family were sent on a visit to Fishkill; and on Thursday, the 21st, at about midnight, Smith, with two of his tenants as boatmen, was despatched by Arnold without a flag to the Vulture, while himself, accompanied by Smith's negro servant, both mounted, proceeded to an appointed spot some two miles from the house, down on the river's bank.

A favorable tide, and a calm sea in the bay, soon brought the boat with muffled oars alongside of the Vulture. The object of his mission was quickly made known, and after a slight delay, Anderson, in his uniform, entered the boat with Smith, and was swiftly rowed to the western bank. On its arrival Arnold was found— " *hid among the firs*"—and, leaving Anderson in consultation with him, Smith was dismissed, to return to the boat and its oarsmen.

The interview was prolonged until the morning of Friday approached, when Smith sought the conspirators and proclaimed that concealment was no longer practicable.

The difficulty of returning to the Vulture was here increased by an insurmountable obstacle : the boatmen, weary, and alarmed at the risk before them, positively refused to act, nor were the inducements or threats of Smith or Arnold sufficient to change their purpose.

Leaving Smith and the remainder of the party to return by' the boat to the starting-place, Arnold, accompanied by Anderson, mounted on the servant's horse, returned to Smith's house.

The day had fully dawned when Smith joined his two companions, and while waiting within the house for breakfast to be served, attention was directed down the river by the report of artillery. The proximity of the Vulture, and her prolonged stay so near the works at Verplanck's Point, aroused the anger of the vigilant commander,* who, planting a field-piece upon the lesser of the two promontories known as Gallows Point, opened such an incessant fire upon the vessel that for a time she seemed to have been set on fire by the shot.

From the window of Smith's house, the Vulture was

---

* The ammunition for this purpose was furnished from West Point, accompanied by the following letter to Colonel Livingston, commanding at Verplanck's Point:—

"WEST POINT, *Sept. 20th*, 1780.

"SIR:—I have sent you the ammunition you requested, but at the same time I wish there may not be a wanton waste of it, as we have little to spare. Firing at a ship with a four-pounder is, in my opinion, a waste of powder; as the damage she will sustain is not equal to the expense. Whenever applications for ammunition are made, they must be through the commanding officer of artillery, at the Post where it is wanted.

"I am, Sir, yours, &c.,   JOHN LAMB."
[Life John Lamb, 258.—Leake.]

seen to swing off her anchorage, and slowly drop down
the river with the ebbing tide.   Breakfast was despatched,
when the two plotters, ascending to a chamber, passed
the greater part of the day in perfecting their plans.
Late in the afternoon, Arnold, bidding an adieu to his
companion, returned in his barge to the Robinson House.

REGION OF ARNOLD'S TREACHERY.

The shadows of evening sunset were fast disappearing
when Smith, accompanied by Anderson, disguised in a
coat belonging to the former, rode forth on horseback

and crossed King's Ferry, in the hazardous attempt to reach New York by the land route, on the east side of the river.

Furnished with the necessary passes, in Arnold's own writing, to go by any of the practicable routes, the party pursued the road in a northeast direction to the little village of Crompond, six miles from Verplanck's Point, where they passed the night. On the morning of Saturday, the 23d, the journey was resumed in a direction almost due south, until Pine's Bridge, crossing the Croton River, was reached, where Smith, separating from his companion, returned tó the Robinson House, dined with Arnold, and pushed on up to join his family at Fishkill the same night.

At this time a local war raged over the thirty miles of territory along the river separating the two armies, between two factions known as the *Cow-Boys* and *Skinners*.

The former ostensively affected to be in the interest of the enemy, and the latter were supposed to be identified with the Americans. Both parties were in truth unprincipled robbers and perfidious villains, plundering alike the inhabitants, the enemy, each other, Congress, and the King.

The country below Pine's Bridge, in the direction of Tarrytown having been represented to the travellers at Crompond as infested with *Cow-Boys*, Anderson, after parting from Smith, resolved to leave the road to White Plains, whither his pass took him, and trust himself on the Tarrytown road, doubtless in the belief that protection would be secured from partisans in the friendly faction.

He had advanced so far as to have left the Bridge some ten miles behind him, when, descending a hill, and crossing a little rivulet at its foot, three armed men sprang from the bushes and interrupted his further progress.

CHAPTER VII.

NARRATIVE OF ONE OF THE CAPTORS.—ANDERSON CONVEYED TO
NORTH CASTLE.—THE PAPERS FOUND ON HIS PERSON.—ANDER-
SON'S APPEARANCE DESCRIBED.—HE IS TRANSFERRED TO THE
"ROBINSON HOUSE."—ARRIVAL OF WASHINGTON.—THE PLOT DIS-
COVERED.—FLIGHT OF ARNOLD.—ANDRÉ CONVEYED TO WEST
POINT AND FROM THENCE TO TAPPAN.—BOARD OF GENERAL OFFI-
CERS CONVENED.

FROM the many published accounts of the scene
which ensued, the narrative of David Williams is
selected, part of which is sworn evidence, and the
remainder given by him at a later day.

"Myself, Isaac Van Wart, and John Paulding were
lying in the bushes in the morning, about 9 or 10
o'clock, on Saturday, the 23d of September last, about
half a mile, as near as I recollect, above Tarrytown,
on the east side of the North River.   Several persons came along whom we knew, and let pass, and
presently came along a person whom we told Mr.
Paulding to stop.   Mr. Paulding stepped out and presented his piece to his breast, and bid him stand, which
he did.   The person said, ' Gentlemen, I hope you belong to our party.'   Mr. Paulding made answer, ' What
party ?'   He said, ' The lower party,' which Mr.
Paulding told him we did.   The person said, ' I am
glad to see you ; I am an officer in the British service,
and have now been on particular business in the coun

try, and I hope you will not detain me.' And for a token, to let us know he was a gentleman, he pulled out his watch. Mr. Paulding told him to dismount, on which the person found out that we belonged to the upper party. He said, 'My God, I must do any thing to get along,' on which he pulled out General Arnold's pass, and gave it to Mr. Paulding, who read it, on which Mr. Paulding again told him to dismount. The person said he was to pass down as far as Dobb's Ferry, and was to meet another gentleman there, and was to get intelligence for General Arnold; he told us we would bring ourselves into trouble if we did not let him go." Williams further says : " We were about allowing him to proceed, and he was reining his horse into the road, when Paulding, in an under-tone, exclaimed : ' D—n him, I do not like his looks.' He was then ordered again to stop, and one of the party asked him what he had done with the paper he had in his hand when first discovered (this, it afterwards appeared, was a sketch of the route). The question produced a momentary hesitation, and his embarrassment being noticed by the party, he was told that the circumstance of his first avowing himself to be of the lower party, required their searching his person. They led his horse into a field, partly covered with underwood. His person was strictly searched, including his hat, coat, vest, shirt, and breeches ; even his hair, which was done up in a queue, in the fashion of the day, was untied without creating any unusual anxiety in André until he was told to take off his boots, when he changed color, and manifested fear in his countenance. The papers were then discovered. He had eighty dollars in Continental money."

Mr. Williams, in his sworn statement, goes on to say: " Mr. Paulding looked at the papers, and said he was a spy. We made him dress himself, and I asked him what he would give us to let him go; he said he would give us any sum of money. I asked him whether he would give us his horse, saddle, bridle, watch, and one hundred guineas, upon which he said yes, and told us he would direct it to any place, even if it was that very spot, so that we could get it. I asked him whether he would not give us more; he said he would give us any quantity of dry goods, or any sum of money, and bring it to any place that we might pitch upon, so that we might get it; upon which Mr. Paulding answered no; if you would give us ten thousand guineas you shall not stir one step. While the search was going on the horse had strayed some distance, grazing on the underbrush; when it was completed, one of us led up the horse, and he was permitted to mount, and he was then taken to the military post commanded by Colonel Jameson."*

North Castle at this time was a cavalry outpost, and, with some Connecticut militia, constituted Lieutenant-Colonel Jameson's command. This officer, following the usual channel of military correspondence, despatched the captive with a note to his immediate commanding officer (Arnold), detailing the occurrence; but the papers being, as he expressed it, " of a very dangerous tendency," were forwarded to the Commander-in-chief, in the hope of intercepting him on his return from Hartford.

Late in the afternoon, Major Benjamin Tallmadge, an officer of rare merit and sterling patriotism, arrived at

---

*Capture of André.—John Paulding, Esq., N. Y. Hist. Mag., 334, Nov., 1857.

the Post, and, learning the whole occurrence, prevailed with much entreaty on Jameson to order the return of Anderson, who was brought back that night; while the note to Arnold, to the chagrin of Tallmadge, was permitted to proceed to its destination. This error* in the decision of Jameson saved the life of Arnold.

The following papers were in the possession of Anderson. All, except the first, were found disposed inside of his stockings and beneath his feet.

These documents have been carefully corrected from the originals, which are preserved in the N. Y. State Library at Albany.

No. 1.

[In Arnold's handwriting.]

"HEAD QUARTERS ROBINSON'S HOUSE,
"*Sept.* 22*d*, 1780.

"Permit Mr. John Anderson to pass the Guards to the White Plains, or below if he Chuses. He being on Public Buisness by my Direction.

"B. ARNOLD, M. Gen'¹."

No. 2.

[In Arnold's handwriting.]

"W'ST POINT, *September* 5*th*, 1780.

"*Artillery Orders.*

"The following disposition of the corps is to take place in case of an alarm: [The enemy were to give the alarm.]

---

* On the 27th of September, Jameson wrote Washington: "I am very sorry that I wrote to General Arnold. I did not think of a British ship being up the river, and expected that, if he was the man he has since turned out to be, he would come down to the troops in this quarter, in which case I should have secured him." —[Correspondence of the Revolution, III., 102.—Sparks.]

" Capt. Dannills with his Comp'y at Fort Putnam, and to detach an officer with 12 men to Wyllys's Redoubt, a Non Commissioned officer with 3 men to Webb's Redoubt, and the like number to Redoubt No. 4.

" Capt. Thomas and Company to repair to Fort Arnold.

", Captain Simmons and Company to remain at the North and South Redoubts, at the East side of the River, until further Orders.

" Lieutenant Barber, with 20 men of Capt. Jackson's Company, will repair to Constitution Island; the remainder of the Company, with Lieut. Mason's, will repair to Arnold.

" Capt. Lieut. George and Lieut. Blake, with 20 men of Captain Treadwell's Company, will Repair to Redoubt No. 1 and 2; the remainder of the Company will be sent to Fort Arnold.

" Late Jones's Company, with Lieut. Fisk, to repair to the South Battery.

" The Chain Battery, Sherburn's Redoubt, and the Brass Field pieces, will be manned from Fort Arnold, as Occation may require.

" The Commissary and Conductor of Military Stores will in turn wait upon the Commanding Officer of Artillery for Orders.

" The artificers in the garrison, (agreeable to former Orders), will repair to Fort Arnold, and there receive further Orders from the Command'g Officer of Artillery.

" S. BAUMAN,* Major Comm't Artillery."

* Major Sebastian Bauman was, early in 1776, appointed a captain of artillery. He served throughout the war, and was afterwards the Postmaster of the city

This document gave the British full information of what would be the disposition of the Americans on the occasion; and as Sir Henry Clinton and many of his officers were acquainted with the ground, they would know at what particular points to make their attacks.

No. 3.

[In Arnold's handwriting.]

"ESTIMATE OF FORCES AT W'ST POINT AND ITS DEPENDENCIES,
September 13, 1780.

" A brigade of Massachusetts Militia, and two regiments of Rank and File New Hampshire, Inclusive of 166 Batteaux Men at Verplanck's and Stony Points	992
"On command and Extra Service at Fishkills, New Windsor, &c., &c., who may be called in occationally	852
" 3 regiments of Connecticut Militia, under the Com'd of Colonel Wells, on the lines near N. Castle	488
" A detachment of New York levies on the lines...............	115
Militia....	2,447

"Colonel Lamb's Regiment	167	
" Colonel Livingston's, at Verplank and Stony Pts.	80	
Continent :		247

"Colonel Sheldon's Dragoons, on the lines, about one half mounted................................	142
" Batteaux Men and Artificers	250
Total....	3,086

of New York. He died October 19th, 1803. The following correspondence with Colonel Lamb is inserted to show a trait in his character:

"FORT ARNOLD, *June* 7, 1779.

   * * * *   " I should be exceedingly obliged to you if you could procure me a Horsemans Tent, as I am without Quarters, without any Bedding, and sometime without eating, and if nature had not provided Water, [which is in great plenty here] would be without drink, too." * * * *

"S BAUMAN."

Again he says:

"WEST POINT, *June* 30, 1779.

"I should be exceedingly happy if you would pay me a visit. I have at present middling good quarters. I could accomodate you in a manner so as to afford you a nights lodging, and give you Continental fare. As for liquors I have none, my daily drink is Water, which I think rather hard for a man in years, and who is on continual fatigue, and who never before experienced so mean nutriment."
* * * *   "S. BAUMAN."

[Lamb MSS., N. Y. Hist. Col.]

No. 4.

[In the handwriting of Villefranche, a French engineer.]

"ESTIMATE OF THE NUMBER OF MEN NECESSARY TO MAN THE WORKS AT WEST POINT AND IN THE VICINITY.

" Fort Arnold ...	620	Redoubt No. 2....	150	Redoubt No. 7....	78
—— Putnam.....	450	ditto 3....	120	North Redoubt ...	120
— Wyllys	140	ditto 4....	100	South Redoubt ...	130
—— Webb	140	ditto 5....	139	——	
Redoubt No. 1....	150	ditto 6....	110	Total.....	2,438

" VILLEFRANCHE, *Engineer.*

" N. B.—The Artillery Men are not included in the above estimate."

No. 5.

RETURN OF THE ORDNANCE IN THE DIFFERENT FORTS, BATTERIES, &c., AT WEST POINT AND ITS DEPENDENCIES,

[In the handwriting of Major Bauman.]

Sept. 5, 1780.

Calibres	Metal.	24 Garrison Carriages.	18 Garrison Carriages.	18 Traveling Carriages.	12 Garrison Carriages.	12 Stocked Carriages.	9 Garrison Carriages.	6 Garrison Carriages.	6 Stocked Carriages.	— Traveling Carriages.	4 Garrison Carriages.	4 Traveling Carriages.	3 Traveling Carriages.	Mortars 10 Inches.	Mortars 5¼ Inches.	Mortars 4⅗ Inches.	Howitzers 8.	Total.
Fort Arnold	Brass. / Iron.	1	6			1				2		1	8	5	4	1	1	23
Fort Putnam	Brass. / Iron.		5		2		1	5							5			14
Constitution Island	Iron.				4	2									2			10
South Battery	Iron.		4	2	1		2						3					8
Chain Battery	Iron.				3			4										8
Lanthorn Battery	Iron.				1			1	1									4
Webb's Redoubt	Iron.				1		2		2		1							5
Sherman's Redoubt	Iron.								2									2
Megg's Redoubt	Iron.								3									6
South Redoubt	Iron.																	5
North Redoubt	Iron.						4	2										5
Wyllys's Redoubt	Iron.		2	2														5
Rocky Hill, No. 4	Iron.				1													2
" No. 1	Iron.																	3
Verplank's Point No. 2	Iron.																	8
" No. 1	Brass. / Iron.																	8
Stony Point	Iron.	1		1		2												4
Total	Brass. / Iron.	1	18	3	14	5	9	14	5	2	1	8	6	5	11	2	1	100

N. B.—The following ordnance not distributed:

No. 6 Iron 12 Pounder.
4 do. 9 do.
1 do. 6 do.
2 do. 3 do.
———
14

8 Brass 24 Pounders.
7 do. 12 do.
1 do. 8 inch howitzer.
———
11

S BAUMAN,
Major Com'd of Artillery.

No. 6.

[In Arnold's handwriting.]
[ENDORSEMENT.]

"Remarks on Works at West Point. A copy to be transmitted* to His Excellency General Washington, Sep'r, 1780.

" Fort Arnold is built of Dry Fascines and Wood, is in a ruinous condition, incompleat, and subject to take Fire from Shells or Carcasses.

" Fort Putnam, Stone, wanting great repairs, wall on the East side broke down, and rebuilding From the Foundation. At the West and South side have been a Chevaux-de-Frise; on the West side broke in many Places. The East side open; two Bomb Proofs and Provision Magazine in the Fort, and Slight Wooden Barrack. A commanding piece of ground 500 yards West, between the Fort and No. 4—or Rocky Hill.

" Fort Webb, built of Fascines and Wood, a slight Work, very dry, and liable to be set on fire, as the approaches are very easy, without defenses, save a slight Abattis.

" Fort Wyllys, built of stone, 5 feet high, the Work above plank filled with Earth, the stone work 15 feet, the Earth 9 feet thick.—No Bomb Proofs, the Batteries without the Fort.

" Redoubt No. 1.—On the South side wood 9 feet thick; the Wt., North and East sides 4 feet thick, no cannon in the works; a slight and single Abattis, no ditch or Pickett. Cannon on two Batteries. No Bomb Proofs.

" Redoubt No. 2.—The same as No. 1. No Bomb Proofs.

" Redoubt No. 3, a slight Wood Work 3 Feet thick,

* This was intended to deceive, should it fall into improper hands.

very Dry, no Bomb Proofs, a single Abattis, the work easily set on fire—no cannon.

"Redoubt No. 4, a wooden work about 10 feet high and fore or five feet thick, the West side faced with a stone wall 8 feet high and four thick.   No Bomb Proof, two six pounders, a slight Abattis, a commanding piece of ground 500 yards Wt.

"The North Redoubt, on the East side, built of stone 4 feet high; above the stone, wood filled in with Earth, very Dry, no Ditch, a Bomb Proof, three Batteries without the Fort, a poor Abattis, a Rising piece of ground 500 yards So., the approaches under cover to within 20 yards.—The Work easily fired with Faggots diptd in Pitch, &c.

"South Redoubt, much the same as the North, a Commanding piece of ground 500 yards due East—3 Batteries without the Fort."

These "Remarks" were accompanied by the report of the Council of War held at Washington's head-quarters, September 6, 1780, which document, setting forth the weakness, wants, and gloomy prospects of the American army, is as follows :—

"At a Council of War, held in Camp Bergen County, Sept. 6th, 1780.

"Present—the Commander-in-Chief

"The Commander-in-Chief states to the Council, that since he had the honor of laying before the General Officers, at Morristown, the 6th of June last, a general view of our circumstances, several important events have occurred, which have materially changed the prospects of the Campaign.

" That the success [assistance] expected from France, instead of coming out in one body, and producing a Naval Superiority in these Seas, has been divided into two Divisions, the first of which only consisting of seven ships of the line, one forty-four and three smaller Frigates, with five thousand land Forces, had arrived at Rhode Island.

" That a Reinforcement of six ships of the line from England having reinforced the Enemy, had made their Naval Force in these seas amount to Nine Sail of the Line, Two Fifties, two forty-fours, and a number of smaller Frigates, a Force completely superior to that of our Allies, and which has in consequence held them Blocked up in the harbor of Rhode Island till the 29th ult., at which Period the British Fleet disappeared, and no advice of them has since been received.

" That Accounts received by the Alliance Frigate, which left France in July, announces the Second Division to be confined in Brest with several other Ships by a British Fleet of thirty-two Sail of the line, and a Fleet of the Allies of Thirty-six, or thirty-eight Ships of the line ready to put to sea from Cadiz to relieve the Port of Brest.

" That most of the States in their answers to the requisitions made of them, give the strongest assurances of doing every thing in their power to furnish the men and supplies required for the expected Co-operation. The effect of which, however, has been far short of our expectations, for not much above one-third of the Levies demanded for the Continental Battalions, nor above the Same proportion of Militia have been assembled, and the Supplies have been so inadequate that there was a

9

necessity for dismissing all the Militia, whose immediate services could be dispensed with to lessen our consumption, notwithstanding which the Troops now in the Field are severely suffering for want of Provision.

" That the army at this Post and in the vicinity in opperating Force consists of 10,400 Continental Troops, and about 400 Militia, besides which is a Regiment of Continental Troops of about 500 at Rhode Island, left there for the assistance of our Allies, against any attempt of the enemy that way, and two Connecticut State Regiments amounting to 800 at North Castle.

" That the Times of Service for which the Levies are Engaged will expire the first of January, which, if not replaced, allowing for the usual Casualties, will reduce the Continental Army to less than 6,000 men.

" That since the state[ment] to the Council above Referred to, the Enemy have brought a detachment of about 3,000 men from Charles Town to New York, which makes the present opperating Force in this Quarter between Ten and Eleven Thousand men.

" That the Enemies Force now in the Southern States has not been lately ascertained by any distinct accounts, but the General supposes it cannot be less than 7,000 (of which about 2,000 are at Savannah) in this estimate the Diminution by the Casualties of the Climate, is supposed to be equal to the increase of Force derived from the Disaffected.

" That added to the loss of Charles Town and its Garrison accounts of a recent misfortune are just arrived from Major-General Gates, giving advice of a general action which happened on the 16th of August near Campden, in which the army under his Command met with a total defeat, and in all probability the whole of the Continental Troops, and a considerable part of the Militia would be cut off.

"That the State of Virginia has been some time exerting itself to raise a Body of 3,000 Troops to serve till the end of December, 1781, but how far it has succeeded is not known.

"That Maryland had Resolved to raise 2,000 Men, of which a sufficient number to compose one Battalion was to have come to this army. The remainder to recruit the Maryland line—but in consequence of the late advices, an order has been sent to march the whole Southward.

"That the Enemies Force in Canada, Halifax, St. Augustine, and at Penobscot, remains much the same as stated in the preceding Council.

"That there is still reason to believe the Court of France will prosecute its original intention of giving effectual succor to this Country, as soon as circumstances will permit; and it is hoped the second Division will certainly arrive in the course of the fall.

"That a Fleet greatly superior to that of the Enemy in the West Indies, and a formidable land Force had sailed sometime since from Martinique to make a combined attack upon the Island of Jamaica, that there is a possibility of a reinforcement from this quarter also, to the Fleet of our Ally at Rhode Island.

"The Commander-in-Chief having thus given the Council a full view of our present Situation and future prospects, requests the Opinion of each Member, in writing, what plan it will be advisable to pursue, to what objects Our Attention ought to be directed in the course of this fall and winter, taking into consideration the alternative of having or not having a Naval Superiority, whether any Offensive operations can be immediately undertaken and against what Point, what ought to be our immediate Preparations and dispositions, particularly whether we can afford or ought to send any Reinforcements from this Army to the Southern States, and to what amount. The General requests to be favored with these opinions by the 10th instant at farthest."[*]

On Sunday, the 24th, Anderson was conveyed to Lower Salem, and committed to the custody of a guard under Lieutenant King, who thus describes the prisoner:

"He looked somewhat like a reduced gentleman. His small clothes were Nankeen, with handsome whitetop boots—in fact his undress military clothes. His coat purple, with gold lace, worn somewhat threadbare, with a small brimmed, tarnished beaver on his head. He wore his hair in a queue, with long black beard, and his clothes somewhat dirty. In this garb I took charge of him. After breakfast my barber came in to dress me, after which I requested him to undergo the same operation, which he did. When the ribbon was taken from his hair I observed it full of powder; this circumstance, with others that occurred, induced me to believe I had no ordinary person in charge. He requested permission to take the bed whilst his shirt and small clothes could be washed. I told him that was needless, for a shirt was at his service, which he accepted. We were close pent up in a bed-room, with a Vidette at the door and

---

[*] Arnold's reply in writing, to the foregoing, is given in the "Correspondence of the Revolution," III., 85.—Sparks.

window. There was a spacious yard before the door, which he desired he might be permitted to walk in with me. I accordingly disposed of my guard in such a manner as to prevent an escape. Whilst walking together he observed he must make a confidant of somebody, and he knew not a more proper person than myself, as I had appeared to befriend a stranger in distress. After settling the point between ourselves, he told me who he was, and gave me a short account of himself, from the time he was taken in St. John's in 1775, to that time. He requested a pen and ink, and wrote immediately to General Washington, declaring who he was. [Page 132, "Proceedings of the Board."]

About midnight the express returned with orders from General Washington to Colonel Sheldon to send Major André immediately to Head-Quarters."*

In the midst of a drenching rain, on this dark and dismal night a strong escort, commanded by Major Tallmadge, set out, and with the unfortunate captive reached the Robinson House about daylight on Tuesday morning, the 26th.

Returning to the papers which had been forwarded to Washington, and the note sent to Arnold by Jameson, it was supposed that the former would return from Hartford by the same route he had pursued in going to that point; but, for some reason not explained, he took the upper road which approached the Hudson at Fishkill, thirteen miles, as the road then ran, above the Robinson House, arriving there in the afternoon of Sunday, the 24th.

It was the intention of Washington to press on that

* N. Y. Hist Mag., 293, Oct., 1857.

evening and pass the night at Arnold's Head-Quarters ;
but meeting the French envoy, then on his way to meet
Rochambeau, he decided to pass the night at Fishkill.

That evening the Chief and his staff were entertained
at a festive board where sat Joshua Hett Smith, little
thinking that the stroke arrested from one, would so
completely overwhelm the other.

Early on Monday, the 25th, Washington set out for
the Robinson House, designing to reach there in time
for breakfast. Arriving opposite West Point, he despatched two of his aides to announce his arrival, while
he with his remaining staff, ascended the hill to inspect
the North and Middle Redoubts.*

Breakfast was served on the arrival of the two aides,
and while seated at the table with Arnold and his
family, the note from Jameson announcing the capture
of André was placed in Arnold's hand. With a slight
apology, and but little discomposure, he left the table,
summoned the cockswain of his barge, ordered a horse,
and ascended to the northeast chamber, followed by
Mrs. Arnold.

There he informed her of his danger, and leaving her
in a swoon, he pressed a kiss upon his sleeping infant
boy,† and returning to his guests, he informed them that
it was necessary for him to repair to West Point, to make
arrangements for the reception of his Commander ; then
mounting his horse, followed by the cockswain on foot,
he dashed down the path yet called "Arnold's path," to

---

* Heath's Memoirs.

† *James Robertson Arnold* was born at Philadelphia, March 19th, 1780, and,
passing through several grades in the English Service, is finally enrolled as a
Lieutenant-General in the British Army List for March, 1853.

the dock on the south side of the point, a little below the Robinson House, through which the Hudson River Railroad now cuts its way. A barge with the breathless, panting renegade, under cover of a white handkerchief raised upon a stick, sped its way down the river to the Vulture.

Upon completing the inspection of the Redoubts, Washington repaired to the Robinson House, and learning that Arnold had crossed to West Point, he proceeded after a hasty breakfast, accompanied by all his staff except Hamilton, to examine the works at that garrison, while the General Commanding was on the spot.

On his arrival, he found, to his astonishment, that Arnold had not been there, and after a general inspection of the works, the party returned to the east side of the river. Jameson's courier, with the papers of a " dangerous tendency," had arrived during the absence of the Chief at West Point, and while ascending the path to the Robinson House, Hamilton placed them in his hand.

A few moments later, La Fayette and Knox were made acquainted with the traitor's design, and to them the Chief tearfully and pathetically appealed, "Whom can we trust now?"

The moment was indeed a trying one, and measures were promptly taken to prevent further disastrous results.

That night every camp and garrison in the army was warned of approaching danger, fatigue parties were called in, and the troops held in hand to move to the assistance of the garrison at West Point at a moment's warning.

At midnight, Joshua Hett Smith* was arrested at
Fishkill, and on the morning of Tuesday, the 26th, both
André and himself were prisoners in the Robinson
House.

In the afternoon of the same day, André and Smith
were removed for greater security to West Point,† and
on Thursday morning, the 28th, both were conveyed in
separate barges, under a guard commanded by Major
Tallmadge, down the river to Tappan, where the main
body of the army lay encamped.

A Board of General Officers constituting a Court of
Inquiry, instructed to report the facts and give an
opinion, was convened to investigate the case of André.
Their proceedings, as published by Congress, are herewith given.

* *Smith* was tried by a Court-Martial, which failing to convict him, he was
conveyed to Goshen and turned over to the civil authorities. He escaped from
jail at this point, and made his way in disguise to New York. At the close of
hostilities he went to England; but afterwards returned and died in New York,
in 1818.—[Field-Book of the Revolution, I., 752.—Lossing.]

† The traditions extant, that *André* was confined in the magazine in Fort Putnam,
have no official authority. The work at that time was undergoing demolition and
rebuilding. The present work was for the most part enlarged from the old one,
and rebuilt, fifteen years later. The regard shown André in the measures elsewhere adopted for his security, affords reason to believe that no deprivation of
light or society attended his confinement at West Point.

CHAPTER VIII.

PROCEEDINGS OF THE BOARD OF GENERAL OFFICERS.—LETTERS OF
WASHINGTON TO CONGRESS.—ANDRÉ TO WASHINGTON AND SHEL-
DON.—LETTER FROM ARNOLD TO WASHINGTON.—ROBINSON TO
WASHINGTON.—CLINTON TO WASHINGTON.—ARNOLD TO CLINTON.
—REPORT OF THE BOARD.—ANDRÉ TO CLINTON.—WASHINGTON TO
CLINTON.—ROBERTSON TO WASHINGTON.—REPLY OF WASHINGTON.
—CLINTON TO WASHINGTON.—ARNOLD TO WASHINGTON.—ROB-
ERTSON TO WASHINGTON.—ARNOLD TO WASHINGTON.—ANDRÉ TO
WASHINGTON.

[*Fac-Simile.*]

PROCEEDINGS

OF A

BOARD

OF

GENERAL OFFICERS,

HELD BY ORDER OF

His Excellency Gen. WASHINGTON,

Commander in Chief of the Army of the United States
of AMERICA.

RESPECTING

Major *JOHN ANDRÈ*,

Adjutant General of the British Army.

SEPTEMBER 29, 1780.

PHILADELPHIA:

Printed by FRANCIS BAILEY, in Market-Street.

M.DCC.LXXX.

EXTRACTS of LETTERS

from General WASHINGTON, *to the* PRESIDENT *of* CONGRESS.

Robinſon's Houſe, in the Highlands, Sept. 26, 1780.

S I R,

I HAVE the honor to inform Congreſs, that I arrived here yeſterday about twelve o'clock on my return from Hartford. Some hours previous to my arrival Major General Arnold went from his quarters, which were this place, and, as it was ſuppoſed, over the river to the garriſon at Weſt Point, whither I proceeded myſelf, in order to viſit the poſt. I found general Arnold had not been there during the day, and on my return to his quarters he was ſtill abſent. In the mean time, a packet had arrived from Lieut. Colonel Jameſon, announcing the capture of a John Anderſon, who was endeavouring to go to New-York with ſeveral intereſting and important papers, all in the hand writing of general Arnold. This was alſo accompanied with a letter from the priſoner, avowing himſelf to be major John Andrè, Adjutant General to the Britiſh army, relating the manner of his capture, and endeavouring to ſhew that he was not come under the deſcription of a *ſpy*. From theſe ſeveral circumſtances, and information that the General ſeemed to be thrown into ſome degree of agitation, on receiving a letter a little time before he went from his quarters, I was led to conclude immediately that he had heard of major Andrè's captivity, and that he would, if poſſible, eſcape to the enemy, and accordingly took ſuch meaſures as appeared the moſt probable to apprehend him. But he had embarked in a barge and proceeded down the river, under a flag, to the Vulture

ſhip

(4)

fhip of war, which lay at fome miles below Stoney and Verplank's Points.   He wrote me a letter after he got on board.
Major Andrè is not arrived yet, but I hope he is fecure,
and that he will be here to-day.   I have been and am taking
precautions, which I truft will prove effectual to prevent the
important confequences which this conduct, on the part of
General Arnold, was intended to produce.   I do not know
the party that took Major Andrè, but it is faid that it con-
fifted only of a few militia, who acted in fuch a manner upon
the occafion, as does them the higheft honor, and proves them
to be men of great virtue.   As foon as I know their names,
I fhall take pleafure in tranfmitting them to Congrefs.

Paramus, October 7, 1780.

S I R,

I HAVE the honour to enclofe Congrefs a copy of the
proceedings of a Board of General Officers in the cafe of
Major Andrè, Adjutant General to the Britifh army.   This
officer was executed in purfuance of the opinion of the board,
on Monday, the 2d inftant, at 12 o'clock, at our late camp at
Tappan.——Befides the proceedings I tranfmit copies of fundry letters refpecting the matter, which are all that paffed on
the fubject, not included in the proceedings.

I have now the pleafure to communicate the names of the
three perfons who captured Major Andrè, and who refufed to
releafe him, notwithftanding the moft earneft importunities and
affurances of a liberal reward on his part.   Their names are
John Paulding, David Williams, and *Ifaac Van Wert.*

PROCEEDINGS

PROCEEDINGS

OF A

Board of General Officers,

Held by order of his Excellency General WASHINGTON, commander in chief of the army of the United States of America, refpecting Major Andrè, Adjutant General of the Britifh army, September the 29th, 1780, at Tappan, in the State of New-York.

PRESENT,

Major General Greene, Prefident,
Major General Lord Stirling,
Major General St. Clair,
Major General The Marquis de la Fayette,
Major General Howe,
Major General The Baron de Steuben,
Brigadier General Parfons,
Brigadier General Clinton,
Brigadier General Knox,
Brigadier General Glover,
Brigadier General Patterfon,
Brigadier General Hand,
Brigadier General Huntington,
Brigadier General Starke,
John Lawrence, Judge-Advocate General.

MAJOR Andrè, Adjutant General to the Britifh army was brought before the Board, and the following letter from General Wafhington, to the Board, dated Head Quarters, Tappan, September 29th, 1780, was laid before them, and read.

" *Gentlemen,*
" Major Andrè, Adjutant General to the Britifh army,
" will be brought before you for your examination. He
" came within our lines in the night, on an interview
" with Major General Arnold, and in an affumed charac-
" ter ; and was taken within our lines, in a difguifed ha-
" bit, with a pafs under a feigned name, and with the
" inclofed papers concealed upon him. After a careful
examination,

(6)

"examination, you will be pleafed, as fpeedily as poffible,
"to report a precife ftate of his cafe, together with your
"opinion of the light in which he ought to be confidered,
"and the punifhment that ought to be inflicted. The Judge-
"Advocate will attend to affift in the examination, who has
"fundry other papers, relative to this matter, which he will
"lay before the Board.
        "*I have the honour to be,*
          "*Gentlemen,*
              "*Your moft obedient and humble fervant,*
                      "G. WASHINGTON."
"*The Board of General Officers,*
    convened at Tappan."

The names of the officers compofing the board were read
to Major Andrè, and on his being afked whether he confeffed
the matters contained in the letter from his Excellency General
Wafhington to the board, or denied them, *he faid, in addition to his letter to general Wafhington, dated Salem, the
24th September,* 1780, (which was read to the board and
acknowledged by Major Andrè, to have been written by him,
which letter is as follows:

                            Salem, 24th Sept. 1780.
    "S I R,
    "*What I have as yet faid concerning myfelf, was in the
"juftifiable attempt to be extricated; I am too little accuf-
"tomed to duplicity to have fucceeded.*
    "*I beg your Excellency will be perfuaded, that no alter-
"ation in the temper of my mind, or apprehenfion for my
"fafety, induces me to take the ftep of addreffing you, but
"that it is to fecure myfelf from an imputation of having
"affumed a mean character for treacherous purpofes or
"felf intereft. A conduct incompatible with the principles
"that actuated me, as well as with my condition in life.*
    "*It is to vindicate my fame that I fpeak and not to fo-
"licit fecurity.*
    "*The perfon in your poffeffion is Major John Andre,
"Adjutant General to the Britifh army.*
    "*The influence of one commander in the army of his
"adverfary is an advantage taken in war. A correfpon-
"dence for this purpofe I held; as confidential (in the pre-
"fent inftance) with his Excellency Sir Henry Clinton.*
    "*To favour it, I agreed to meet upon ground not
"within pofts of either army, a perfon who was to give
"me intelligence; I came up in the Vulture man of war*
                                            for

(7)

" for this effect, and was fetched by a boat from the shore to
" the beach: Being there I was told that the approach of day
" would prevent my return, and that I must be concealed
" until the next night. I was in my regimentals and had
" fairly risked my person.

   " Against my stipulation, my intention and without my
" knowledge before hand, I was conducted within one of
" your posts. Your Excelleucy may conceive my sensation
" on this occasion and will imagine how much more I must
" have been affected, by a refusal to reconduct me back
" the next night as I had been brought. Thus become a
" prisoner I had to concert my escape. I quitted my uni-
" form and was passed another way in the night without
" the American posts to neutral ground, and informed I was
" beyond all armed parties and left to press for New-York.
" I was taken at Tarry Town by some volunteers.

   " Thus as I have had the honor to relate was I betrayed
" (being adjutant general of the British army) into the
" vile condition of an enemy in disguise within your posts.

   " Having avowed myself a British officer I have nothing
" to reveal but what relates to myself, which is true on
" the honor of an officer and a gentleman.

   " The request I have to make your Excellency and I am
" conscious I address myself well, is, that in any rigor
" policy may dictate, a decency of conduct towards me may
" mark, that though unfortuuate I am branded with no-
" thing dishonourable, as no motive could be mine but the
" service of my king and as I was involuntarily an impostor.

   " Another request is, that I may be permitted to write
" an open letter to Sir Henry Clinton and another to a
" friend for cloaths and linen.

   " I take the liberty to mention the condition of some
" gentlemen at Charles-Town, who being either on parole
" or under protection were engaged in a conspiracy against
" us. Though their situation is not similar, they are objects
" who may be set in exchange for me, or are persons whom
" the treatment I receive might affect.

   " It is no less Sir in a confidence in the generosity of your
" mind than on account of your superior station that I have
" chosen to importune you with this letter.

   " I have the honour to be, with great respect, Sir,
       " Your Excellency's most obedient
           " and most humble servant,
              " JOHN ANDRE,
" His Excellency   adjutant general."
   " General Washington
      " &c. &c. &c.")
         10   That

(8)

That he came on fhore from the Vulture floop of war in *the night* of the twenty firft of September inftant, fomewhere under the Haverftraw Mountain That the boat he came on fhore in carried *no flag*, and that he had on a furtout coat over his regimentals, and that he wore his furtout coat when he was taken. That he met general Arnold on the fhore and had an interview with him there. He alfo faid that when he left the Vulture floop of war, it was underftood he was to return that night ; but it was then doubted, and if he could not return he was promifed to be *concealed on* fhore in a place of fafety, until the next *night*, when he was to return in the fame manner he came on fhore ; and when the next day came he was folicitous to get back, and made enquiries in the courfe of the day, how he fhould retnrn, when he was informed he could not return that way and muft take the rout he did afterwards. He alfo faid, That the firft notice he had of his being within any *of our pofts*, was, being challenged by the fentry, which was the firft night he was on fhore. He alfo faid, that the evening of the twenty-fecond of September inftant, he paffed *King's Ferry between our pofts of Stoney and Verplank's Points*, in the *drefs he is at prefent in and which he faid was not his regimentals*, and which drefs he procured, after he landed from the Vulture and when he was within *our poft*, and that he was proceeding to New-York, but was taken on his way, at Tarry Town, as he has mentioned in his letter, on Saturday the twenty-third of September inftant, about nine o'clock in the morning.

The following papers were laid before the board and fhewn to major Andrè, who confeffed to the board that they were found on him when he was taken, and faid they were concealed in his boot, except the pafs :———
A pafs from general Arnold to *John Anderfon*, which *name* major Andrè *acknowledged he affumed :*
Artillery orders, September 5, 1780.
Eftimate of the force at Weft Point and it's dependencies. September 1780.
Eftimate of men to man the works at Weft Point, &c.
Return of ordnance at Weft Point, September 1780.
Remarks on works at Weft Point.
Copy of a ftate of matters laid before a council of war, by his Excellency general Wafhington, held the 6th of September 1780.

A letter

(9)

A letter figned *John Anderfon*, dated Sept. 7, 1780, to Colonel Sheldon*, was alfo laid before the Board, and fhewn to Major Andrè, which *he acknowledged* to have been written by *him*, and is as follows:

"S I R,   "*New-York, the 7th Sept.* 1780.

"I AM told *my name* is made known to you, and that "I may hope your indulgence in permitting me to meet "a friend near your out pofts. *I* will endeavour to obtain "permiffion to go out *with a flag* which will be fent to "Dobb's Ferry on Monday next, the 11th, at twelve o'clock, "when I fhall be happy to meet Mr G---§. Should I not "be allowed to go, the officer who is to command the efcort, "between whom and myfelf no diftinction need be made, can "fpeak on the affair.

."Let me entreat you, Sir, to favour a matter fo intereft-"ing to the parties concerned, and which is of fo private a "nature that the public on neither fide can be injured by it.

"I fhall be happy on my part in doing any act of kindnefs "to you in a family or property concern of a fimilar nature.

"I truft I fhall not be detained, but fhould any old "grudge be a caufe for it, I fhall rather rifk that, than neg-"lect the bufinefs in queftion, *or affume a myfterious cha-"racter* to carry on an innocent affair, and, as friends have "advifed, get to your lines by ftealth. I am, Sir, with all "regard,

"*Your moft obedient humble fervant,*

"JOHN ANDERSON."

"*Col.* SHELDON."

---

* *Left it fhould be fuppofed that Colonel Sheldon, to whom the above letter is addreffed, was privy to the plot carrying on by general Arnold, it is to be obferved, that the letter was found among Arnold's papers, and had been tranfmitted by Colonel Sheldon, who, it appears from a letter of the 9th of September to Arnold, which inclofed it, had never heard of John Anderfon before. Arnold in his anfwer on the 10th, acknowledged he had not communicated it to him, though he had informed him that he expected a perfon would come from New-York, for the purpofe of bringing him intelligence.*

(§) *It appears by the fame letter that Arnold had written to Mr. Anderfon, under the fignature of Guftavus. His words are* "I was obliged to write with great caution to him, my letter was figned Guftavus to prevent any difcovery in cafe it fell into the hands of the enemy."

B

(10)

Major Andrè obferved that this letter could be of no force in the cafe in queftion, as it was written in New York, when he was under the orders of General Clinton, but that it tended to prove that it was not his intention to come within our lines.

The Board having interrogated Major Andrè about his conception of his coming on fhore under the fanction of a flag, *he faid, That it was impoffible for him to fuppofe he came on fhore under that fanction;* and added, *That if he* came on fhore under that fanction, he certainly might have returned under it.

Major Andrè having acknowledged the preceeding facts, and being afked whether he had any thing to fay refpecting them, anfwered, He left them to operate with the Board.

The examination of Major Andrè being concluded, he was remanded into cuftody.

The following letters were laid before the Board, and read :——Benedict Arnold's letter to General Wafhington, dated September 25, 1780, Col. Robinfon's letter to General Wafhington, dated September 25, 1780, and general Clinton's letter, dated the 26th September, 1780, (inclofing a letter of the fame date from Benedict Arnold) to General Wafhington.

" On board the Vulture, Sept. 25, 1780.

SIR,

" THE heart which is confcious of its own rectitude, cannot attempt to palliate a ftep which the world may cenfure as wrong; I have ever acted from a principle of love to my country, fince the commencement of the prefent unhappy conteft between Great-Britain and the Colonies; the fame principle of love to my country actuates my prefent conduct, however it may appear inconfiftent to the world, who very feldom judge right of any man's actions.

" I have no favour to afk for myfelf. I have too often experienced the ingratitude of my country to attempt it: but from the known humanity of your Excellence, I am induced to afk your protection for Mrs. Arnold, from every infult and injury that the miftaken vengeance of my country may expofe her to. It ought to fall only on me; fhe is as good and as innocent as an angel, and is incapable of doing wrong. I beg fhe may be permitted to return to her friends in Philadelphia, or to come to me as fhe may choofe : from your Excellency I have no fears

on

(11)

on her account, but she may suffer from the mistaken fury of the country.

"I have to request that the inclosed letter may be delivered to Mrs. Arnold, and she permitted to write to me.

"I have also to ask that my cloaths and baggage, which are of little consequence, may be sent to me, if required their value shall be paid in money.

"*I have the honour to be, with great regard and esteem,*
"*Your Excellency's most obedient humble servant,*
"B. ARNOLD."

"*His Excellency*
"*General* WASHINGTON."

"N. B. In justice to the gentlemen of my family, Col. Varrick and Major Franks, I think myself in honour bound to declare, that they, as well as Joshua Smith, Esq, (who I know is suspected) are totally ignorant of any transactions of mine, that they have reason to believe were injurious to the public."

"*Vulture, off Sinsinck, Sept.* 25, 1780.

"S I R,

"I AM this moment informed that Major Andrè, Adjutant General of his Majesty's army in America, is detained as a prisoner, by the army under your command. It is therefore incumbent on me to inform you of the manner of his falling into your hands: He went up with a flag at the request of General Arnold, on public business with him, and had his permit to return by land to New-York: Under these circumstances Major Andrè cannot be detained by you, without the greatest violation of flags, and contrary to the custom and usage of all nations; and as I imagine you will see this matter in the same point of view as I do, I must desire you will order him to be set at liberty and allowed to return immediately: Every step Major Andrè took was by the advice and direction of General Arnold, even that of taking a feigned name, and of course not liable to censure for it.

"*I am, Sir, not forgetting our former acquaintance,*
"*Your very humble servant,*
BEV. ROBINSON, Col.
Loyl. Americ."

"*His Excellency*
"*General* WASHINGTON."

"*New-*

(12)

"*New-York, Sept.* 26, 1780.

"*S I R,*

"BEING informed that the King's Adjutant General in America has been ſtopt under Major General Arnold's paſſports, and is detained a priſoner in your Excellency's army, I have the honour to inform you, Sir, that I permitted Major Andrè to go to Major General Arnold at the particular requeſt of that general officer. You will perceive, Sir, by the incloſed paper, that a flag of truce was ſent to receive Major Andrè, and paſſports granted for his return, I therefore can have no doubt but your Excellency will immediately direct, that this officer has permiſſion to return to my orders at New-York.

"*I have the honour to be your Excellency's*
"*moſt obedient & moſt humble ſervt.*
"H. CLINTON."

"*His Excellency General* Washington."

"*New-York, Sept.* 26, 1780.

"*S I R,*

"IN anſwer to your Excellency's meſſage, reſpecting your Adjutant General, Major Andrè, and deſiring my idea of the reaſons why he is detained, being under my paſſports, I have the honour to inform you, Sir, that I apprehend a few hours muſt reſtore Major Andrè to your Excellency's orders, as that officer is aſſuredly under the protection of a flag of truce ſent by me to him for the purpoſe of a converſation which I requeſted to hold with him relating to myſelf, and which I wiſhed to communicate through that officer to your Excellency.

"I commanded at the time at Weſt Point, had an undoubted right to ſend my flag of truce for Major Andrè, who came to me under that protection, and having held my converſation with him, I delivered him confidential papers in my own hand writing, to deliver to your Excellency, thinking it much properer he ſhould return by land, I directed him to make uſe of the feigned name of John Anderſon under which he had by my direction come on ſhore, and gave him my paſſports to go to the White Plains on his way to New-York. This officer cannot therefore fail of being immediately ſent to New-York, as he was invited to a converſation with me, for which I ſent him a flag of truce, and finally gave him paſſports for his ſafe return to your Excellency; all which I had then a right to do, being in the actual ſervice of America, under the orders of General

ral

(13)

ral Wafhington, and commanding general at Weft Point and
its dependencies.

> "*I have the honour to be, your Excellency's*
> "*moft obedient and very humble fervant,*
>   "B. ARNOLD."

"*His Excellency Sir* HENRY CLINTON."

The Board having confidered the letter from his Excellency General Wafhington refpecting Major Andrè, Adjutant
General to the Britifh army, the confeffion of Major Andrè,
and the papers produced to them, REPORT to His Excellency, the Commander in Chief, the following facts, which
appear to them relative to Major Andrè.

Firft, That he came on fhore from the Vulture floop of
war in the *night* of the twenty-firft of September inftant, on
an interview with General Arnold, *in a private and fecret
manner.*

Secondly, That *he changed his drefs within our lines, and
under a feigned name, and in a difguifed habit,* paffed our
works at Stoney and Verplank's Points, the evening of the
twenty-fecond of September inftant, and was taken the morning of the twenty-third of September inftant, *at Tarry Town,
in a difguifed habit,* being then on his way to New York, *and
when taken,* he had in his poffeffion feveral papers which contained *intelligence for the enemy.*

The Board having maturely confidered thefe facts, DO
ALSO REPORT to His Excellency General Wafhington,
That Major Andrè, Adjutant General to the Britifh army,
ought to be confidered as a Spy from the enemy, and that
agreeable to the law and ufage of nations, it is their opinion,
he ought to fuffer death.

> NATH. GREENE, *M Genl.* Prefident.
> *Stirling, M. G.*
> *Ar. St. Clair, M. G.*
> *La Fayette, M. G.*
> *R. Howe, M. G.*
> *Stuben, M. G.*
> *Saml. H. Parfons, B. Genl.*
> *James Clinton, B. Genl.*
> *H. Knox, Brigr. Genl. Artillery.*
> *Jno. Glover, B. Genl.*
> *John Patterfon, B. Genl.*
> *Edwd. Hand, B. Genl.*
> *J. Huntington, B. Genl.*
> *John Starke, B. Genl.*
>   JOHN LAWRENCE, *J. A. Genl.*

APPENDIX.

Copy of a Letter from Major André, Adjutant General, to
Sir Henry Clinton, K. B. &c. &c.

Tappan, Sept. 29, 1780.

SIR,

YOUR Excellency is doubtleſs already appriſed of the
manner in which I was taken, and poſſibly of the ſerious
light in which my conduct is conſidered, and the rigorous
determination that is impending.

Under theſe circumſtances, I have obtained General Waſhington's permiſſion to ſend you this letter; the object of which
is, to remove from your breaſt any ſuſpicion, that I could
imagine I was bound by your Excellency's orders to expoſe
myſelf to what has happened. The events of coming within
an enemy's poſts, and of changing my dreſs, which led me to
my preſent ſituation, were contrary to my own intentions, as
they were to your orders; and the circuitous route, which I
took to return, was impoſed (perhaps unavoidably) without
alternative upon me.

I am perfectly tranquil in mind, and prepared for any fate,
to which an honeſt zeal for my King's ſervice may have devoted me.

In addreſſing myſelf to your Excellency on this occaſion,
the force of all my obligations to you, and of the attachment and gratitude I bear you, recurs to me. With all the
warmth of my heart, I give you thanks for your Excellency's
profuſe kindneſs to me; and I ſend you the moſt earneſt
wiſhes for your welfare, which a faithful, affectionate, and
reſpectful attendant can frame.

I have a mother and three ſiſters, to whom the value of
my commiſſion would be an object, as the loſs of Grenada
has much affected their income. It is needleſs to be more
explicit on this ſubject; I am perſuaded of your Excellency's
goodneſs.

I receive

(15)

I receive the greateſt attention from his Excellency General Waſhington, and from every perſon, under whoſe charge I happen to be placed.

I have the honour to be,
With the moſt reſpectful attachment,
Your Excellency's moſt obedient
and moſt humble ſervant,
JOHN ANDRE,
Adjutant General.

(Addreſſed)
His Excellency
General Sir Henry Clinton, K. B.
&c. &c. &c.

Copy of letter from His Excellency General Waſhington, to His Excellency Sir Henry Clinton.

Head Quarters, Sept. 30, 1780.

S I R,

IN anſwer to your Excellency's letter of the 26th inſtant, which I had the honour to receive, I am to inform you that Major André was taken under ſuch circumſtances as would have juſtified the moſt ſummary proceedings againſt him. I determined, however, to refer his caſe to the examination and deciſion of a Board of General Officers, who have re-ported, on his free and voluntary confeſſion and letters,----"That he came on ſhore from the Vulture ſloop of war in "the night of the twenty-firſt of September inſtant," &c. &c. as in the report of the Board of General Officers.

From theſe proceedings it is evident Major André was employed in the execution of meaſures very foreign to the objects of flags of truce, and ſuch as they were never meant to authoriſe or countenance in the moſt diſtant degree; and this gentleman confeſſed, with the greateſt candor, in the courſe of his examination, "That it was impoſſible for him "to ſuppoſe he came on ſhore, under the ſanction of a "flag."

I have the honour to be your Excellency's
Moſt obedient and moſt humble ſervant,
G. WASHINGTON.

(Addreſſed)
His Excellency Sir Henry Clinton.

In this letter, Major André's of the 29th of September to Sir Henry Clinton, was tranſmitted.

New-York,

(16)

New-York, 29, Sept. 1780.

S I R,

    PERSUADED that you are inclined rather to promote than prevent the civilities and acts of humanity, which the rules of war permit between civilized nations, I find no difficulty in reprefenting to you, that feveral letters and meffages fent from hence have been difregarded, are unanfwered, and the flags of truce that carried them, detained. As I ever have treated all flags of truce with civility and refpect, I have a right to hope, that you will order my complaint to be immediately redreffed.

    Major André, who vifited an officer commanding in a diftrict at his own defire, and acted in every circumftance agreeable to his direction, I find is detained a prifoner; my friendfhip for him leads me to fear he may fuffer fome inconvenience for want of neceffaries; I wifh to be allowed to fend him a few, and fhall take it as a favour if you will be pleafed to permit his fervant to deliver them. In Sir Henry Clinton's abfence it becomes a part of my duty to make this reprefentation and requeft.

        I am, Sir, your Excellency's
            Moft obedient humble fervant,
              JAMES ROBERTSON,
                Lt. General.

His Excellency
General Wafhington.

Tappan, Sept. 30, 1780.

S I R,

    I HAVE juft received your letter of the 29th. Any delay which may have attended your flags has proceeded from accident, and the peculiar circumftances of the occafion,---not from intentional neglect or violation. The letter that admitted of an anfwer, has received one as early as it could be given with propriety, tranfmitted by a flag this morning. As to meffages, I am uninformed of any that have been fent.

    The neceffaries for Major André will be delivered to him, agreeable to your requeft.

        I am, Sir,
           Your moft obedient humble fervant,
              G. WASHINGTON.

His Excellency
Lieut. General Robertfon,
    New-York.

                      New-York,

(17)

New-York, Sept. 30, 1780.

S I R,

FROM your Excellency's letter of this date, I am per-
fuaded the Board of General Officers, to whom you referred
the cafe of Major Andrè, can't have been rightly informed
of all the circumftances on which a judgment ought to be
formed. I think it of the higheft moment to humanity, that
your Excellency fhould be perfectly apprized of the ftate of
this matter, before you proceed to put that judgment in execution.

For this reafon, I fhall fend His Excellency Lieut. General Robertfon, and two other gentlemen, to give you a
true ftate of facts, and to declare to you my fentiments and
refolutions. They will fet out to-morrow as early as the wind
and tide will permit, and will wait near Dobbs's ferry for your
permiffion and fafe conduct, to meet your Excellency, or fuch
perfons as you may appoint, to converfe with them on this
fubject.

I have the honour to be, your Excellency's
Moft obedient and moft humble fervant,

H. CLINTON.

P. S. The Hon. Andrew Elliot, Efq. Lieut. Governor,
and the Hon. William Smith, Chief Juftice of this province, will attend His Excellency Lieut. General Robertfon.

H. C.

His Excellency General Wafhington.

Lieut. General Robertfon, Mr. Elliot, and Mr. Smith
came up in a flag veffel to Dobbs's ferry, agreeable to the
above letter. The two laft were not fuffered to land. General Robertfon was permitted to come on fhore, and was
met by Major General Greene, who verbally reported that
General Robertfon mentioned to him in fubftance what is
contained in his letter of the 2d of October to General
Wafhington.

New-York, Oct. 1, 1780.

S I R,

I TAKE this opportunity to inform your Excellency,
that I confider myfelf no longer acting under the commiffion
of Congrefs: Their laft to me being among my papers at
Weft-point, you, Sir, will make fuch ufe of it, as you think
proper.

C   At

(18)

At the fame time, I beg leave to affure your Excellency, that my attachment to the true intereft of my country is invariable, and that I am actuated by the SAME PRINCIPLE which has ever been the GOVERNING RULE of my conduct, in this unhappy conteft.

I have the honour to be, very refpectfully,
    Your Excellency's moft obedient humble fervant,
                        B. ARNOLD.

His Excellency General Wafhington.

                Greyhound Schooner, Flag of Truce,
                    Dobbs's Ferry, October 2, 1780.

SIR,

A NOTE I have from General Greene, leaves me in doubt if his memory had ferved him, to relate to you with exactnefs the fubftance of the converfation that had paffed between him and myfelf, on the fubject of Major André. In an affair of fo much confequence to my friend, to the two armies, and humanity, I would leave no poffibility of a mif-underftanding, and therefore take the liberty to put in writing the fubftance of what I faid to General Greene.

I offered to prove, by the evidence of Colonel Robinfon and the officers of the Vulture, that Major André went on fhore at General Arnold's defire, in a bbat fent for him with a flag of truce ; that he not only came afhore with the know-ledge and under the protection of the General who commanded in the diftrict, but that he took no ftep while on fhore, but by direction of General Arnold, as will appear by the inclofed letter from him to your Excellency.

Under thefe circumftances I could not, and hoped you would not, confider Major André as a fpy, for any improper phrafe in his letter to you.

The facts he relates correfpond with the evidence I offer ; but he admits a conclufion that does not follow. The change of cloaths and name was ordered by General Arnold, under whofe directions he neceffarily was, while within his com-mand. As General Greene and I did not agree in opinion, I wifhed, that difinterefted gentlemen of knowledge of the law of war and nations, might be afked their opinion on the fubject ; and mentioned Monfieur Knyphaufen, and General Rochambault.

I related that a Captain Robinfon had been delivered to Sir Henry Clinton as a fpy, and undoubtedly was fuch : but that it being fignified to him that you were
                                    defirous

(19)

desirous that this man should be exchanged, he had ordered him to be exchanged.

I wished that an intercourse of such civilities, as the rules of war admit of, might take off many of its horrors. I admitted that Major André had a great share of Sir Henry Clinton's esteem, and that he would be infinitely obliged by his liberation; and that if he was permitted to return with me, I would engage to have any person you would be pleased to name set at liberty.

I added, that Sir Henry Clinton had never put to death any person for a breach of the rules of war, though he had, and now has, many in his power. Under the present circumstances, much good may arise from humanity, much ill from the want of it. If that could give any weight, I beg leave to add, that your favourable treatment of Major André, will be a favour I should ever be intent to return to any you hold dear.

My memory does not retain with the exactness I could wish, the words of the letter which General Greene shewed me from Major André to your Excellency. For Sir Henry Clinton's satisfaction, I beg you will order a copy of it to be sent to me at New-York.

I have the honour to be, your Excellency's
Most obedient and most humble servant,
JAMES ROBERTSON.
His Excellency General Washington.

New-York, October 1, 1780.
S I R,

THE polite attention shewn by your Excellency and the Gentlemen of your family to Mrs. Arnold, when in distress, demand my grateful acknowledgment and thanks, which I beg leave to present.

From your Excellency's letter to Sir Henry Clinton, I find a Board of General Officers have given it as their opinion, that Major André comes under the description of a spy: My good opinion of the candor and justice of those Gentlemen leads me to believe, that if they had been made fully acquainted with every circumstance respecting Major André, that they would by no means have considered him in the light of a spy, or even of a prisoner. In justice to him, I think it my duty to declare, that he came from on board the Vulture at my particular request, by a flag sent on purpose for him by Joshua Smith Esq. who had permission to go to Dobbs's ferry to carry letters, and for other purposes not mentioned, and

(20)

and to return. This was done as a blind to the spy boats: Mr. Smith at the same time had my private directions to go on board the Vulture, and bring on shore Col. Robinson, or Mr. John Anderson, which was the name I had requested Major André to assume: At the same time I desired Mr. Smith to inform him, that he should have my protection, and a safe passport to return in the same boat, as soon as our business was compleated. As several accidents intervened to prevent his being sent on board, I gave him my passport to return by land. Major André came on shore in his uniform (without disguise) which with much reluctance, at my particular and pressing instance, he exchanged for another coat. I furnished him with a horse and saddle, and pointed out the route by which he was to return. And as commanding officer in the department, I had an undoubted right to transact all these matters; which, if wrong, Major André ought by no means to suffer for them.

But if, after this just and candid representation of Major André's case, the Board of General Officers adhere to their former opinion, I shall suppose it dictated by passion and resentment; and if that Gentleman should suffer the severity of their sentence, I shall think myself bound by every tie of duty and honour, to retaliate on such unhappy persons of your army, as may fall within my power, that the respect due to flags, and to the law of nations, may be better understood and observed.

I have further to observe, that forty of the principal inhabitants of South-Carolina have justly forfeited their lives, which have hitherto been spared by the clemency of His Excellency Sir Henry Clinton, who cannot in justice extend his mercy to them any longer, if Major André suffers; which in all probability will open a scene of blood at which humanity will revolt.

Suffer me to intreat your Excellency, for your own and the honour of humanity, and the love you have of justice, that you suffer not an unjust sentence to touch the life of Major André.

But if this warning should be disregarded, and he suffer, I call heaven and earth to witness, that your Excellency will be justly answerable for the torrent of blood that may be spilt in consequence.

I have the honour to be, with due respect, your Excellency's
Most obedient and very humble servant,

B. ARNOLD.

His Excellency General Washington.

Tappan,

(21)

Tappan, Oct. 1, 1780.

S I R,

    BUOY'D above the terror of death by the confcioufnefs of a life devoted to honourable purfuits, and ftained with no action that can give me remorfe, I truft that the requeft I make to your Excellency at this ferious period, and which is to foften my laft moments, will not be rejected.

    Sympathy towards a foldier will furely induce your Excellency and a military tribunal to adopt the mode of my death to the feelings of a man of honour.

    Let me hope, Sir, that if ought in my character impreffes you with efteem towards me, if ought in my misfortunes marks me as the victim of policy and not of refentment, I fhall experience the operation of thefe feelings in your breaft, by being informed that I am not to die on a gibbet.

    I have the honour to be, your Excellency's
      Moft obedient and moft humble fervant,

          J O H N   A N D R E,
          Adj. Gen. to the Britifh army.

    The time which elapfed between the capture of Major André, which was on the morning of the 23d of Sept. and his execution, which did not take place till 12 o'clock on the 3d of October;---the mode of trying him;---his letter to Sir Henry Clinton, K. B. on the 29th of September, in which he faid, "I "receive the greateft attention from his Excellency General "Wafhington, and from every perfon under whofe charge I "happen to be placed;"---not to mention many other acknowledgments, which he made of the good treatment he received;---muft evince, that the proceedings againft him were not guided by paffion or refentment. The practice and ufage of war were againft his requeft, and made the indulgence he folicited, circumftanced as he was, inadmiffible.

        Publifhed by order of Congrefs,

        CHARLES THOMSON, *Secretary.*

CHAPTER IX.

ANDRÉ'S STATEMENT.—HIS EXECUTION.—ASSIGNMENT OF GENERAL
McDOUGALL TO COMMAND AT WEST POINT.—GENERAL GREENE
ORDERED TO RELIEVE HIM.—THE ARMY GO INTO WINTER QUAR-
TERS.—VISIT OF THE MARQUIS DE CHASTELLUX.—CELEBRATION AT
WEST POINT OF THE BIRTH OF THE DAUPHIN OF FRANCE.—GEN-
ERAL KNOX ORDERED TO COMMAND AT WEST POINT.—MAJOR
FLEMING SUCCEEDS HIM.—REMOVAL OF THE GREAT CHAIN FROM
THE HUDSON.—ATTEMPT TO RAISE THE OLD IRON IN THE SUNKEN
FRIGATES.—CAPTAIN MOLLY.—THE ARTILLERISTS AND ENGINEERS.
—ESTABLISHMENT OF A MILITARY SCHOOL.—REPAIRS ON THE FORTI-
FICATIONS.—REPORT OF MAJOR NIVEN.—VISIT OF LIANCOURT.—
WEST POINT NO LONGER OF IMPORTANCE AS A DEFENSIVE POINT.

THESE Proceedings were not followed by the usual
formality of a trial by a court-martial, nor were witnesses summoned; but the following paper, submitted
by André, was placed before the Board:

"ANDRÉ'S STATEMENT.

" On the 20th of September I left New York, to get
on board the Vulture, in order [as I thought] to meet
General Arnold there in the night. No boat, however,
came off, and I waited on board until the night of the
21st. During the day, a flag of truce was sent from
the Vulture to complain of the violation of a military
rule, in the instance of a boat having been decoyed on
shore by a flag, and fired upon. The letter was addressed
to General Arnold, signed by Captain Sutherland, but

11

written in my hand, and countersigned ' J. Anderson, Secretary.' Its intent was to indicate my presence on board the Vulture. In the night of the 21st, a boat with Mr. ——* and two hands came on board, in order to fetch Mr. Anderson on shore, and, if too late to bring me back, to lodge me until the next night in a place of safety. I went into the boat, landed, and spoke with Arnold. I got on horseback with him to proceed to ——* house, and in the way passed a guard I did not expect to see, having Sir Henry Clinton's directions not to go within an enemy's post, or to quit my own dress.

" In the morning A. quitted me, having himself made me put the papers I bore between my stockings and feet. Whilst he did it, he expressed a wish, in case of any accident befalling me, that they should be destroyed, which I said, of course would be the case, as when I went into the boat I should have them tied about with a string and a stone. Before we parted, some mention had been made of my crossing the river, and going by another route; but, I objected much against it, and thought it was settled that in the way I came, I was also to return.

" Mr. ——* to my great mortification persisted in his determination of carrying me by the other route; and, at the decline of the sun, I set out on horseback, passed King's Ferry, and came to Crompond, where a party of militia stopped us and advised we should remain. In the morning I came with ——* as far as within two miles and a half of Pine's Bridge, where he said he must part with me, as the Cow-Boys infested the road thencefor-

* Joshua Hett Smith.

ward. I was now near thirty miles from Kingsbridge, and left to the chance of passing that space undiscovered. I got to the neighbourhood of Tarrytown, which was far beyond the points described as dangerous, when I was taken by three volunteers, who, not satisfied with my pass, rifled me, and, finding papers, made me a prisoner.

" I have omitted mentioning, that, when I found my-self within an enemy's posts, I changed my dress."

" There is a tide " in the annals of war, as well as " in the affairs of men," which must be " taken at its full."

The period was a critical one—distrust, suspicion, and lack of confidence, amounting almost to demoralization, prevailed in the army.

If, in the history of a nation, an hour arrived when a " military necessity" justified the infliction of the penalty of death, the time had surely come.

At 12 o'clock on Monday, the 2d of October, André was executed in the presence of the army, at Tappan.

Dressed with scrupulous neatness, in full uniform, he said to those who, drawn by his gentle, truthful, and candid nature, clustered around him to take his hand : "All I request of you, gentlemen, is, that you will bear witness to the world that I die like a brave man;" and adding, " It will be but a momentary pang," Major André died, " lamented even by his foes."

Eighty-three years have passed, bringing to light the memoirs, incidents, details, and opinions of those who participated on that trying occasion ; but nothing has transpired to indicate that the measure of justice then meted out was not even-handed and impartial.*

* The remains of Major André were interred at Tappan, on the spot where he

On the 27th of September, General McDougall was ordered to assume the command at West Point, until the arrival of General St. Clair.   Three days after, the latter was directed to take command of the Post and its dependencies; his command was to consist of the Pennsylvania division, Meigs's and Livingston's regiments of Continentals, and a body of Massachusetts and New Hampshire militia.*   In the mean time Major-General Greene made application for the command, and on the 6th of October he was directed to repair to West Point, taking with him the Jersey, York, and Starke's Brigades, and on his arrival to relieve General St. Clair.   The latter, with the Pennsylvania division and Meigs's regiment, was directed to join the army.†

General Greene was enjoined to exercise great vigilance in completing the works, and providing magazines and shelter for the troops.

A delegation of the Southern States having applied to have General Greene succeed General Gates in the command of the Southern army, on the 14th of October Major-General Heath was ordered to repair to West Point and relieve General Greene, who left for this purpose on the 19th.‡

On the 28th of November, the army went into winter quarters in the Highlands and its vicinity.   The Jersey brigades returned to that State.   Four Massachusetts brigades were added to the garrison at West Point,

---

was executed; they were exhumed in 1821, under the direction of the British Consul, and conveyed to England.   A very interesting account of this occurrence will be found in the United Service Journal [British], November, 1833.

* Writings of Washington, Sparks, VII., 223.

† Id., Sparks, VII., 232.   ‡ Heath's Memoirs.

and two from Connecticut were stationed on the east
side of the river opposite, and on Constitution Island,
while General Head-Quarters were established at New
Windsor.

It was at this period that the Major-General, the
Marquis de Chastellux, visited West Point, and the following description of the works, at that time, is taken
from his narrative :   *   *   *   *   *.

FORT PUTNAM—FROM THE WEST POINT HOTEL.

" The first fort we met with above West Point, on
the declivity of the mountain, is called Fort Putnam,
from the General* of that name. It is placed on a rock,
very steep on every side ; the ramparts were at first
constructed with trunks of trees ; they are rebuilt with
stone, and are not quite finished. There is a powder
·magazine, bomb-proof, a large cistern, and souterrains
for the garrison. Above this fort, and when we reach

* Named from Colonel Rufus Putnam.

the loftiest summit, there are three strong redoubts, lined with cannon, at three different eminences, each of which would require a formal siege. The day being nearly spent, I contented myself with judging by the eye of the very intelligent manner in which they are calculated for mutual protection. Fort Wyllis, whither General Heath conducted me,* was near and more accessible. Though it be placed lower than Fort Putnam, it still commands the river to the south. It is a large pentagonal redoubt, built of huge trunks of trees; it is picketed and lined with artillery. Under the fire of this redoubt, and lower down, is a battery of cannon, to range more obliquely the course of the river. This battery is not closed at the gorge, so that the enemy may take, but never keep it; which leads me to remark that this is the best method in all field fortifications. Batteries placed in works have two inconveniences: the first is, that if these works be ever so little elevated, they do not graze sufficiently; and the second, that the enemy may at once attack the redoubt and the battery; whereas the latter, being exterior, and protected by the redoubt, must be first attacked; in which case it is supported by troops who have nothing to fear for themselves, and whose fire is commonly better directed, and does more execution. A battery yet lower, and nearer to the river [Fort Meigs], completes the security of the southern part.

"In returning to West Point, we saw a redoubt that is suffered to go to ruin, as being useless, which in fact it is.† It was night when we got home, but what I had

* The General, it appears, did not visit Fort Webb.
† Probably on Block-House Point, near Mr. Kinsley's.

to observe did not require daylight. It is a vast souter-
rain, formed within the Fort of West Point [Fort Clin-
ton], where not only the powder and ammunition necessary for this Post are kept in reserve, but the deposit of
the whole army.

"These magazines completely filled, the numerous
artillery one sees in these different fortresses, the prodi-
gious labour necessary to transport, and pile up on steep
rocks, huge trunks of trees, and enormous hewn stones,
impress the mind with an idea of the Americans very
different from that which the English ministry have
laboured to give to Parliament."†   *   *   *

With the exception of Fort Putnam, upon which
repairs were commenced fourteen years later, these works
remain at this moment, with no change other than that
wrought by neglect and decay.

The age of progress and the march of empire have left
these monuments of the labor and skill of that patriot
band, not one of whom, it is believed, is still among the
living inhabitants of the present day.

One incident only, of interest, occurred from the date
last mentioned until the close of hostilities, and this was
the celebration of the birth of the unfortunate Louis the
XVII. of France.

The army had passed the winter in the Highlands,
and the following extracts explain the character of the
rejoicing held over the event referred to :

"HEAD-QUARTERS, NEWBURG,
"*Tuesday*, *May* 28*th*, 1782.
" *Orders :*
"The Commander-in-Chief is happy in the opportu-

† Travels in North America.—Chastellux.

nity of announcing to the Army, the birth of the *Dauphin of France ;* and desirous of giving a general occasion of testifying the satisfaction which he is convinced, will pervade the breast of every American officer and soldier, on the communication of an event so highly interesting to a monarch and nation, who have given such distinguishing proofs of their attachment, is pleased to order a *feu de joie* on Thursday next; and requests the company of all the General, Regimental, and Staff Officers of the Army, who are not necessarily detained by duty, at West Point on that day at four o'clock. Commanding Officers of Brigades and Corps will receive particular instructions for their government."

"Head-Quarters, Newburg,
" *Wednesday, May 29th,* 1782.

" The Troops are to be supplied with an extra gill of Rum per man to-morrow.

" Memorandum.

" The Commander-in-Chief desires his compliments may be presented to the Officers' Ladies, with and in the neighborhood of the Army, together with a request that they will favor him with their company at dinner on Thursday next, at West Point. The General will be happy to see any other Ladies of his own or his friends' acquaintance, on the occasion, without the formality of a particular invitation."

"Inspector-General's Order,
[West Point,] " *May* 30, 1782.

" The Regimental Quarter-Masters will instantly apply to the Conductor of Military Stores for three blank cartridges for each man and Non-commissioned officer ; they will be careful that all the other cartridges are taken out of the boxes, and delivered to the men as soon as the *feu de joie is over*.   Colonel Crane will please to direct that the thirteen cannon which are to compose the Park are furnished with two hundred and eight blank cartridges; Fort Sherburne* six; the South Redoubt with three; and the Garrison at Stoney Point† with thirteen.

"Colonel Crane's Regiment of Artillery will parade and receive his Excellency on his arrival; after which, one Captain, Captain-Lieutenant, and two Sub-Lieutenants, with sixty privates of the same Regiment, will form a Guard of Infantry, and receive the Inspector-General's particular orders; the remainder of the Regiment will man the Batteries.

"The discharge of thirteen cannon from the Park, after the first toast, will be followed by a similar discharge from the Garrison of Stoney Point.

"The signal for the commencement of the *feu de joie* will be given by the cannon from Fort Sherburne, and, in each volley, as soon as the Regiment on the left of the Line has finished to fire, one cannon from the South Redoubt will be given, as a signal for the Park to renew the firing, which will be repeated three times.

"After the fire-works are played off, the ceremony will be concluded by a discharge of three cannon from Fort Sherburne.

"The Officers will pay the most minute attention to the arms of the Troops, that they may be in the best possible order."

---

* Where the Mexican Trophy Guns now rest.   † Gee's Point.

"Head-Quarters, Newburg,
" *Thursday, May* 30, 1782.

"The celebration of the birth of the Dauphin of France, which was to have taken place this day, is to be postponed until to-morrow, the 31st inst.

"A Plan for conducting the Rejoicing on Thursday, the 31st May, 1782.*

"The Troops, having previously cooked their provisions, will march from their Cantonments at such an hour as will admit of their being at the places severally assigned them by half after two o'clock, *post meridian*, where they will remain in columns under cover, until the discharge of three pieces of cannon at West Point, which will be a signal for the columns to advance and display in full view of the Point, and stack their arms.   That done,

* It appears, by several orders issued at "Highlands," [the Head-Quarters of General Heath were at the "Robinson House"] between the dates, May 28 and the above date, that large fatigue parties had been constantly at work in procuring "small timber and some other materials," from the neighborhood of West Point. On the 24th it was ordered that "the 30 fatigue men now with the Engineer at West Point, having some particular knowledge of a particular piece of business which the Engineer has on hand, are not to be relieved until the 31st inst."— On the 25th it was stated in orders, that "All the Carpenters and Joiners in the Army are wanted for a few days at West Point, to assist in erecting and completing an arbor; they are to be immediately draughted and sent for that purpose." On the 26th it was ordered, that "the Connecticut Line, and 3d Massachusetts Brigade, are to cover the arbor building at West Point.   The Commanding Officers of the Brigades will appoint an officer from each to attend Major Villefranche this evening, who will designate the part they are severally to perform, and when it is to be completed. The Superintending Officers are to be furnished with such numbers of men from their respective Brigades, as they think necessary to finish the Bower in the time limited, for which they are responsible." On the 27th it was ordered, that "2 captains, 4 subalterns, 6 sergeants, and 150 rank and file, be for fatigue to-morrow; a Captain, Subaltern, and 50 men of which are to parade at reveille beating, and work until 8 o'clock in the morning, at which time the remainder are to turn out, and work until 6 o'clock in the evening; then the others are to work again until dark. This is to be done until the Bower is completed." "They are to be under the direction of Major Villefranche."

all the Officers (except one Field Officer to each Brigade, and one Battalion Officer to each Regiment on the east side of the river, who are to remain with their Corps) are requested to repair to West Point, where the General expects the pleasure of their company at dinner.

" Dinner will be on the table at four o'clock, at which time a proportion of liquor will be distributed to each Regiment and Corps by their respective Quarter-Masters.

" After dinner thirteen Toasts will be drank, and each Toast announced by a discharge of Artillery.

" As soon as the thirteenth is drank, the Officers will rise from the table, and join their respective Regiments.

" At half after seven, the *feu de joie* will commence with the discharge of thirteen pieces of cannon from the Park, succeeded by a fire of musketry from the Infantry, in the following order, viz. :—

2d   Massachusetts Brigade.

1st   ditto   ditto

1st Connecticut   ditto

2d   ditto   ditto

10th Massachusetts Regiment.

3d   ditto   Brigade.

" The firing being three times repeated in the same order, the Officers commanding Corps will, with an audible voice, pray to God to bless the Dauphin of France, and grant him long life and happiness, and the Troops give three cheers.

" The fireworks will then be displayed from Fort Webb, and the ceremony concluded by a discharge of three pieces of cannon from the Park, which will also serve as a signal for the Troops to return to their cantonment."*

The expectations which these preparations gave rise to were amply realized, and are thus fully described:

" The 31st of May being the day appointed for the celebration, between 12 and 1 o'clock P. M., His Excellency General Washington and Lady, and Suite, His Excellency Governor Clinton, with his Lady, Major-General Knox and Brigadier-General Hand, with their Ladies, Mr. Benson, the Attorney-General, Mrs. Livingston [of the lower Manor], Mrs. Montgomery [widow of the Hero who fell at Quebec], and a great number of ladies and gentlemen from the States of New York and New Jersey, arrived in their barges at West Point, and were conducted through the grand colonnade which had been erected for the entertainment, situated on the gently rising ground in the rear of Fort Clinton, commanding the level of the Plain with a variegated view of all the barracks, encampments, and fortifications of the garrison.

" The situation was romantic, and the occasion novel and interesting. Major Villefranche,† an ingenious

* Revolutionary Orders.—Colonel Whiting, U. S. A.

† Major *Villefranche* was one of the many French Officers who came to America early in the autumn of 1777, after the news of Burgoyne's overthrow reached Europe, to seek employment in the army. On the 4th of October of that year, Congress "Ordered," That there be paid to Mons. Villefranche, who has tendered his services to the United States, $100, for which he was to be accountable.* In the following winter, Mons. Villefranche laid a memorial before Congress, setting forth that though he had received a " gratification" and money, to return to France, he would prefer to remain, if he could be employed as an Engineer, under General Du Portail. Whereupon, on January 1st, 1778, Congress " *Resolved*, That the Chevalier de Villefranche be appointed a Major of Engineers under Brigadier Du Portail."† [The Corps of Engineers was organized as a distinct branch of the army, March 11, 1779.]‡ He built the stone magazine on the west end of Con-

* Journals of Congress, II., 274.   † Journals of Congress, II., 390.
‡ Journals of Congress, III., 224.

(Fac Simile)

A Colonade built at West Point During the American War To Celebrate the birth of the
Dauphin of France our great and good Ally as then styled May 31. 1782 By
Major Villefranche [Eng.]

French Engineer, had been employed with one thousand men about ten days, in constructing the curious edifice. It was composed of the simple materials which the common trees in the vicinity afforded, being about two hundred and twenty feet in length, and eighty feet wide, supported by a grand colonnade of one hundred and eighteen pillars, made of the trunks of trees. The covering of the roof consisted of boughs, or branches of trees curiously interwoven, and the same materials formed the walls, leaving the ends entirely open. On the inside, every pillar was encircled with muskets and bayonets, bound round in a fanciful and handsome manner, and the whole interior was decorated with evergreens, festoons of flowers, garlands, emblematical devices, Fleur-de-lis, and other ornaments significant of the existing alliance.

"This superb structure in symmetry of proportion, neatness of workmanship and elegance of arrangement, has seldom perhaps been surpassed on any temporary

stitution Island in 1782. [Heath, 351.] On the 2d of May, 1783, Congress "*Resolved*, That Major Villefranche be a Lieutenant-Colonel by Brevet in the Corps of Engineers."* It is probable that he returned to France on the close of the war. The numerous drawings he left, show him to have been an officer of great value as an Engineer and Draughtsman.

Major *Peter Charles L'Enfant*, Engineer, was born in France, in 1755. He was appointed a lieutenant in the French provincial forces, which position he vacated, and tendered his services to the United States in the autumn of 1777, as an Engineer. He was appointed Captain of Engineers on 18th February, 1778, and was at the siege of Savannah, where he was wounded and left on the field of battle. He afterwards served in the army under the immediate command of Washington, and was promoted Major of Engineers, May 2, 1783. He was employed as the Engineer at Fort Mifflin in 1794, and appointed Professor of Engineering at the United States Military Academy in July, 1812 (declined). He died in Prince George's County, Md , June, 1825. He was an accomplished draughtsman and made himself greatly respected. It is worthy of remark, that both he and Major Villefranche expended their fortunes in the service of the United States.†

* Journals of Congress, IV., 219.
† Army Dict., Journals Congress, III., 243; IV., 219. French Archives, Hon. Richard Rush.

occasion; it affected the spectators with admiration and pleasure, and reflects much credit on the taste and ability of Major Villefranche. Several appropriate mottoes decorated the grand edifice, pronouncing benedictions on the Dauphin and happiness to the two allied nations. The whole army was paraded on the contiguous hills on both sides of the river, forming a circle of several miles in open view of the public edifice, and in the following order. The 2d Brigade of Massachusetts on the ridge of the hills beneath Fort Putnam, with its right extending towards the river; the 1st Brigade continuing the line on the left, stretched its flank to the Red House in the valley, and enveloped the point. On the eastern shore, the 1st and 2d Connecticut Brigades were drawn up on the high grounds in the rear of Constitution Island; the 10th Massachusetts regiment, on the cleared fields above Nelson's Ferry; and the 3d Massachusetts Brigade on the heights, between the North and Middle Redoubts.

"At the signal designated, by firing three cannon, the regimental officers all left their commands, and repaired to the building to partake of the entertainment which had been prepared by order of the Commander-in-Chief. At five o'clock, dinner being on the table, his Excellency General Washington, and his Lady and suite, with the invited guests, moved from Major-General McDougall's quarters through the line formed by Colonel Crane's regiment of Artillery, to the Arbor which was guarded by the Commander-in-Chief's Guard, where more than five hundred gentlemen and ladies partook of a magnificent festival. A martial band charmed the senses with music; and while the appetite feasted, all gazed with admiration on the illustrious guests, and the novel spectacle presented to the view. The cloth being removed, thirteen appropriate toasts were drank, each one being announced by the discharge of thirteen cannon and accompanied by music. The guests retired from the table at seven o'clock, and the regimental officers repaired to their respective commands.

"The Arbor, in the evening, was illuminated by a vast number of lights, which, being arranged in regular and tasteful order, exhibited a scene vying in brilliancy with the starry firmament. The Officers having rejoined their regiments, thirteen cannon were again fired as a prelude to a general *feu de joie*, which immediately succeeded throughout the whole line of the army on the surrounding hills, and being three times repeated, the mountains resounded and echoed like tremendous peals of thunder, and the flashing from thousands of fire-arms in the darkness of evening, could be compared only to the most vivid flashes of lightning from the clouds. The *feu de joie* was immediately followed by three shouts of acclamation and benediction for the Dauphin, by the united voices of the whole army on all sides. The celebration was concluded by the exhibition of fireworks, consisting of rockets, wheels, fountains, trees, bee-hives, balloons, stars and fleur-de-lis, admirably constructed and played off at twenty minutes past 11 o'clock.

"His Excellency General Washington was unusually cheerful. He attended the ball in the evening, and with a dignified and graceful air, having Mrs. Knox for his partner, carried down a dance of twenty couple in the Arbor on the green grass."*

* Thacher's Military Journal; New Jersey Gazette, June 12th, 1782.

On the 29th of August, General Knox was ordered to relieve General Heath, and instructed from Head-Quarters at Newburg to visit the redoubts frequently, to see that the garrisons were kept on the alert, and to make them invariably sleep within the works. The care of the public buildings and the repair and alteration of the works were especially enjoined, and a timely order prohibited private buildings from being erected without his knowledge and consent.

General Knox held the command until the latter part of January, 1785, and receiving the appointment of Secretary of War in March of that year, he was succeeded by Major George Fleming,* who commanded the arsenal and ranked as an Ordnance and Military Storekeeper.

Under Major Fleming's administration, the old arms and camp equipage of the army were preserved and stored, or condemned and sold, as opportunities presented. Immense quantities of powder were stored in the magazines at Fort Putnam and on Constitution Island. The work of dismantling the redoubts of their artillery occurred in 1787, at which time a large number of guns were sold for old iron. The time of the removal of the Boom and Chain has not been ascertained, but on the 29th of September, 1783, a memorial from Mark Bird was read in Congress, requesting that the great Chain used for the defence of Hudson's River be delivered to him at a reasonable price. Whereupon Congress *Resolved*, "That at this time it is improper to dispose of the

---

* Major *Fleming* had been a captain of artillery during the war. He remained at West Point until after the establishment of the Military Academy, in charge of the Arsenal of Repairs and Storage. The "Long Barrack" near the present Hotel was used for this purpose.—[Fleming, MSS.]

chain made for the defence of Hudson's River."* Six years afterwards, Major Fleming informed the Secretary of War that he had agreed with a party to raise some cannon and old iron in the river; of which one-half of the cannon and one-fourth of the wrought iron was to revert to the United States. The wrought iron, he stated, "lies in fourteen fathoms of water, besides being fastened to some very large logs which must be hoisted to the surface to cut away the iron."†

In April, 1787, efforts were made to raise the pig-iron used as ballast on the frigates which were burned after the fall of Forts Clinton and Montgomery. "The frigates," said Major Fleming, in his report to the Secretary of War, "were set on fire opposite Constitution Island, and it being ebb tide, they drifted down the river nearly as far as Fort Montgomery, where one burnt to the water's edge and sunk. The other one I have found. She lies fore and aft the channel on the east side of the river, better than three miles from this Point. The timbers of her starboard side are to be seen at low water, and the other side is about ten feet under water at the same time, owing to her listing off as the edge of the channel runs.

" The iron was cast at the ' Forest of Dean', and from the quantity of stone ballast now resting upon it, it cannot be raised short of a round sum."‡

The buildings, magazines, barracks, &c., on Constitution Island, were sold early in 1788, to Gideon Salmon. " Mr. Bunn, who occupied the barrack at the time, was the owner of the Island, and requested that one-fifth of

---

* Jour. Congress, IV., 280.   † Fleming, MSS. U. S. M. A.
‡ Fleming, MSS. U. S. M. A.

the building be given him, for the use of the land on which the Block-house, Forts, and magazines stood."*

Near Swimstown, now called Buttermilk Falls, upon the premises now owned by Mr. Alfred Pell, there lived and died the soldier's wife, "Molly Pitcher," better known as *Captain Molly*. She was in Fort Clinton at the time of its capture by the British, in October, 1777. When the enemy scaled the parapet, her husband, who was an artilleryman, dropped his port-fire and fled, but Molly caught it up, and discharged the last gun fired by the Americans. Nine months afterwards, at the memorable battle of Monmouth, although but twenty-two years of age, she illustrated her devotion to her husband, who was serving a gun, by bringing him water during the action from a neighboring spring. A shot from the enemy killed him at his post, and the officer in command, having no one competent to fill his place, ordered the piece to be withdrawn. Molly saw her husband fall as she came from the spring, and also heard the order. She dropped her bucket, seized the rammer, and vowed she would fill his place at the gun, and avenge his death. She performed the duty with a skill and courage which attracted the attention of all who saw her.

On the following morning, covered with dirt and blood, General Greene presented her to Washington, who, admiring her bravery, conferred upon her the appointment of a Sergeant. By his recommendation her name was placed upon the half-pay list for life. She is described as a stout, red-haired, freckled-faced young Irish woman, with a handsome, piercing eye.† She was a great

---

* Fleming, MSS. U. S. M. A.

† Field-Book of the Revolution.—Lossing, II., 155.

favorite in the army, usually appearing with an artillery-man's coat over her dress, and wearing a cocked hat.

After taking up her residence near West Point, she received her subsistence through the Commissary at the Post, and supplies of various kinds were sent to the family employed to take care of her, direct from the Secretary of War.

The extracts below* are from Major Fleming's MSS., and the letters are addressed to " Major-General Henry Knox, Secretary of War."

Molly, it is believed, died on the spot where she lived for so many years, in 1789, as at that date her name ceases to appear on the Commissary's books.

By the act of May 9th, 1794, Congress authorized the raising of a Corps of Artillerists and Engineers, to consist of four battalions, which Corps was stationed at

---

* " WEST POINT, 7th of October, 1786.

*   *   *   *   " SIR:—I have sent another account of Mrs. Swim's for taking care of Captain Molly up to the 27th of Sept., and have removed her to another place, as I thought she was not so well treated as she ought to be."   *   *   *   *   *

" WEST POINT, 8th of July, 1787.

*   *   *   *   *   " SIR:—I have drawn three orders on you, for the maintainance of Captain Molly, in favor of Mr. Denniston: one is from January 19th to April 12th, the other from April 13th to July 5th, 1786, inclusive, which accounts were lodged in the War Office last fall, and are Mrs. Swim's. The other is from September 28th to July 5th, 1786, inclusive, and will be delivered by Mr. Denniston for Mrs. Randall.

" As Molly is such a disagreeable object to take care of, and I promised to pay them every quarter, I have been obliged to borrow the money to pay the people; if it can possibly be replaced, I should be very glad."   *   *   *

" WEST POINT, April 21st, 1787.

*   *   *   *   " SIR:—I am informed by the woman that takes care of Captain Molly, that she is much in want of Shifts. If you think proper to order three or four, I should be glad."   *   *   *   *

" WEST POINT, June 12th, 1787.

*   *   *   *   " SIR:—If the Shifts which you informed me should be made for Captain Molly are done, I should be glad to have them sent, as she complains much for want of them."   *   *   *   *

West Point, under the command of Lieutenant-Colonel Stephen Rochefontaine,* with Major Lewis Toussard, and Major J. J. U. Rivardi as the field officers. In the summer of this year, the work of repairing Fort Putnam was commenced, under Colonel Vincent, a French Engineer, assisted by Major Niven. The following report, rendered by Colonel Vincent in August, 1794, represents the condition and progress of the works :—

"FORTIFICATIONS AT WEST POINT.

"STATE OF THE WORKS ORDERED AT WEST POINT, N. Y., AUGUST 31ST, 1794. BY COLONEL VINCENT.

"*Fort Putnam.*—The repairing of the enclosure of the fort is now going on; one part has been altered, according to the strong reasons reported in one memorial, which has not yet been seen by the minister; but, as that part of the enclosure to be changed was to be new built, it will be a very trifling expense to make the useful proposed alteration.

"*Fort Clinton.*—It will not be possible for this year to begin any works; and it will be sufficient to collect every necessary material, during this season, in order to be ready to begin very early in the beginning of the spring. It should be also very useful to begin this year the digging of the foundations, in employing the diggers at the task by cubic fathoms. We think that this way is the only one to be used in the works ordered by the General Government, inasmuch as the laborer's day's work is very high.

"*Observations.*—The works at West Point are directed by the Major Niven, who may hardly be sufficient for

---

* Colonel *Rochefontaine* had been an officer of the army of France, and served in the Revolutionary war in America.

so great a business. It will be necessary to employ one engineer more, principally for the important masonry to be erected there, which will require great knowledge in that line. The manner of carrying on all the necessary diggings by task, requires also one man accustomed to such works, and daily upon the spot. The able commander and clever man, Captain Fleming, ought also obtain the first superintendency upon these important works."*

"REPORT OF MAJOR DANIEL NIVEN TO THE SECRETARY OF WAR. RELATIVE TO THE FORTIFICATIONS AT WEST POINT, DECEMBER 12, 1794.

" SIR :—I conceive it my duty to make the following report : That, from the 20th of May to the 18th day of July last, I was employed in superintending lime-burning, collecting stone to Fort Clinton, making and repairing roads, making and repairing tools, and repairing such parts of the rear wall of Fort Putnam as I judged sufficient. On the said 18th day of July, Colonel Vincent, Captain Fleming, and myself, concluded that all the old wall of Fort Putnam, facing Fort Clinton, be taken down and rebuilt; enclosing the point, for the advantage of enlarging the battery facing the ridge, where Forts Webb and Wyllis stood. Accordingly, I proceeded, and employed as many miners, masons, laborers, and teams, as I could find, that would work to advantage, and have taken away the old wall and built a new one, with the foundation on the rock, agreeably to your instructions, on durable principles of masonry. The said new wall is raised from twenty to twenty-five feet high, except the gate-way, for want of free-stone to face the arch. Nine

* S. P. Mil. Affairs, I., 104.

bomb-proof arches are closed over the barracks and
magazines. I had hopes to finish four more, but the
days are so short and cold, and the frost would damage
the masonry so much, if the mortar could be worked,
that I judged it best to discharge the workmen on the
22d day of November, except a very few under the
direction of Captain Fleming. It was impossible to
carry on the works without great damage to the public
service.

RUINS OF FORT PUTNAM—INTERIOR VIEW.

"Several arrangements ought to be made this winter,
that the works may be carried on to advantage the
ensuing season; that the laborers be hired by the month,
and forfeit something if they leave the works without
timely notice; that a forage store be established; that
the brick be moulded in the shape of a key-stone, to
turn the arches. This will make strong work, and save
great labor.*

(Signed)   " D. NIVEN."

* S. P. Mil. Affairs, I., 104.

In 1796, Liancourt visited West Point, and remarks that thirty-five thousand dollars had been uselessly expended in repairing Fort Putnam, because forty-five thousand more, necessary to complete the work, were refused by Congress. The same traveller found the four battalions of artillerists and engineers, composed of about two hundred and fifty men each, mostly made up of foreigners. But ten officers were present, representing " all nations ;" they were, however, better provided than the officers in the French service.*

A Military School, through the instrumentality of President Washington, was established in 1794, for the instruction of this corps, and books and apparatus were supplied. The building used for this purpose, called the " Old Provost," was situated on the northwest side of the " Ice-House Hollow;" it was two stories high, and built of stone. It was destroyed by fire, with its books and contents, in 1796, and the School was suspended until 1801.†

The importance of West Point for defensive purposes in a military point of view belongs to the past; but the soil hallowed by the footsteps of Washington, Greene, Knox, and almost every General officer of the Revolution, secluded in its mountain position, as it were purposely for retirement and study, was henceforth to be consecrated by the Nation to the education of her chosen youth, for the advancement and welfare of the Republic.

---

* Travels in the United States.—Liancourt.
† MSS. Gen. J. G. Swift.

PART II.

—

THE ORIGIN AND PROGRESS

OF THE

UNITED STATES MILITARY ACADEMY.

CHAPTER X.

EARLY NECESSITY FOR A MILITARY ACADEMY RECOGNIZED AT THE
COMMENCEMENT OF THE REVOLUTION.—APPOINTMENT OF A COM-
MITTEE TO VISIT THE ARMY BY CONGRESS, AND THEIR REPORT IN
FAVOR OF SUCH AN INSTITUTION.—RESOLUTION OF CONGRESS UPON
THE SUBJECT.—NECESSITY FOR A MILITARY ACADEMY ON THE
ESTABLISHMENT OF PEACE.—ARGUMENTS OF GENERALS HUNTING-
DON AND PICKERING.—VALUE OF THEIR EXPERIENCE AND OPIN-
IONS.—OFFICIAL REPORT OF GENERAL KNOX ON MILITARY EDUCA-
TION.—BRIEF CAREER OF MILITARY MEN.—CITIZEN GRADUATES
AND THEIR SERVICES.—OPINIONS OF WASHINGTON AND JEFFERSON
ON THE ESTABLISHMENT OF A MILITARY ACADEMY.—ORGANIZATION
OF THE CORPS OF ARTILLERY AND ENGINEERS, AND APPOINTMENT
OF CADETS THERETO, IN 1794.—INCREASE OF THE CORPS AND OF THE
NUMBER OF CADETS IN 1798.—PROVISION FOR THEIR EDUCATION.
—INADEQUATE MEANS FOR THIS PURPOSE.—VIEWS OF PRESIDENT
ADAMS AND MR. McHENRY, THE SECRETARY OF WAR.—ORGANIZA-
TION OF THE MILITARY ACADEMY BY CONGRESS, TO BE STATIONED
AT WEST POINT.—MESSAGE OF PRESIDENT JEFFERSON RELATIVE
TO THE SUBJECT.—REPORT OF COLONEL WILLIAMS, THE FIRST
SUPERINTENDENT OF THE ACADEMY.

THE idea of establishing a National MILITARY ACADEMY
dates back to an early period in our history; indeed, at
the very outset of the struggle for independence, it
forced its claims upon the attention of those invested
with the control and direction of provincial authority.

On the 20th of September, 1776, the Continental
Congress appointed a Committee, consisting of Messrs.
Sherman, Gerry, and Lewis, in accordance with a
resolution of the same date, " to repair to Head-Quarters

near New York, to inquire into the state of the army, and the best means of supplying its wants."*

On the 3d of October this Committee submitted a report, which was read, and ordered to lie on the table. The following extracts are taken from the report:

" The Committee appointed to inquire into the State of the Army at New York, left on the 21st, and arrived at Camp on the 24th of September; and after three days' conference with the General officers, and an interview with many of the Staff, they found the following to be a statement of the facts   *   *   *   *   *
*   *   *   "That some of the troops in Camp were badly officered, and not subject to the command which good troops ought ever to be. The Articles of War and General Orders were frequently transgressed, and the Commander-in-chief had the mortification to see, that some of his officers, instead of suppressing disorderly behavior, encouraged the soldiers by their examples to plunder and commit other offences, or endeavored to screen them from just punishment by partial trials."

These and other practices and evils, so deeply impressed the Committee with the importance of having officers of known honor, ability, and education, to officer the regiments, that they earnestly called on the States to resort to more effective measures for the purpose; and among many resolutions then adopted, the following is to be found:

" *Resolved*, That the Board of War be directed to prepare a Continental Laboratory, and a *Military Academy*, and provide the same with proper Officers."   *   *   *

This Committee, while at the camp, among others,

* Am. Archives, V., II., 1373.

conferred with Colonel Henry Knox, of the Artillery, and on the 27th of September, 1776, this afterwards greatly distinguished officer furnished the Committee with "Hints for the Improvement of the Artillery of the United States," from which the following extract is taken, under the belief that it is the earliest record of a plan for a United States Military Academy bearing any resemblance in its design to the one now in existence :

*   *   *   *   "And as officers can never act with confidence until they are masters of their profession, an Academy established on a liberal plan would be of the utmost service to the Continent, where the whole theory and practice of fortification and gunnery should be taught; to be nearly on the same plan as that at Woolwich, making allowance for the difference of circumstances; a place to which our enemies are indebted for the superiority of their artillery to all who have opposed them."*

Three days after these "Hints" were furnished, and two days before the Committee submitted their report, the following entry is to be found on the Journal :

"CONTINENTAL CONGRESS,
Oct. 1, 1776.

"*Resolved*, That a Committee of five be appointed to prepare and bring in a plan of a *Military Academy* at the Army.

" The members chosen, Mr. Hooper, Mr. Lynch, Mr. Wythe, Mr. Williams, and Mr. J. Adams."†

It does not appear that this Committee ever reported, or that any further active measures were ever devised to carry out the intention so clearly disclosed, and so distinctly recognized as necessary to the welfare of the

---

* Am. Archives, V., II., 1387.   † Am. Archives, V., II., 1383.

army, until the termination of the Revolutionary War. The Proclamation for a cessation of hostilities was adopted in Congress on the 11th day of April, 1783; on the same day Colonel Alexander Hamilton, the chairman of the Committee for Peace Arrangements, communicated to the General-in-chief a wish to be furnished with his opinions, as to what ought to constitute a proper peace establishment.

This request was laid before the officers of the army, then encamped at Newburg and New Windsor, who were requested to report to the Commander, in writing, their views; and, guided by the experience of eight years in active field service, the necessity for a Military Academy was not overlooked in the voluminous papers submitted.

Brigadier-General Huntingdon declared that "West Point has been held as the key to the United States. The British viewed it in the same point of light, and will, it is presumed, keep their eye upon it as long as they regret the loss of the country, or have a passion for power and conquest.

"West Point is exposed to a *coup-de-main*, and ought therefore to be always in a complete condition of defence. With a little more expense than that of maintaining a garrison of five hundred or six hundred men, it may be made a safe deposit, where every military article may be kept in good order and repair; and, with a small additional expense, an academy might be here instituted for instruction in all the branches of the military art."*

Colonel Timothy Pickering, the Quartermaster-General of the army, after combating the idea of instituting aca-

* Correspondence of the Revolution.—Sparks, IV., 27.

demies for military purposes at the different arsenals in the United States, a scheme that had found favor with some of the officers, proceeds to say : " If any thing like a military academy in America be practicable at this time, it must be grounded on the permanent military establishment for our frontier posts and arsenals, and the wants of the States, separately, of officers to command the defences on their seacoasts.

" On this principle it might be expedient to establish a military school or academy at West Point. And that a competent number of young gentlemen might be induced to become students, it might be made a rule, that vacancies in the standing regiment should be supplied from thence ; those few instances excepted where it would be just to promote a very meritorious sergeant.

" For this end the number, which shall be judged requisite to supply vacancies in the standing regiment, might be fixed, and that of the students, who are admitted with an expectation of filling them, limited accordingly.

" They might be allowed subsistence at the public expense If any other youth desired to pursue the same studies at the Military Academy, they might be admitted, only subsisting themselves.

" Those students should be instructed in what is usually called military discipline, tactics, and the theory and practice of fortification and gunnery.

" The Commandant and one or two other officers of the standing regiment, and the Engineers, making West Point their general residence, would be the masters of the Academy ; and the Inspector-General superintend the whole." *

* Writings of Washington.—Sparks VIII., 417.

These suggestions, although not productive of immediate results, did not fail to arrest the attention of statesmen and legislators on the general subject of military
education at a later day.

" They perceived that although the ordinary, subordi-
nate, and mechanical duties of a soldier and officer might
be performed without especial training, the higher class
of duties, and the capacity for command, could be understood and exercised only by those whose intellectual
faculties had been carefully cultivated. They felt that
the common interpretation of the axiom that, 'knowledge is power,' significant and important as it is, was
not its noblest and worthiest interpretation.

" Power over matter, and over the minds of others, is
not the choicest gift of knowledge, enviable and glorious
though it be; it is, in truth, a dangerous gift. But
power over the mind of its possessor, purifying and elevating it, subduing all that is low or selfish to the
authority of duty and virtue, this is the distinguishing,
the kingly gift of knowledge. They felt, therefore, that
the moral, as well as the intellectual nature should be
sedulously nurtured. They were convinced, also, that
in a free state, it was most impolitic and unsafe for the
army to be separated, in habits, interests, and feelings,
from the other orders of society; and they recognized
in knowledge, which is, in a great measure, the result of
mutual interchange of thoughts, the true principle of
amalgamation.

" Many of them had been observers or partakers of
the moral dangers of a military life; they were aware of
the impoverished means of the members of the army,
and of the probable inability of the country, for a long

period, to provide more for them than a mere support; and they were, consequently, solicitous to impart to them knowledge, 'in itself an economical possession,' the pursuit of which is inconsistent with, and destroy the desire for indulgence in, idle or vicious amusements. To these general considerations were added others, growing out of our peculiar form of government, and the sentiments and prepossession of the people.

" As an almost necessary consequence of the national experience during the war of the Revolution, the subject of military education first presented itself, in connection with the organization and improvement of the militia. While they bore grateful testimony to the services and valor of those of their countrymen who upheld the standard of the United Colonies in the hours of darkest gloom, they could not be insensible that the struggle for independence would have been sooner triumphantly closed, if those gallant men had been disciplined, or had been led on by officers accomplished in the various branches of the art of war. They accorded a cordial tribute to the few brave spirits who devoted all the skill and science they had acquired in the 'seven years' war,' which commenced in 1754, to the formation of military habits in the new levies, which were raised in rapid succession, during the whole progress of the contest. But they had before them the admissions of these officers, and of their beloved commander, that the difficulties of their perilous undertaking would have been greatly diminished, if a knowledge of the theory and science of war had been more generally diffused through the army.

" A striking illustration of the justness of these views

13

is contained in an official report, made by General Knox, then Secretary of War, to the President, January 21st, 1790. In this report the position is laid down, that 'all discussions on the subject of a powerful militia, will result in one or other of the following principles.'*

"1. Either efficient institutions must be established for the military education of youth, and the knowledge acquired therein be diffused throughout the country by the means of rotation ; or,

"2. The militia must be formed of substitutes, after the manner of the militia of Great Britain.

" 'If the United States possess the vigor of mind,' says the Secretary, 'to establish the first institution, it may reasonably be expected to produce the most unequivocal advantages; a glorious national spirit will be introduced, with its extensive train of political consequences.'

"The only provision immediately applicable [in this able state paper] to the present inquiry is that, which required the young men, from the age of 18 to 20 years, to be disciplined for thirty days successively in camps of instruction, where, in addition to their military tuition, they were to receive lectures from the chaplains, explanatory of the value of free governments, and of their dependence upon the knowledge and virtue of the youth of the country. A proposition similar to this, with the exception that the term of instruction was limited to six days instead of thirty, was submitted to the House of Representatives in 1821. And it may induce those who are inclined to adopt this course, to be reminded how soon it was abandoned by its first projectors. The

* Penn. Daily Adv. Feb. 3d, 1790.

obvious objections arising from the expenditure of time and money, from the loss occasioned by the periodical abstraction of labor, and from the but too probable formation of licentious or indolent habits, seem to have been justly regarded as decisive."

But the principle underlying all these propositions continued to germinate, and stimulated those intrusted with the direction of national affairs, to labor for the establishment of an institution at which young men might receive a military education, who, when separated from it, and scattered throughout the length and breadth of the land, might serve as instructors of the untrained militia in times of peace, and, upon the outbreak of war, furnish a powerful aid in organizing and concentrating the enormous military resources of the country.

Herein lies the chief, and by far the most valuable and comprehensive motive, which gave origin to the Military Academy. Remote from foreign jealousies and hostile powers, save those hidden in our own forests, it was foreseen that the presence of large standing armies was inimical to republican development, and that an army small as that of the United States has always been, and ought ever to be, could only supply an insignificant quota upon emergencies of great magnitude.

Absorbed in the temptations and allurements to the acquisition of wealth which the numerous fields of American enterprise and labor afford, it is vain, in time of peace, to expect civilians to qualify themselves for the performance of military duties, with little or no prospect of pecuniary remuneration or military renown; and were there even any such inclined, there are no institutions where the necessary qualifications could be secured.

In the few conflicts, happily, in which the nation has been engaged, from the first period of its existence to the present, scarcely more than three or four who were not resigned graduates of the Military Academy, came into service, possessed of any marked aptitude or acquaintance with the art of war. Even in the unexampled successful war with Mexico, all who were appointed to high commands from civil life, without an exception, sought and invited those, who by their education and professional skill were fitted to become their aides, and staff officers, and military advisers.

In all our wars, but very few indeed of those who have been actively engaged, and who have thereby qualified themselves for after service, remain in the profession of arms. From the wear and fatigue of camp life, from the hope of political advancement, or from broken health, they disappear after the lapse of a few years. It is thus that the war of 1812 exhibits but few names conspicuous during the Revolution; that the names familiar in 1812 are seldom found in the history of our Indian conflicts; and that the heroes of the war in Mexico, save the graduates of the Military Academy, constitute but a small proportion of those now actually engaged in the present melancholy internal strife.

The roll of *citizen* graduates of the Military Academy, who responded at the nation's call in 1846, affords an impressive illustration of the wisdom of those who labored for the establishment of an institution, whose principal design was to diffuse and disseminate among the people a class of military educated citizens, whose services might be relied on, when encroachments upon or non-fulfilment of treaty stipulations rendered resistance necessary by an appeal to arms. To the names of *Clay*, *McKee*, *Davis*, and upwards of a hundred others who entered the volunteer service, may be added by the score those who proffered services to such an extent, that the Government declined to receive them.

But brighter yet, in the present civil war, does the usefulness of the Military Academy gleam forth, in impelling from the secluded and lucrative pursuits of civil life nearly every living graduate, including those long disconnected with the soldier's profession, to struggle, with *Halleck*, *McClellan*, *Rosecrans*, *Burnside*, *Grant*, *Hooker*, and the lamented *Stevens*, *Sill*, and *Mitchel*, for the maintenance of the unity of the nation.

In every State, and upon every tented field, the *citizen* graduates of the Military Academy are found, with their thousand former associates who failed to meet the rigid requirements of the institution, repaying their indebtedness for an education, and offering themselves as willing victims at the shrine of duty.

"In 1793, the establishment of a military academy is known to have been a favorite object of the Executive. In the annual message, dated the 3d of December of that year, General Washington suggests the inquiry,[*] 'whether a material feature in the improvement' of the system of military defence 'ought not to be, to afford an opportunity for the study of those branches of the art which can scarcely ever be attained by practice alone.'

[*] Journal House Reps., 3d and 4th Cong., 7.

"Mr. Jefferson has informed us,* that when the preparation of this message was discussed in the Cabinet, the President mentioned a military academy as one of the topics which should be introduced, and that he himself raised the objection, that there was no clause in the Constitution which warranted such an establishment : that the above sentence was nevertheless incorporated in the message, and was again the subject of special deliberation. The reply of Washington was, that he would not recommend any thing prohibited by the Constitution, 'but if it was doubtful, he was so impressed with the necessity of the measure that he would refer it to Congress, and let them decide for themselves whether the Constitution authorized it or not.'

"An authentic exposition of the views of Congress is contained in the Act of the 7th of May, 1794, which provided for a corps of Artillerists and Engineers, to consist of four battalions, to each of which eight cadets were to be attached; and made it the duty of the Secretary of War to procure, at the public expense, the necessary books, instruments, and apparatus, for the use and benefit of said corps. The result of his subsequent reflection upon the opinions of Washington him-

* "November 28, 1793.—Met at the President's, * * * Randolph had prepared a draught of the speech. The clause recommending fortifications was left out, but that for a Military Academy was inserted. I opposed it, as unauthorized by the Constitution. Hamilton and Knox approved it without discussion. Randolph was for it, saying that the words of the Constitution authorizing Congress to lay taxes, &c., for the common defence, might comprehend it. The President said he would not choose to recommend any thing against the Constitution, but if it were doubtful, he was so impressed with the necessity of the measure that he would report it to Congress, and let them decide for themselves whether the Constitution authorized it or not. It was therefore left in."—Jefferson's Memoirs; Correspondence, &c., Vol. IV., p. 499.

self, whose attachment to the national charter was too pure and firm to be perverted by any prepossessions for a particular object, is manifested by his declaration in December, 1796,* that 'the desirableness of this institution had constantly increased with every new view he had taken of the subject.' 'The institution of a military academy,' he observes in this annual communication to Congress, 'is also recommended by cogent reasons. However pacific the general policy of a nation may be, it ought never to be without an adequate stock of military knowledge for emergencies. The first would impair the energy of its character, and both would hazard its safety, or expose it to greater evils, when war could not be avoided. Besides, that war might not often depend upon its own choice. In proportion as the observance of pacific maxims might exempt a nation from the necessity of practising the rules of the military art, ought to be its care in preserving and transmitting, by proper establishments, the knowledge of that art. Whatever argument may be drawn from particular examples, superficially viewed, a thorough examination of the subject will evince that the art of war is extensive and complicated; that it demands much previous study; and that the possession of it in its most improved and perfect state is always of great moment to the security of a nation. This, therefore, ought to be a serious care of every government; and for this purpose, an academy, where a regular course of instruction is given, is an obvious expedient, which different nations have successfully employed.'"

---

* Journal House Reps., 3d and 4th Cong., 610.

In 1798, Congress authorized the raising of an additional regiment of artillerists and engineers, and increased the number of cadets to fifty-six. Provision was also made to secure books and apparatus for their instruction. In July of the same year the President was empowered by another act to appoint four teachers of the arts and sciences necessary for the instruction of this corps.

Thus far the legislative proceedings had been in accordance with Executive recommendation, except that they did not provide for the collection of the regiment of artillerists and engineers at one point, and the erection of buildings adapted to the purposes of education. But the principle upon which the institution as at present organized rests was fully sanctioned : a new grade [cadet] was created in the army, to which young men were exclusively entitled to be admitted, and means were appropriated for their education in the science of war, that they might be fitted for stations of command.

It was soon apparent, however, that something more was required to afford a fair opportunity for imparting systematic instruction. The subject seems to have been carefully investigated in 1800, by Mr. McHenry, then the head of the War Department, and his report was communicated to Congress by President Adams, on the 13th of January, with a special message, in which it was characterized as containing ' matter in which the honor and safety of the country are deeply interested;'* and a supplemental one of the 31st of January, which

* American State Papers, 1800, I., 299, 485.

are equally illustrative of the comprehensive and discriminating talent of their author, and of the beneficial consequences to be anticipated from the establishment of a military academy.

"No sentiment can be more just than this: that, in proportion as the circumstances and policy of a people are opposed to the maintenance of a large military force, it is important that as much perfection as possible be given to that which may at any time exist.

"It is not however enough, that the troops it may be deemed proper to maintain be rendered as perfect as possible in form, organization, and discipline; the dignity, the character to be supported, and the safety of the country further require, that it should have military instructions capable of perpetuating the art of war, and of furnishing the means for forming a new and enlarged army, fit for service in the shortest time possible, and at the least practicable expense to the State.

"Since, however, it seems to be agreed that we are not to keep on foot numerous forces, and it would be impossible on a sudden to extend to every essential point our fortifications, military science, in its various branches, ought to be cultivated with peculiar care, in proper nurseries; so that a sufficient stock may always exist, ready to be imparted and diffused to any extent, and a competent number of persons be prepared and qualified to act as engineers, and others as instructors to additional troops, which events may successively require to be raised. This will be to substitute the elements of an army to the thing itself, and will greatly tend to enable the Government to dispense with a large body of standing forces, from the facility which it will give of procuring officers and forming soldiers promptly, in all emergencies.

"To avoid great evils, we must either have a respectable force always ready for service, or the means of preparing such a force with certainty and expedition. The latter, as most agreeable to the genius of our Government and nation, is the object of the following propositions."

The laws which have been framed having proved inadequate, he adds, "to afford the requisite instruction to officers and others in the principles of war, the exercises it requires, and the sciences upon which they are founded, it is proposed that the academy shall include four schools: one to be called the Fundamental School; another the School of Engineers and Artillerists; a third, the School of Cavalry and Infantry; and a fourth, the School of the Navy. The Fundamental School, it is supposed, will be the only one required for the first two years. It is designed to form in this engineers (including geographical engineers), miners, and officers for the artillery, cavalry, infantry, and navy; consequently, in this school are to be taught all the sciences necessary to a perfect knowledge of the different branches of the military art.

"These schools to be provided with proper apparatus and instruments for philosophical and chemical experiments, for astronomical and nautical observations, for surveying, and such other processes as are requisite to the several branches of instruction. Barracks and other proper buildings must be erected for the accommodation of the directors, professors, and students, and for the laboratories and other works to be carried on at the respective schools. These selections demonstrate, that the conception the Secretary of War had formed of the true character of a national institution for military education, was in very near accordance with the character of the one, which has been long sustained by the beneficent and wise legislation of Congress. The whole report contemplates certain military schools as an essential mean, in conjunction with a small military establishment, to prepare for, and perpetuate to the United States, at a very moderate expense, a body of scientific officers and engineers, adequate to any emergency, qualified to discipline for the field, in the shortest time, the most extended armies, and to give the most decisive and useful effects to their operations."

These reports were referred to a committee of seven in the House of Representatives, who submitted a bill,* creating a Military Academy, which, in the absence of the chairman, was postponed to a day beyond the close of the session, one member only of the committee voting for the postponement. The Secretary of War was called upon by a resolution, dated 22d December, 1801,† to lay before the House a statement of the existing military establishment, which was furnished accordingly on the 24th. Out of these proceedings grew the act of the 16th of March, 1802, by which the military peace establishment was determined. By this act, the Artillerists and Engineers were made to constitute two distinct corps. To one regiment of Artillery, forty cadets were attached; and to the Corps of Engineers, ten cadets. The 27th section provided that the said Corps, when organized, shall be stationed at West Point, in the State

* Journal House Reps., 5th and 6th Cong., 634.
† Ibid., 7th Cong., 1st Ses., 56.

of New York, and shall constitute a Military Academy. It also provided that the senior Engineer officer present shall be the Superintendent of the Academy, and authorized the Secretary of War to procure, at the public expense, the necessary books, implements, and apparatus for the use and benefit of the Institution. In the following year, another act, dated 28th of February, 1803, empowered the President to appoint one teacher of the French language, and one teacher of Drawing.

These acts afforded some of the desired facilities for developing the tendencies of the principle, which had been sanctioned by the previous acts of 1794 and 1798. At the expiration of six years, however, further legislation was considered necessary. And the attention of Congress was called to the subject by Mr. Jefferson in the following Message, which evinces not only his deep interest in the Institution, but that he no longer entertained the opinion of its unconstitutionality, which he expressed while a member of General Washington's cabinet, in 1793.

" The scale on which the Military Academy at West Point was originally established, is become too limited to furnish the number of well-instructed subjects in the different branches of artillery and engineering, which the public service calls for. The want of such characters is already sensibly felt, and will be increased with the enlargement of our plans of military preparation. The Chief Engineer having been instructed to consider the subject, and to propose an augmentation, which might render the establishment commensurate with the present circumstances of the country, has made his report, which I now transmit for the consideration of Congress. The plan, suggested by him, of removing the Institution to this place, is also worthy of attention. Besides the advantage of placing it under the immediate eye of the Government, it may render its benefits common to the Naval department, and will furnish opportunities of selecting, on better information, the characters most qualified to fulfil the duties which the public service may call for."*

The following Report on the condition of the Academy, by Colonel JONATHAN WILLIAMS,† head of the Corps of Engineers, dated March 14th, 1808, accompanied the Message.

" This Institution was established at West Point, in the year 1801, under the direction of a private citizen [George Barron], and was nothing more than a mathematical school for the few cadets that were then in service. It was soon found that the government of young military men was incompatible with the ordinary system of schools, and, consequently, this Institution ran into disorder, and the Teacher into contempt.

" When the peace establishment was made, the Corps of Engineers was created, and the *twenty-seventh* section enacts that the Corps 'shall be stationed at West Point, in the State of New York, and shall constitute a Military

---

* Journal House Reps., 10th Cong., 234.

† *Jonathan Williams* was born in Boston, 1750. During the Revolution he resided abroad, acting part of the time as Commercial Agent for the United States. In 1790 he returned and resided near Philadelphia.

Appointed Major of Artillery and Engineers, Feb. 16, 1801. Inspector of Fortifications and Superintendent at West Point, Dec. 4, 1801. Retained, at reorganization of the Army, as Major of the Corps of Engineers, and Superintendent of the *Military Academy*, April, 1802. Lieutenant-Colonel Engineers, April 10, 1805. Colonel and Chief Engineer, Feb. 23, 1808 ; resigned July 31, 1812. Representative in Congress from Philadelphia; died May 20, 1815.*

* National Port. Gallery, vol I.; Gardner's Army Dict.

Academy, and the Engineers, assistant Engineers, and Cadets, shall be subject to do duty at such places, and on such service, as the President of the United States may direct.' It was not probably foreseen, that although the head-quarters of the Corps might be at West Point, yet the duties of the individual officers necessarily spread them along our coast from one extremity of the United States to the other; and as the whole number of officers can be no more than sixteen, they could not, in their dispersed state, constitute a Military Academy. The incongruity of a stationary and errant existence, in the same Corps, has been amply exemplified by experience. Indeed, it never can be supposed that Engineers, as such, could be efficient elementary teachers; their capability, consistent with other duties, is confined to practical teaching, by combining example with precept, and carrying the rudiments of the art into practical execution; in the same manner as other professional men do who have youth under their tuition, after they have gone through every branch of elementary learning relating to their profession.

"A part only of the officers were appointed soon after the passage of the act, of whom the Major, [Williams] who was *ex-officio* the Chief Engineer, and two Captains [Barron and Mansfield] took charge of the Academy, the students of which were the cadets belonging to the regiment of Artillery. The Major occasionally read lectures on fortifications, gave practical lessons in the field, and taught the use of instruments generally. The two Captains taught mathematics; the one in the line of geometrical, the other in that of algebraical demonstrations.

"As the Corps was small, as it had little or nothing to do in its more appropriate professional duties, and as the students were few, the institution went on producing all the effect in its power, and all that could be expected on its limited scale. It was soon discovered that mere mathematics would not make either an Artillerist or an Engineer, and a power was given, by law, to appoint a teacher of Drawing and of the French language. Had this law, instead of absolutely limiting the number of teachers and designating their duties, left it general in the discretion of the President to appoint such and so many as he might find requisite to produce the effect contemplated by the establishment, and left the internal organization to him, who, from constant observation, could judge of the most expedient one, with a reasonable but ample appropriation, we should, at this day, have a greater number of well-instructed young officers than we can boast of. From that time to this, however, the Academy has progressed beyond what could have been expected from its means; but now the first mathematical teacher has resigned, and the second has, for several years, been employed as Surveyor-General of the United States in the Western country.

"During the last year, a citizen, of eminent talents as a mathematician, has been employed as principal teacher, and a first lieutenant of Engineers performed the duties of assistant teacher, while the professor of French and Drawing confined his abilities to these branches. So far as talents can go, nothing is wanting as to these teachers; they are all capable in the highest degree; the subscriber is only apprehensive that he shall not be able to retain them. Mr. Hassler, the chief mathematician, is already designated for a survey of the coast when circumstances shall permit that business to be undertaken, and it could not be committed to more able hands. Mr. de Masson, the professor of French and Drawing, being the only teacher designated by the law, he is the only one that, exclusive of the Corps of Engineers, can be said to belong to the Institution.

" In short, the Military Academy, as it now stands, is like a foundling, barely existing among the mountains, and nurtured at a distance out of sight, and almost unknown to its legitimate parents. The questions that have been frequently put to the subscriber, by members of Congress, evidently show that the little interest the Institution has excited arises solely from its being unknown to those who ought to be, and doubtless would willingly become, its generous guardians and powerful protectors. Had it been so attached to the Government (its real and only parent), as to be always with it, always in sight, and always in the way of its fostering care, it would probably have flourished, and have become an honorable and interesting appendage to the national family."

CHAPTER XI.

Action taken by Congress and Increase of the Number of Cadets.—Urgent Recommendations in Favor of the Institution by President Madison.—Reorganization of the Institution in 1812, by which it became a Branch of the Army.—Reduction of the Latter, and Recommendation of the President to Enlarge the Academy.—Inquiry into the Constitutionality of the Institution.—Unanimity of Boards of Investigating Committees on the Subject.—Progress of the Institution, and the Difficulties it Encountered—Changes among the Teachers.—Organization under the Law of 1812.—Resignation of Colonel Williams; Colonel Swift his Successor.—Introduction of the Inspector.—Rules with respect to the Promotion of Cadets.—Appointment of a Board of Visitors.—Uniform of the Cadets.—Report of the Chief-Engineer.

The Message before mentioned was referred to Messrs. Nicholas, of Virginia, Troup, of Georgia, Desha, of Kentucky, Upham, of Massachusetts, and Milner, of Pennsylvania. The names of some of these gentlemen are identified with republican principles, and they will not be suspected of having lost sight of or disregarded the strict requirements of the Constitution. This Committee reported a bill on the 12th of April, 1808, which added one hundred and fifty-six members to the corps of cadets, and which passed in the House by a vote of 95 to 16.

Under the succeeding administration, the welfare and interests of the Institution were repeatedly recommended

14

to the favorable consideration of Congress by the Executive. In his annual communication, dated 5th December, 1810, Mr. Madison maintains its usefulness with
great earnestness and power, and combats successfully
a popular impression, that such establishments were
only suited to nations whose policy was, to a considerable extent, and by the necessity of their position, warlike.

"The Corps of Engineers, with the Military Academy,
are entitled to the early attention of Congress. But a
revision of the law is recommended, principally with a
view to a more enlarged cultivation and diffusion of the
advantages of such institutions, by providing professor-
ships for all the necessary branches of military instruction, and by the establishment of an additional Academy
at the seat of government or elsewhere.

"The means by which wars, as well for defence as
offence, are now carried on, render these schools of the
more scientific operations an indispensable part of every
adequate system. Even among nations whose large
standing armies and frequent wars afford every other
opportunity of instruction, these establishments are
found to be indispensable for the due attainment of military science, which requires a regular course of study and
experiment.

"In a country, happily without the other opportunities,
seminaries, where the elementary principles of the art of
war can be taught without actual war, and without the
expense of extensive and standing armies, have the
precious advantage of uniting an essential preparation
against external dangers, with a scrupulous regard to internal safety. In no other way, probably, can a pro-

vision of equal efficiency for the public defence be made at so little expense, or more consistently with the public liberty."* It seems almost superfluous to remark, that the recommendation for creating a new Academy, as well as the whole tenor of this extract, is conclusive evidence that the constitutionality of these institutions was considered by Mr. Madison to be unquestionable. The maintenance of an unconstitutional establishment could not, with any propriety, be said to be consistent " with a scrupulous regard to internal safety," and " with public liberty." In 1811, Congress was again reminded by the President " of the importance of these military seminaries, which, in every event, will form a valuable and frugal part of our military establishment."†

And before the close of the session, the Act of April 29, 1812, was passed, which declares that the Military Academy shall consist of the Corps of Engineers, and the following professors and assistants, in addition to the teachers of French and Drawing already provided for : viz., a Professor of Natural and Experimental Philosophy; a Professor of Mathematics; a Professor of Engineering; with an assistant for each. A Chaplain was also to be appointed, and required to officiate as Professor of Geography, Ethics, and History. The number of cadets was limited to two hundred and sixty; the requirements for admission, the term of study and service, and the rate of pay and emoluments were prescribed.

The broad basis of the Military Academy was thus laid; and as the Act of 1802 expressly declares, " that the Corps of Engineers *shall constitute* a Military Academy," and the Act of 1812 reiterates "that the Military Academy *shall consist of* the Corps of Engineers and the following professors and assistants, in addition," &c.; it will be perceived that the Military Academy, as designed by its founders, does not consist in buildings, apparatus, and location, where instruction is communicated, but in a regularly constituted military body, whose officers and professors are appointed, confirmed, and commissioned, in the same manner and form as other army officers, and subjected to the same Rules and Articles of War as govern all the land forces of the United States.[*]

By the Act of March 3, 1815, the Army was reduced to ten thousand men, a number deemed to be sufficiently large, in view of the segregation of this country from Europe, and the diminished strength of the Indian tribes. In his last Message, dated December 5, 1815, Mr. Madison urged "an enlargement of the Military Academy, and the establishment of others in sections of the Union. "If experience has shown in the recent splendid achievements of the militia the value of this resource for public defence, it has shown, also, the importance of that skill in the use of arms, and that familiarity with the essential rules of discipline, which cannot be expected from the regulations now in force."

During the sessions of Congress in 1815 and 1817, bills were introduced in the House of Representatives for creating additional Military Academies, which, however, received no decisive action. In 1821 the Army

---

[*] Attorney Gen. U. S., Aug. 26, 1819; Sect. of War, May 6, 1846.

was further reduced to six thousand men, but the act of this year, as well as that of 1815, authorized the retaining of the Corps of Engineers as already organized.

These legislative enactments in relation to the Academy, considered in connection with the army, clearly indicate it to have been the settled policy of that day not to rely upon the rank and file of the army, which were enlisted for a short period, and could never be thoroughly disciplined, but to educate officers, so that instructors could always be found ready and competent to teach new levies, whenever changes in the political condition of the country might require them to be raised.

The proceedings in the House of Representatives in 1821, demonstrate most conclusively that public sentiment, so far as it could be expressed through the representatives of the people, was strongly and almost unanimously in favor of the perpetuity of this method of providing for future military instruction.

On February 6th, of that year, a resolution was introduced, proposing an inquiry into the constitutionality of the Military Academy. Ten days after, a motion was made to discontinue the pay and rations of the Cadets, and discharge them from the Academy and the service of the United States—a motion, the certain effect of which would have been the abolition of the Institution.

The opinion of the House upon the subject in general, and the two propositions in particular, was emphatically shown in the vote on the last, which was rejected by a majority of eighty-nine. Subsequent to these proceedings in the popular branch of the government, President Monroe, in his annual message in 1822, pronounced this strong commendation upon the discipline and management of the Academy : " Good order is preserved in it, and the young men are well instructed in every science connected with the great objects of the Institution. They are also well trained and disciplined in the practical parts of the profession. It has always been found difficult to control the ardor inseparable from that early age, in such a manner as to give it a proper direction. The great object to be accomplished is the restraint of that ardor by such wise regulation and government as will keep it within a just subordination, and at the same time elevate it to the highest purposes. This object seems to be essentially obtained in this Institution, and with great advantage to the nation.

" The Military Academy forms the basis in regard to science, on which the military establishment rests. It furnishes annually, after due examination, and on the report of the Academic Staff, many well-informed youths, to fill the vacancies which occur in the several corps of the army; while others, who retire to private life, carry with them such attainments, as, under the right reserved to the several States to appoint the officers and to train the militia, will enable them, by affording a wider field for selection, to promote the great object of the power vested in Congress of providing for the organizing, arming, and disciplining the militia."

It has been mentioned that, during the inception of the Military Academy, *Mr. Jefferson* entertained doubts as to the constitutional power of the Government to create a Military Academy, and that in the end, he not only yielded them, but, during his administration, gave his active support to the legislative measures for creating and adding to the efficiency of the one existing.

Like objections have been raised from time to time, which have met with little or no success.

On this subject it may be briefly observed, that Congress, in the exercise of its constitutional power " to raise and support armies," and " to make rules for the government and regulation of the land and naval forces," has enacted, that a number of cadets may be appointed as a part of the army, "at no time to exceed two hundred and fifty." Under this law it will be conceded, that these cadets, on receiving their warrants, could be assigned to companies as in other armies, and instructed in such way as would best qualify them for the duties for which they are candidates, and that the expense could be provided for by Congress in the usual manner.

Economy would dictate that these cadets should be embodied, and that all requisite means to effect the proper training and instructing of them, as officers and soldiers, were included in the powers granted by the Constitution. The only question to be decided then is, What are the necessary means for this purpose ? In other military States, military schools are found to exist, provided not only with every thing necessary for military instruction, but with professors for all those branches of science connected with the military profession.

The most strict constructionist would hardly question the power to provide masters of Riding, of the Sword, and of Gymnastics ; and yet these are no more a part of a military education than a knowledge of Surveying, of

Ballistics, and of the composition and fabrication of Gunpowder, of the construction of Ordnance, and of the art of Fortification,—all of which require for their attainment and practice scientific culture of the highest order.

It is the fate of every institution of National importance, which is fostered and sustained by our Government, to undergo, periodically, probing and investigation. *Nothing*, established by the legislators of one day, is exempt from inquiry and examination by those who follow them in after-life.

In looking over the lists of the Boards of Visitors, who, for more than forty years, have attended the annual examinations at the Military Academy, the names of individuals known throughout the country, as eminent in Arts, Sciences, and Literature, are found to be conspicuous.

These Boards have been composed of men of all political parties, and from all sections of the Union; men whose reputation was of such a character, as to forbid the imputation of rendering false testimony as to the merits of the Institution; and yet, whatever may have been their prejudices or predilections, they have melted away, and been converted into the strongest approbation, in the crucibles of personal inquiry and conscientious judgment.

No Institution in the land has undergone such an ordeal of investigations from Boards and Congressional Committees, and none courts closer examination and scrutiny.

" The history of the origin of the Military Academy, and the opinions and action of the Executive and Legislative Departments in regard to it, exhibits the correctly balanced mind of Washington, passing from doubt to assured conviction, upon the question of its constitutionality ; the philosophic mind of Jefferson, who was ever biased against free constructions, relinquishing the confident opinion he had expressed in the negative upon the same question, and proposing an enlargement of the Institution ; the clearly discriminating mind of Madison, exerting its great powers to perpetuate the existing, and create new establishments, untrammelled by a doubt of the constitutional authority of the Government, and his example imitated by his friend and successor.

" It shows the recognition by Congress of the soundness of the principle, constituting the basis of such an Institution in the Acts of 1794 and 1798 ; the distinct and not to be mistaken expression of the conviction of the same body, of their power, and of the expediency of exercising their power, to establish a Military Academy in the Act of 1802 ; and this, too, after the *projet* of such an institution had been fully developed in all its extent, in the official report of 1800, and had been two years open for their consideration, and that of their constituents ; and, lastly, it exhibits an unbroken series of legislative enactments for the support and extension of the Academy, running through a period of twenty years, and the failure of the attempts which have been made to induce an opposite course of legislation."

It will be difficult to find in the recorded history of the country, a question upon which public sentiment has been more fully and fairly tested, and one which has so closely approached unanimity in its settlement.

Under the Act of July 16, 1798, the President was authorized to appoint four teachers of the "Arts and Sciences," for the instruction of the regiment of Artillerists and Engineers; and accordingly, a number of officers and men from that regiment were collected at West Point, and the attempt made to organize a school for military instruction at that place. It soon became apparent, however, that the want of a preparatory induction into the "Arts and Sciences," rendered it difficult for the officers to impart the necessary instruction. The school, as a consequence, progressed slowly, and with little success.*

Of the four teachers, none were appointed prior to January 6, 1801; at which time Mr. George Barron was appointed teacher of Mathematics, and served as such until his dismissal from service, February 11, 1802.

On December 4, 1801, Major JONATHAN WILLIAMS, of the regiment of Artillerists and Engineers, assumed the command of the Post and the duties of instruction,† assisted by Captain W. A. Barron, of the same corps. It was soon discovered that the regiment of Artillerists and Engineers could not combine with effect the two duties assigned to its members, and a law was therefore framed, separating them into two corps, and declaring that the Corps of Engineers should be stationed at West Point, N. Y., and should constitute a Military Academy. The following extracts include all the law that relates to the subject under consideration :

* Seventeenth Cong., First Session, No. 226.
† Williams's Report.—General Swift, MSS.

" SEC. 2.—That the regiment of Artillerists shall consist of one colonel, one lieutenant-colonel, four majors, one adjutant, and twenty companies, each company to consist of one captain, one first lieutenant, one second lieutenant, two cadets, four sergeants, four corporals, four musicians, eight artificers, and fifty-six privates ; to be formed into five battalions.   *   *   *   *

" SEC. 26.—That the President of the United States is hereby authorized and empowered, when he shall deem it expedient, to organize and establish a Corps of Engineers, to consist of one engineer, with the pay, rank, and emoluments of a major ; two assistant engineers, with the pay, rank, and emoluments of first lieutenants ; two other assistant engineers, with the pay, rank, and emoluments of second lieutenants ; and ten cadets, with the pay of sixteen dollars per month, and two rations per day ; and the President of the United States is in like manner authorized, when he shall deem it proper, to make such promotions in the said Corps, with a view to particular merit, and without regard to rank, so as not to exceed one colonel, one lieutenant-colonel, two majors, four captains, four first lieutenants, four second lieutenants, and so that the number of the whole Corps shall at no time exceed twenty officers and cadets.

" SEC. 27.—That the said Corps, when so organized, shall be stationed at West Point, in the State of New York, and shall constitute a Military Academy ; and the Engineers, assistant Engineers, and cadets of the said Corps, shall be subject, at all times, to duty in such places, and on such service, as the President of the United States shall direct.

" Sec. 28.—That the principal Engineer, in his absence the next in rank, shall have the Superintendence of the said Military Academy, under the direction of the President of the United States ; and the Secretary of War is hereby authorized, at the public expense, under such regulations as shall be directed by the President of the United States, to procure the necessary books, implements, and apparatus for the use and benefit of the said Institution."

Under the foregoing Act the following officers were appointed :*

Jonathan Williams, Major of Engineers and Superintendent of the Military Academy, April, 1802.

William A. Barron, Captain Engineers, Teacher Mathematics, April, 1802.

Jared Mansfield, Captain Engineers, Teacher Natural and Experimental Philosophy, May, 1802.

James Wilson, First Lieutenant Engineers, *Student.*

Alexander Macomb, First Lieutenant Engineers, *Student.*

Joseph G. Swift, Second Lieutenant Engineers, *Student.*

Simon M. Levi, Second Lieutenant Engineers, *Student.*

By the Act of February 28, 1803, there were added to the Academy, a teacher of French and a teacher of Drawing ;† but both positions were filled by Francis De Masson from July, 1803, until September, 1808, at which time Christian E. Zoeller was appointed teacher of Drawing. Upon the resignation of the latter, in April, 1810, De Masson again resumed the duties.

* Mil. Affairs, II., 634.   † Mil. Affairs, II., 634.

The same Act authorized forty Cadets from the Artillery, in addition to the ten from the Engineers already provided ; and by another Act, passed April 12, 1808, twenty Cadets from the Light Artillery, one hundred from the Infantry, sixteen from the Cavalry, and twenty from the Riflemen, were authorized. But few, if any, of the Cadets thus designated were appointed. No law attached them to the Military Academy ; no provision existed for the reception or instruction of such a number at West Point, and to order them to their regiments without instruction was deemed useless.

Thus, at this early period, the Military Academy was recognized as a Scientific Institution for the education of the Corps of Engineers, and as such, its existence was not made contingent upon the presence or absence of Cadets appointed in the army. Some changes occurred among the teachers meanwhile ; Captain Barron having been relieved in February, 1807, by Ferdinand R. Hassler; and the latter, having been called on the Coast Survey in February, 1810, was succeeded by Captain Alden Partridge, of the Engineers, who discharged the duties until his appointment as Professor, under the Act of 1812. Captain Mansfield was relieved in 1805, leaving his position vacant until his return as Professor, under the same Act.

The Cadets were quartered in the old "Long Barrack"*

* " WAR DEPARTMENT, *Dec.* 8, 1813.

" The Cadets of the Military Academy shall, as early as possible, be fed at a common table. The present method of boarding at different and private houses, ought to be discontinued; you are accordingly authorized to take measures necessary to this end, making a report of what you do to this Department.*

[Signed]   " J. ARMSTRONG."

" To CAPT. PARTRIDGE."   [*Sect. of War.*]

* Order-Book, 1813, U. S. M. A.

of the Revolution, boarded promiscuously, and instructed in a two-story wooden building, serving as the "Academy," and at the same time as the quarters of the Superintendent. It stood on the site now occupied by the latter.

In this embryonic condition the Military Academy furnished but seventy-one graduates during the first ten years of its existence, and was indeed appropriately compared to "a foundling barely existing among the mountains, nurtured at a distance, out of sight of, and almost unknown to, its legitimate parents."

The urgent recommendation of Mr. Madison, in 1810, and its repetition the following year, at length awakened Congress to the necessity of revising the existing laws relative to the Institution.

On April 29th, 1812, an Act was passed, entitled,

"AN ACT MAKING FURTHER PROVISION FOR THE CORPS OF ENGINEERS.

"SEC. 2.—That the Military Academy shall consist of the Corps of Engineers, and the following professors, in addition to the teachers of the French language and Drawing, already provided, viz.: one professor of Natural and Experimental Philosophy, with the pay and emoluments of lieutenant-colonel, if not an officer of the Corps, and, if taken from the Corps, then so much in addition to his pay and emoluments as shall equal those of a lieutenant-colonel; one professor of Mathematics, with the pay and emoluments of a major, if not an officer of the Corps, and, if taken from the Corps, then so much in addition to his pay and emoluments as shall equal those of a major; one professor of the art of Engineering in all its branches, with the pay and emoluments of a major, if not an officer of the Corps, and, if taken from the Corps, then so much in addition to his pay and emoluments as shall equal those of a major; each of the foregoing professors to have an assistant professor, which assistant professor shall be taken from the most prominent characters of the officers or cadets, and receive the pay and emoluments of captains, and no other pay or emoluments while performing these duties. Provided, That nothing herein contained shall entitle the Academical Staff, as such, to any command in the army separate from the Academy.

" SEC. 3.—That the cadets heretofore appointed in the service of the United States, whether of Artillery, Cavalry, Riflemen, or Infantry, or that may in future be appointed as hereinafter provided, shall at no time exceed two hundred and fifty; that they may be attached, at the discretion of the President of the United States, as students, to the Military Academy, and be subject to the established regulations thereof; that they shall be arranged into companies of non-commissioned officers and privates, according to the direction of the commandant of Engineers, and be officered from the said Corps, for the purpose of military instruction; that there shall be added to each company of cadets four musicians, and the said Corps shall be trained and taught all the duties of a private, non-commissioned officer, and officer; be encamped at least three months of each year, and taught all the duties incident to a regular camp; that the candidates for cadets be not under the age of fourteen, nor above the age of twenty-one years; that each cadet, previously to his appointment by the President of the United States, shall be well versed in reading, writing, and arithmetic, and that he shall sign articles, with the consent of his parent or guardian, by which he shall engage to serve five years, unless sooner discharged; and all such cadets shall be entitled to and receive the pay and emoluments now allowed by law to cadets in the Corps of Engineers.

" Sec. 4.—That when any cadet shall receive a regular degree from the Academic Staff, after going through all the classes, he shall be considered as among the candidates for a commission in any Corps, according to the duties he may be judged competent to perform; and in case there shall not, at the time, be a vacancy in such Corps, he may be attached to it at the discretion of the President of the United States, by brevet of the lowest grade, as a supernumerary officer, with the usual pay and emoluments of such grade, until a vacancy shall happen. Provided, That there shall not be more than one supernumerary officer to any one company at the same time.

" Sec. 5.—That $25,000 be appropriated for erecting buildings, and for providing an apparatus, a library, and all necessary implements, and for such contingent expenses as may be necessary and proper, in the judgment of the President of the United States, for such an institution."

This law furnished the principles upon which the Military Academy has been conducted and controlled, without change to the present moment. In addition to the Departments of Engineering, Philosophy, Mathematics, French, and Drawing, provided for, there have been added in later years, as the Academy progressed in usefulness, a Department of Geography, History, and Ethics;

a Department of Chemistry, Mineralogy, and Geology;
a Department of Infantry Tactics,* a Department of
Practical Engineering, a Department of Artillery and
Cavalry, a Department of Spanish, a Department of
Ordnance and Gunnery, a Department for Equitation
and Cavalry instruction, and a Department of Fencing
and Bayonet exercise.

Upon the resignation of Colonel Williams, July 31, 1812,
he was succeeded by Colonel JOSEPH G. SWIFT, as senior
officer of Engineers, and Superintendent. Although
the law had contemplated that the Corps of Engineers
should be stationed at West Point, its duties soon
became so extensive that the chief of the Corps could
not be present continuously at the Academy; but by
the direction of the President he was, previous to 1815,
charged with the administration of its affairs, conveying
his orders, when absent, to the senior Engineer officer at
the Institution, who thus exercised the functions of
Superintendent.

The Regulations of the Military Academy, dated
"War Department, January 3, 1815, Approved, James
Monroe," and an Order from the War Department, dated
February 28, 1815, approved in like manner, provided
that, "'A Permanent Superintendent' shall be appointed
to the Military Academy, who, under the direction of
the Secretary of War, shall have exclusive control of
the Institution and of those connected with it, and who

* A General Order, dated "Dec. 8, 1813, signed, John Armstrong [Sect. of
War], directs three hundred short muskets to be forwarded from the Springfield,
Mass., Armory to West Point, for the use of the Cadets—and another of the same
date, requires the Ordnance Officer at Albany to furnish one 18-Pounder, one 10½-
inch Mortar, and one 5½-inch Howitzer, for the use of the Academy at the same
place." [Order-Book, 1813, U. S. M. A.]

15

will be held responsible for its conduct and progress:
he will direct the studies, field exercises, and other academic duties.   The Commandant of the Corps of Engineers shall be the 'Inspector' of the Academy, and
shall visit it officially and report thereon to the War
Department, with such alterations and improvements as
he and the Superintendent may deem necessary.   The
Superintendent will réceive orders from the Inspector,
and will make all returns and communications relative
to the Academy to him only."   The Order declared
that no officer of the Army, of any rank whatever,
should exercise command at West Point, unless subor-
dinate to the Inspector or the Superintendent of the
Academy.   These orders have remained in force to the
present day.

During the following year, the " Rules with respect
to the Promotion of the Cadets at the Military Academy"
were approved by Mr. Monroe, by which their distribu-
tion to the different Corps in the army and their relative rank were made to depend on their general merit,
to be determined by a competent Board of Examiners,
and that no Cadet should be promoted until after completing his course of studies, and receiving his diploma,
&c.   It does not appear that these "Rules" were operative until November, 1818, at which time they were
published in Orders at the Academy, and the Academic
Staff constituted the examining Board.

Another series of Regulations for the Government of
the Military Academy, dated West Point, May 22,
1816, was transmitted to the Inspector by Mr. Crawford, the Secretary of War, "approved" July 1, 1816,
which contained, in addition to the foregoing, a pro-

vision for the appointment of a "Board of Visitors," to consist of five competent gentlemen, who should attend at each general examination, and report thereon to the War Department through the Inspector. Of this Board the Superintendent was constituted the President. It was also provided that annual and semi-annual examinations should be held in June and January, and that new Cadets should present themselves in the month of September, and be examined in spelling, reading, writing, and arithmetic.* During the same year a course of studies for each of the four years was drawn up, and received the sanction of the Secretary of War.

A General Order on September 4, 1816, prescribed the uniform of the Corps of Cadets, the same as now worn, except that the hat and cockade have been displaced by a dress and fatigue-cap, and the pants are without the Austrian knot. Regulations and orders alike seemed unavailing in producing the expected results, for the Chief Engineer, in his report dated March 30th, 1822, declared that "the Military Academy may be considered as having been in its infancy until about the beginning of 1818, prior to which there was but little system or regularity. Cadets were admitted without examination, and without the least regard to their age or qualifications, as required by the law of 1812. Hence the Institution was filled with Cadets who were more or less unfit for their situations. It is not surprising, therefore, that a large portion of them have been under the necessity of leaving the Academy without completing their education."†

---

* Niles's Reg., XVI., Supplement.   † Mil. Affairs, II., 381.

The Cadets were not regarded as amenable to martial law; no class-rank was established; no register of the classes was published; and in the assignment to positions in the Army, they demanded the *right* to elect such Corps as seemed to them most satisfactory.

CHAPTER XII.

Appointment of Brevet-Major Thayer as Superintendent.—Impetus imparted to the Institution.—Organization of the Battalion of Cadets.—Improvements in the System of Education.—The Secretary of War directs Five most Distinguished Cadets in each Class, to be Annually Reported.—Amenability of Cadets to Martial Law.—Cadet Assistant Professors.—General Examinations in January and June.—Furloughs.—Major De Russy Appointed to Succeed Colonel Thayer as Superintendent.—Destruction by Fire of the Academic Building.—New one Erected.—Organization of the Department of Chemistry, &c.—The Cadets Sworn to Serve Eight Years.

Submerged under these and other chaotic influences, Brevet-Major Sylvanus Thayer, of the Corps of Engineers, on July 28, 1817, assumed command as Superintendent of the Military Academy, and from this period the commencement of whatever success as an educational institution, and whatever reputation the Academy may possess throughout our country and abroad, for its strict, impartial, salutary, elevating, and disciplinary government, must be dated.

Major Thayer was an early graduate of the Academy; he had served with distinction in the War of 1812, and had studied the Military Schools of France, and profited by the opportunity to acquire more complete and just views concerning the management of such an institution than were generally entertained among educational and military men of that day. The field before him was

uncultivated; the period was one when rare qualifications for position were not regarded as valueless; and
blessed with health, devotion to the cause, and firmness,
of purpose, he was permitted to organize a system, and
remain sixteen years to perfect its operation.

Immediately after entering upon his duties, the Cadets
were organized into a Battalion of two Companies, with
a *Colonel** of Cadets, an Adjutant and Sergeant-Major, for
its Staff; and within the year he created a "Commandant of Cadets," to be an instructor of Tactics, and
superintend their instruction.   The office thus introduced has recently been recognized by Congress, though
it had, from its origin, continuously existed with no
other sanction than a Regulation.

The division of Classes into sections,† the transfers between the latter,† the weekly rendering of class reports,
showing the daily progress, the system and scale of
daily marks,‡ the establishment of relative class rank
among the members, the publication of the Annual
Register, the introduction of the Board of Visitors,§ the
Check-book system,‖ the preponderating influence of
the "Black-board," and the essential parts of the Regu-
lations‖ for the Military Academy, as they stand to

---

* *Battalion Orders*, Sept. 23, 1817.—"For the designation of rank, chevrons will
be worn on the arms of the Battalion Officers and non-commissioned Officers.
The *Colonel* shall wear three on each arm, the *Captain* shall wear two on each
arm, the *Adjutant* one on each arm, the *Lieutenant* one on the left arm; the
Sergeant-Major two on each arm, the *Sergeants* one on each arm, the *Corporals* one
on the left arm.   Those worn by the officers to be of gold lace, and those of the
non-commissioned officers to be of yellow ribbon."—[Order-Book U. S. M. A., 1817.]

† Order-Book, Oct., 1817, U. S. M. A.   ‡ Mil. Affairs, II., 659

§ Although authorized by the "Crawford" Regulations of March 6, 1816, no
record exists of the proceedings of such a Board previous to 1819.—[Off. Records,
U. S. M. A.]

‖ Order-Book, 1818, U. S. M. A.

this day, are some of the evidences of the indefatigable efforts of Major Thayer to insure method, order, and prosperity to the Institution. It was through the agency of Major Thayer that Professor Claude Crozet, the parent of Descriptive Geometry in America, and one of the first successful instructors of the higher Mathematics, permanent Fortifications, and Topographical Curves, became attached to the Academy.

On February 14, 1818, a communication from John C. Calhoun, Secretary of War, to the Superintendent, declares that it is the determination of the Department to aid in elevating the system of discipline, and create a spirit of emulation among the cadets; and further discloses the belief, "that in future wars the Nation must look to the Academy for the skill to conduct valor to victory;" it also adds, that as " publishing in the Army Register the names of cadets who are most distinguished for attainments and meritorious conduct, may inspire attention to study, and create emulous exertion, you will report to this Department annually in November for that object, the names of those who have most distinguished themselves in the examination, not exceeding five in each class, specifying the studies in which they may excel."*

This order has fully sustained the object of its originator; and few among those thus honored have in after-life experienced a higher feeling of gratified ambition, than accompanied the annual publication, now presented in the appendix, for a period of forty-five years.

The Department of Geography, History, and Ethics was organized by the Act of April 14, 1818; on the 18th,

* Order-Book, 1818, U. S. M. A.

the Chaplain, Rev. Cave Jones, was appointed Professor. The clerical and secular duties thus combined have remained inseparable to the present period.

In November of this year, there occurred a series of events which resulted in the memorable trial of Cadets F., H., L., R., and V., and established the amenability of the Corps of Cadets to martial law, and trial by garrison courts.

The cadets referred to composed a committee representing one hundred and eighty-nine others, who had formed a combination, under the impression that they had, as a corps in the army, rights to defend; and that as cadets at the Military Academy, they were entitled to a free expression of opinion in regard to its management. A General Court-Martial, of which Brevet-Colonel J. Hindman, Corps of Artillery, was president, convened at West Point in May following, for the trial of the cadets named; and upon the completion of the first case [Cadet R.], the court decided that, according to their construction of the Rules and Articles of War, they *had no authority to try cadets.*

Upon this decision, August 21, 1819, Hon. William Wirt, then Attorney-General,* delivered an elaborate opinion, wherein the following views are supported:

" It is suggested by Colonel Hindman, on behalf of the court-martial, that these cadets are merely students. In one sense they are so, and so was the old corps, known under the name of ' Artillerists and Engineers ;' so was

* A decision of the Attorney-General, dated July 13th, 1837, places the sojourn of any person at West Point not connected with the Military Academy (denying the right of a citizen, even to visit the hotel, post-office, or use of the public wharf) subject to a prohibition by the Superintendent, if in his opinion the public interest requires it.—[Official Records U. S. M. A.]

the original corps of engineers who constituted the Military Academy; for both 'books, instruments, and apparatus for study,' were expressly provided by law; yet this character of students did not exempt them from liability to martial law. But if the suggestion is intended to place cadets on the footing of civil students, clothed with all their civil privileges and immunities, it is proper to remark, that these cadets occupy a very different ground; they are enlisted soldiers; they engage, like soldiers, to serve five years unless sooner discharged; * * * * they are bound to perform military duty in such places, and on such service, as the Commander-in-chief of the army of the United States shall order; and, finally, by the Act of the 3d of March, 1815, fixing 'the military peace establishment of the United States,' the corps to which they are attached, and of which they form a part, is expressly recognized as a part of that military establishment. * * * After every allowance for the genius of our Constitution and laws, and after rejecting every thing like implication and inference from the consideration of this question, I come to the conclusion that the corps at West Point form a part of the land forces of the United States, and have been constitutionally subjected by Congress to the Rules and Articles of War, and to trial by courts-martial."*

This opinion was confirmed by President Monroe and Mr. Calhoun, Secretary of War, and has prevailed from that day to this, as supreme law.

An order from the Engineer Department, dated April 13, 1818, authorized the employment of cadets as acting

---

* Mil. Affairs, II., 30.

Assistant Professors, " each cadet so detailed to receive
ten dollars per month," and the appointment, declared
an " honorable distinction," was further marked by the
order of the Superintendent, dated September 10, 1823,
which prescribed the additional number of buttons on
the uniform of such as held these positions.*

Practical instruction at this time was conveyed not
only at the Academy, but excursion marches, under
Major William J. Worth, the Commandant of Cadets,
were made at different times by the cadets to Boston,
Philadelphia, Princeton, and other points, during which
all the duties incident to camp-life and field-service were
regularly performed.

A Regulation, approved by the Secretary of War,
dated July 23d, 1818, introduced the following radical
changes in the existing code :

" I. There shall be two general examinations in each
year; the first to commence on the 1st of January, and
the second on the 1st of June.

" II. All newly appointed cadets will be ordered to
join the Military Academy for examination by the 25th
of June in each year, and no cadet shall be examined for
admission after the first day of September following, unless he shall have been prevented from joining at the
proper time by sickness or some other unavoidable
cause; in which case he may be examined with the fourth
class at the general examination in January, and if then
found qualified to proceed with that class, may be admitted accordingly.

" III. Until a revision of the laws relating to the

Military Academy, there shall be, in lieu of the vacation authorized by the existing regulations, an annual encampment, to commence on the 1st of July and end on the 31st of August.

" IV. The Superintendent is authorized to grant furloughs to the cadets, at the request of their parents, during the period of their encampment, provided that not more than one-fourth of the whole number be absent at any one time, and provided also that every cadet, previously to his receiving a diploma, shall have been present at not less than two entire encampments."*

At his own request, on July 1, 1833, Colonel Thayer was relieved as Superintendent by Major R. E. DE RUSSY, of the Corps of Engineers. The upward impetus given to the Institution by the former, had attracted general observation. Cadet appointments became a matter of greater importance and patronage. The asperities of party were aroused; politics invaded the Military Academy; and the decisions of its controlling authorities were subject to reversion, by those who sought to perpetuate influence rather than uphold discipline.

Under Colonel De Russy the present Academic Hall was commenced; and while yet in progress, on February 19, 1838, the old two-story stone Academy, facing the north, and in front of the present Barracks, was destroyed by fire.

The books and records of the Adjutant's Office, containing the history of the Academy, and of the Post since the Revolution, were entirely consumed, and a loss

---

* Order-Book, Aug., 1818, U. S. M. A.

was thereby sustained which can never be replaced. The contents of the Library, Engineering Department, and Chemical Laboratory, were rescued by the cadets in a seriously damaged condition.

By the Act of July 5, 1838, it was provided, " That an additional professor be appointed to instruct in the studies of Chemistry, Mineralogy, and Geology," and the Secretary of War was authorized to assign an assistant professor, " to be taken from the officers of the line or cadets, and who should receive the same pay as the other assistant professors."

The Department thus created was organized by the appointment of Lieutenant Jacob W. Bailey, as Professor.

Section 28 of the same Act declared : " That the term for which Cadets hereafter admitted into the Military Academy at West Point shall engage to serve be, and the same is hereby, increased to eight years, unless sooner discharged."

This engagement has remained unchanged ; and by it the United States claims the services of those who have been educated at the expense of the nation, though the latter is by no means bound to provide commissions to the cadets after passing the prescribed four years at the Military Academy. No instances, however, have occurred where the services were refused, or the graduates left unprovided with commissions.

CHAPTER XIII.

Major Delafield Appointed to Succeed Colonel De Russy as Superintendent.—Progress in Improvements.—Establishment of Cavalry Instruction.—Commandant of the Post.—Method of Appointing the Cadets.—Principles Regulating it.—Not Controlled by the Wealthy.—Open to all.—Substitutes for the Present System of making Appointments.—Enormous Expense of the Proposed Change.—Comparison of a Cadet and Citizen Applicant for Grade of Lieutenant.—The Military Academy said to be "Only a School of Art," and Accused of having Produced no "Great Military Genius."—An Appeal to its Records.—Term of Service of Graduates, and of Citizens in the Army.

On September 1, 1838, Colonel De Russy was succeeded by Major Richard Delafield, of the Corps of Engineers, as Superintendent. Endowed with administrative abilities of a high order, and an inflexible resolution to maintain the discipline of the Institution, one of the earliest efforts of this officer was directed towards defining and establishing the boundaries of the public lands at West Point, and removing all unauthorized individuals who had settled thereon. Various suits of ejectment were successfully instituted against those who, under divers pretences, occupied portions of the public domain. Under his direction, Lieutenant Knowlton was employed to search the State and County records; and the result was most successful in effecting the removal of the offending parties, and the establishment by a new survey, in 1839, of the boundaries before described, and which have remained ever since unchanged. The erection of the Library Building and Artillery Laboratory, the enlargement of the Library, the improvement of the Chemical Laboratory, many acquisitions to the Drawing department, and the construction of the roads leading towards Canterbury, to the North Wharf, and the Chain battery walk, are some of the efforts which attest Major Delafield's untiring energy.

The repeated representations of the successive Boards of Visitors induced Mr. Poinsett, the Secretary of War, on June 12, 1839, to transfer a sergeant and five dragoons from Carlisle Barracks, to aid in the introduction of exercises in Riding at the Academy. Twelve horses were supplied by the Quarter-Master's Department in the ensuing week. In September following, the Sergeant was appointed Riding-Master; and at the same time authority was given the Superintendent to recruit the detachment, purchase thirty additional horses with equipments, and the harness necessary for a battery of Light Artillery.

From this period new life was infused into the Light Artillery and mounted corps of the army, and instruction in both of these branches has continued without interruption.

By the Act of July 20, 1840, it was declared that the Commandant of Cadets should be either the instructor of Artillery, Cavalry, or Infantry tactics, or the instructor of practical Engineering; and by the same Act, an Assistant professor was authorized in the department of Ethics as in other departments.

Section 6th of the Act of August 23, 1842, declared,

that the Superintendent of the Military Academy should be the Commandant of the Post; and thus a vexatious question of rank and command was definitively settled.

Up to this period, the mode of selecting and appointing the Cadets had constituted a grave subject of inquiry and discussion in different sections of the country. An examination of the method, and the comparative merit of the system which was proposed as a substitute, admit of a brief description.

Prior to 1817, various circumstances connected with the condition of the country and of the Academy, contributed to render admission to it far less an object of ambition than it has since become. The openings for the aspiring, before the commencement of the second war of 1812, were indicated by the pacific policy of the country. The talents of the young were exerted in achieving pre-eminence in the legislative or judicial halls, or in acquiring the wealth to be gained in commercial intercourse with foreign lands. Undoubtedly military science and skill assumed more important aspects in the public mind during the progress of that war; but the sure means of obtaining this science and skill were not as perceptible in the then imperfect organization of, and instruction at the Military Academy, as they have been since the year 1817.

From that period the increasing reputation of the Institution attracted towards it public attention; and young men of ardent minds and strong powers sought a participation in its privileges and advantages. This general emulation imposed upon the Department, by which the selection of candidates was to be made, the necessity of adopting some general rule, which should exclude the imputation of favoritism, and be equitable for all. One principle was admitted to be fundamental —that the doors of an institution which was sustained by the munificence of the country should be first opened to receive the sons of those who had bravely perilled, or who had nobly lost their lives in its defence. Another principle, which naturally suggested itself to the minds of those who wished that the army should be deservedly honored, was, that an uncommon intellectual ability should be a guarantee of success to an applicant. In the application of these principles, however, even upon the supposition that selections were limited to these two classes, there might often occur a serious practical difficulty. The very word, Selection, implies a balancing of claims; and it is not to be supposed that any individual, however extensive his intercourse with society might have been, would be able, from his personal knowledge of candidates, to frame in all classes a just award.

This difficulty increased as the number of admissions to be granted increased, and as the classes from which a selection was to be made were multiplied. To rely entirely upon the representations of individuals residing at a distance, and equally unknown with those whom they recommended, would be obviously most unsafe. It would be reposing confidence under circumstances which would not justify trust in ordinary matters of mere pecuniary interest. The representative branch of the Government, including under this denomination the Senate and the House, afforded a means of obtaining the information prerequisite to a decision, which pro-

mised an effectual security for the rights of all. No
inference could be more legitimate than this : that they
who were intrusted with the higher concerns of the
people, and who were directly responsible to the people,
would be safe counsellors in the administration of this
interest. From these and similar views originated,
probably, the *custom* of selecting one cadet from each
Congressional district, and of allowing great weight
to the recommendation of the representatives of the
respective districts. This rule, while it afforded to the
appointing power the means of judging correctly, or
rather of avoiding error, was acceptable to the representatives and to their constituents. To the former, as
it gave them opportunities of extending their personal
influence, or of gratifying their feelings of personal
regard. To the latter, who could thus present their
claims with the more freedom and confidence through
the medium which the Constitution and their own choice
had provided.

It is true that, in some instances, a representative
might feel himself bound to present the names of several candidates, and that then the final decision must be
made by the head of the Department. But such instances are of rare occurrence; and it is believed the
fact is susceptible of positive proof, that, in a vast
majority of cases, the selections have been determined
by the representative of the district, or by the joint
action of all the members of a delegation from a State.
The necessary operation of this rule leaves but little patronage with the appointing power; and the danger of an
abuse of the privilege allowed them by the representatives is guarded against, not only by their responsibility

16

to their constituents, but by the sense of honor which will forbid them to mislead the judgment of him who relies upon them for the means of deciding rightly. It has been charged, however, that under the influence of the motives which have been alluded to [the extension of their personal interest, and the gratification of personal regard], the representatives have exerted themselves for the success of the *wealthy* or *powerful*. The records of the Academy furnish a complete refutation to this charge. From them it prominently appears, that not more than *one-eighteenth* of those admitted during the last twenty-two years could have received, without this aid, more than a common English school education, and that a still smaller number of the officers of the army possess any income or means of support beyond their regular pay and emoluments. It seems that this accusation underrates the intelligence and moral feeling of both representatives and people. The sentiments of gratitude and veneration for the worthies of the army have not so far subsided, nor the appreciation of uncommon mental power become so rare in any community, that the overlooking, by a representative or an officer of the Government, of a son of the former, or the possessor of the latter, in favor of one whose only recommendations were wealth or influence with a party, would not draw upon him their distrust and contempt.

That appointments have been, and may again be made, without consulting those peculiar interests for which the Institution was designed, it is not unreasonable to suppose; but the Academy itself furnishes the best possible corrective for abuses of this kind, in rejecting incompetent and unworthy members; while, from the legal authority* with which it is clothed, it can accomplish what no executive authority has hitherto been able to effect, by resisting all political and other influences for the restoration of such subjects. It thus secures the public interests, and the rightful claims of those of its members who faithfully perform their duties.

All will readily admit that the military profession, like that of every other calling in life, requires a peculiar training and special qualifications to exercise it successfully. In most of the other vocations of life, the welfare of the individual is the chief object—in this, the safety and honor of the State are involved. It is true that there are other bodies upon whom this guardianship rests, as the Executive, the Legislative, and the Judiciary; but the acts of these, if erroneous, are seldom irreparable, and most of them are easily remedied. But this is far from being true in regard to the acts of armies. A battle lost, besides the effusion of blood, often entails an immense destruction of property, and other annihilating results; but a far greater and more momentous loss—that of national existence—may depend upon victory or defeat.

Hence the State has the greatest possible interest in maintaining her armies in the most effective condition; and to neglect any of the means recognized by experience as the best for attaining this purpose, would be not only a culpable, but might prove a fatal remissness. Among these means, there is no one which nations, obliged from their political condition to keep large armies on foot, regard as more important than that of securing a highly educated body of officers, whose instruction has

* Act of Congress, August 3, 1861, Chap. 42, Sec. 8.

been specially designed to qualify them for the performance of the various duties pertaining to the organization and discipline of armies. The inquiry naturally presents itself, in what way can these agents be best obtained?

The solution of this question is one which has claimed the attention of every statesman and political economist in Europe and America.

From the period of disbanding the army of the Revolution on the banks of the Hudson, in 1783, down to the present moment, three methods only have been suggested. It has been urged that individual enterprise might accomplish the end desired; that independent State institutions would fill the necessary requirement; or that the central Government, under the provision "to provide for the common defence," was clothed with all the authority requisite to obtain the desired service.

The enormous outlay required by an individual attempt, the failure to maintain any thing like a system of discipline, from the feeble tie which binds the pupil, and the insignificant pecuniary return when contrasted with other avocations, have produced, in all efforts of this kind, no fruit beyond affording relief to the otherwise sedentary habits of student life.

Nor have the State military institutions enjoyed the measure of success so ardently desired. In every State, when not locally endowed, they have drooped and languished, revived and drooped again. From the diversity of discipline, from the unwillingness to submit to or the inability to maintain it, from the great expense, and from more lucrative attractions, all, save two or three, have failed to enjoy even an ordinary measure of prosperity. And yet the opportunities for advancement in military life have ever remained open.

The commissioned officers of the army are drawn from three sources : 1st, from civil life ; 2d, from the rank and file ; and 3d, from the Cadets, who are warrant officers of the army.

The *first* are appointed without any previous military training, and without any specific examination as to their qualifications.

The *second* are taken from the sergeants,* who have had some practical military training, subject to a preliminary examination on some of the very elementary branches of common school instruction.

The *third*, after four years' practical military instruction, and after two half-yearly rigid examinations, upon branches of science and art connected with his professional pursuits, acquires a claim to the commission only of the lowest grade.

There are thus three doors open to army commissions, embracing all citizens of the proper military age, and no one in theory or practice excludes the others. The President of the United States alone is clothed with the power of selection and nomination from these classes —a power which, thus far in history, he has confined to no one of the three. How little the cadet excludes the citizen, or even his own military inferior, may be

---

* "SEC. 5.—The President of the United States is authorized, by and with the advice and consent of the Senate, to confer the brevet of second lieutenant upon such meritorious non-commissioned officers as may be brought before an army board, composed of four officers of rank, specially convened for the purpose; and if found qualified for the duties of commissioned officers, to attach them to regiments as supernumerary officers, according to the Act of April 29, 1812, entitled 'An Act making further provision for the Corps of Engineers,' Approved August 4, 1854."

shown from the fact, that vacancies have been repeatedly filled only a few days before the graduation of a class of cadets, which, had they been left open, the graduates would in due course have filled.

The average age of admission of the cadet is eighteen years; he then enters the service at a period of life when the mind and the body are in the best condition to be moulded into any form. The State places him on active field service when his frame has become sufficiently matured to bear the wear and rough usage of military life, and thirty years of efficient service may be reasonably counted upon from him. The private citizen or sergeant, particularly the latter, as a general rule, is farther advanced in years; and the cadet is therefore more likely to attain a responsible command when possessed of health and strength sufficient to endure its hardships and fatigue.

For the staff, Engineers, Ordnance, and Artillery, high scientific attainments are indispensable; and it is of the utmost importance to the efficiency of other arms, that a portion at least of its officers should be men of the same acquirements. These the Military Academy has hitherto supplied, and with a degree of economy which may well bear the closest examination.

A recurrence to the remark in regard to the imputation that undue preference has been shown for the *wealthy*, is made because the facts do not support the allegation. But it is by no means conceded, that where there are natural endowments and capacities of a high order, the possession of wealth would be a proper ground of exclusion from the Academy. It should be open to all.

Admitting, for the moment, that the objections of exclusiveness, favoritism, and aristocracy are well founded, the question immediately occurs, how will these objections be removed? While the Academy exists, the rank of cadet is the lowest grade in the army; if it be discontinued, the rank of second lieutenant will be the lowest. The change is simple and apparently unimportant; the consequences are worthy of grave consideration.

The annual average number of vacancies for ten years in the army, just previous to 1861, is 42; the average number of admissions to the Military Academy for the same period is 78.

The opportunities, therefore, for entering the army, being represented by the ratio of 78 to 42, do not, most certainly, render appointments in it less exclusive. But it is said it will be more popular, because the vacancies will be filled by selections from the community at large. Do not the wealthy, and those possessing political influence, constitute a part of the community? and will not the appointing power have the same inducements for preferring their applications for lieutenants' commissions that he now has for preferring their applications for cadets' warrants? Will not these applications be made through the representatives, and will there not be the same reasons for relying upon their recommendations? How then will the opportunities for favoritism be lessened? On the other hand, the vacancies which annually occur are now supplied by those graduates of the Academy who have acquired distinction by their conduct and attainments, and are prepared to undertake the higher duties of their profession.

Assuming that forty-two vacancies are to be filled each year from the mass of our citizens, there will be thus added to the army forty-two lieutenants to whom every branch of duty and service will be new, and who, after four years, instead of being familiar with the theory, science, and practice of war, will be very slightly and imperfectly acquainted with the two first, and only tolerably proficient in the last. And to accomplish this result, a considerable pecuniary expenditure must be made.

The pay of the forty-two lieutenants for the four years will be 212,688 dollars; that of the forty-two cadets for the same time, including every thing for their education, will be 60,480 dollars. The difference, 152,208 dollars, is the amount the nation will be required to pay for a change in the military establishment which will deprive it of its great ornaments of talent, learning, and skill, and effect a general deterioration in the character of the officers and the army. The military and scientific information diffused throughout the country by those who pass two or three years at the Academy, but do not complete the course, is considered in this estimate. But a fair equivalent for the expense of their education is, or may be found, in the employment of their services in perfecting the discipline of the militia, and the construction of works of improvement. A comparison of the results of this change is quite as marked as the expense which would accompany it. In the one case, there stands a cadet graduate awaiting promotion, who has had four years of the very best kind of military instruction. His mind has been engaged in laborious study, affording him a large stock of professional knowledge, and preparing a foundation for all the acquisition his advancement may call for. Not only this: he has been drilled in practical military exercises; he has served as a soldier for years in the ranks, or as a sergeant or corporal; and for a year he has often, if not during that whole period, served as a commissioned officer, performing on the field all the appropriate duties, as Engineers, Infantry, Light infantry, Cavalry, and Artillery, both mounted and on foot.

He can himself drill a Battalion of Infantry, a Battery of Artillery, or a Squadron of Cavalry, with promptitude and exactness. He can take in at a glance an offensive or defensive position, and can stake out and direct the construction of a field fortification, block-house, bridge, building, or roadway. On paper, he can delineate maps and plans, and explain the manœuvres of Battalions, Brigades, Divisions, and Army Corps. He has spent nearly a year in actual field service, under tents, performing all the military duties incident thereto; his mind invigorated by constant exercise; his habits moulded by the observance of order and discipline to a prompt and cheerful execution of duty; his moral character elevated by the practice of virtuous habits, and the honorable emulation in which he has participated; while, from the class which contains him and his fellows, the idle, the stupid, the incapable, and the vicious, have, in the four years passed at the Academy, been thoroughly weeded out.

Admitting that he has been taught theories and saturated with mathematics, and that the genius of Julius Cæsar, Alexander the Great, and Napoleon, has not descended upon him; can there be a doubt as to his superiority over one not thus instructed for appointment into the army? A citizen, after four years in the army, will be inferior even to what the cadet now is ; for his opportunities will have been less ; the stimulants by which the other was both urged and forced will be wanting ; and his mind and character will have passed the period when kindly nature could leave its deepest impress.*

It was to meet the absurd allegations that the cadets were drawn from the wealthy classes in the country, or were principally sons of high functionaries under the government, that the Superintendent, in 1842,† instituted a classification of the circumstances in life of the parents of the cadets ; and, to insure a faithful record, the cadets were separately required to make the necessary entries, under appropriate headings, without affixing names,—to the end that the information might not affect the social relations among the cadets themselves, or be traceable, even by authorities, to the individual who furnished it. In this way, upon the entry annually of each class of new cadets, the information contained in the table in the appendix has been obtained, and is herewith given for a period of twenty-two consecutive years.

Equally derogatory with the charge of favoring the wealthy classes, and alike depreciative, is the oft-repeated declaration that the Military Academy is merely a " School of Art," and that it has never yet produced " a military genius" like Napoleon. Without

* Report of the Chief-Engineer, 1844.

† A similar document, giving the names and parentage of the cadets, was published by order of Congress in the spring of 1830.

enumerating the few great generals that the most military powers of ancient and modern times have furnished—powers which were almost always in a state of war, and whose military luminaries are so few that the number may be reckoned upon the fingers—it may be observed, that the province of the Academy is not to *create* genius, but to bring together the means of aiding its development and storing up its results for the benefit of less powerfully gifted or instructed minds.

Schools are the great storehouses for gathering in all the detached germs of knowledge which would otherwise be lost; for organizing, and systematizing, and diffusing them throughout the masses of society by means of the bodies of able men who, devoted to such objects, are naturally brought to concur to this end. From this point of view, the only true and fair one, the question may properly suggest itself, how does the Military Academy compare with like institutions in fulfilling this object? As it is only by comparison that a correct judgment can be rendered upon the agency of the Academy in accomplishing the end referred to, a brief reference to the results of the workings of other institutions becomes necessary.

Besides our Colleges for preparing young men to enter with advantage upon their chosen professional career, there are many schools specially designed for prosecuting all the pursuits which require a higher order of elementary acquirement, as those for Theology, Law, Medicine, &c. Moreover, every one of these professions is, respectively, a practical school, where men are daily learning from each other. Our law courts, our hospitals, and our halls of legislation, are but so many schools of practical instruction for Oratory, Surgery, and States-manship. Bearing this in view, and starting back from a period fifty years ago, when the Military Academy was fairly organized, how many great lawyers, great orators, great physicians, and great statesmen, have stood forth pre-eminently, as men of commanding genius, from all those institutions, who have left an impress through the country of the period of their existence? Neither their numbers nor their names are long enshrin-ed; yet the world has moved on, and each has added his mite to the general stock of human knowledge, while the external marks of civilization have been more strik-ing within this period than for any like period of the world's history.

Has the Military Academy, which from its organiza-tion has labored under greater disadvantages than any of the institutions referred to, produced no fruits worthy of commendation during this period?

An appeal to its records will demonstrate, that it has diffused military science throughout the country, both by its teachings and through its pupils who have retired to civil life, the results of which were glaringly visible in the war of 1812, in the war with Mexico, and in the present contest for national supremacy. In all these, it contributed its quota to the diffusion of science, and through the industrial pursuits depending upon or springing out of them. It has girdled our extensive sea-coast with permanent fortifications, which will com-pare favorably with the most celebrated of like works in Europe; it has aided in fathoming and mapping our harbors and lakes; it has explored our rivers and territo-ries; it gave its quota to the pioneers of civil engineering; its graduates mainly collected and organized the resources of the country in the Mexican war, and conducted them through a series of unparalleled triumphs; while, in the present struggle for constitutional integrity, its graduates are not less entitled to praise, for the organization of the largest military force ever called into the field by a nation in the same space of time.

These are the recorded results of the agencies emanating from the Military Academy, and it may be fairly claimed that the design of the Institution has not only been attained, by diffusing military knowledge and providing officers conversant with their professional duties, but, incidentally and directly, it has been of the greatest advantage to the public interests.—second alone to the military security of the nation.

If it has thus far produced no "military genius," it has nevertheless furnished the means, without which genius would be to a great extent powerless to effect any great end, and equally helpless, without its intelligent agents, to accomplish momentous designs.

The resignation of the graduates of the Military Academy at different periods has furnished another topic for animadversion; and yet the period of service rendered by such as have separated from the army exceeds that rendered by those appointed from civil life, who have in like manner abandoned the profession.

The average term of service of the graduates of the Academy, including the period of cadet life, who resigned from 1802 to 1860, inclusive, was ten and a half years; while the average term of service for the *eleven* years prior to 1861, was thirteen and a quarter years. The average term of service of those appointed from civil life in this latter period, was only seven and a half years.*

The period of cadet life is properly included in estimating the service of resigned graduates, when it is remembered that their time between the age of eighteen and twenty-two was given to the public, when young men in most of the callings of civil life are embarked upon the future professional career upon which their fortunes depend. And although the Government bears the expense of the cadet's education, the latter fits him specially for the military profession alone, although it enables him to take up advantageously and particularly the pursuit of civil engineering and scientific instruction. The act of resignation does not deprive the country of the acquirements of its citizen graduate; he carries them with him, it is true, but they are for the greater part useless to him as an individual. It is so much capital locked up, or awaiting investment. It is on hand whenever the Government may stand in need of it, and it is ready to yield to the former a far greater interest than if it had been employed in the much more contracted sphere,—to which the graduate would have been assigned had he remained in the army,—which he usually is found to have reached in civil life.

Experience has shown that in every war in which the nation has been engaged since the Academy went into operation, most of the citizen graduates have been returned to the service with a rank superior to that enjoyed by those who have remained continuously in the

* This period of eleven years is selected, because, at its commencement, every inducement was furnished, by the tide of emigration setting toward the newly-discovered gold region of California, to young men to embark in a career promising wealth, reputation, and distinction.

army—a circumstance in itself of advantage to the country, however unfavorably it may operate on individuals, for the professional acquirements of most of the graduates are far beyond the military grades which most of them attain, until after many years of service during peace. In the latter state it is no unfrequent thing to find lieutenants of ten or fifteen years' standing, and captains of over twenty, all of whom possess acquirements and experience, after very few years' service, fitting them for the superior grades of field officers. The war with Mexico and the present contest furnish abundant examples of this kind.

CHAPTER XIV.

THE custom which had so long prevailed of appointing
one cadet from each Congressional district, was, on
March 1, 1843, made a law by Congress, with the condition affixed, that each cadet so appointed should be
an actual resident of the District, State, or Territory from
which the appointment purported to be made; and thus
the number of cadets was limited to the number of members of the House of Representatives.   But as the District of Columbia and the Army and Navy were not represented, the President was empowered to appoint one
cadet from the former and ten cadets " at large;" the
latter to be annually selected by the President from the

Army or Navy, or any other quarter at his option, without being confined to Congressional districts.

The same act declared, that in future a " Board of Visitors" should not be appointed, unless otherwise ordered by Congress.

Thus far the monthly pay of the cadets, as fixed by the law of 1802, was sixteen dollars and two rations, being altogether valued at twenty-eight dollars; but on March 3, 1845, Congress enacted, that in lieu of the pay and rations before allowed, each cadet should receive twenty-four dollars per month, and no more.

Major Delafield was succeeded on August 15, 1845, by Captain HENRY BREWERTON, of the Corps of Engineers. The spirit for improvement which marked the career of this officer as Superintendent, and the faithful discharge of all the duties enjoined upon him, or exacted by him from others, have left their impress upon the Military Academy.

The erection of the spacious Barracks and Mess-Hall, the grading of the surface of the Plain, the iron fences, the South Wharf, with the road leading thereto, the road leading southward to Cozzens' Hotel, the enlargement of the supply of water, and the erection of several cottages, for the accommodation of the officers and their families, had their origin during the administration of Captain Brewerton.

By the Act of May 15, 1846, a company of Engineer soldiers was raised, and assigned, among other duties, to aid in conveying practical instruction in engineering to the cadets at the Military Academy.

The outbreak of the war with Mexico having greatly increased the interest of the public in the necessity for

17

and importance of the Institution, on August 8, of the
same year, Congress authorized the appointment annually of a Board of Visitors, whose duty it was made to
attend each yearly examination, and report to the Secretary of War upon the discipline, instruction, police,
and fiscal affairs of the Academy.   The members of the
Board were to be selected by the President, and taken
from one-half of the number of States, alternating yearly
with the other half, each member being a *bonâ fide* resident of the State from whence appointed, and each Congressional district being in turn designated to furnish
the appointee.

The same act declared that the teachers of French
and Drawing should henceforth be entitled Professors
in their respective departments, and subsequent laws
placed them upon the same footing with regard to pay,
and an Assistant, as all the other Professors.

The brilliant success of the American army in Mexico,
untarnished by a single defeat, or doubtful action, furnished the nation with ample proof of the wisdom of
Knox, Hamilton, McHenry, Huntingdon, Pickering,
Washington, and Madison, in their efforts to establish a
Military Academy wherein officers might be educated
and trained to organize and discipline citizen soldiers,
and lead them to victory;—while a network of railways,
and innumerable public edifices, fortifications, lighthouses, and harbor improvements bear witness to an
educational course of incalculable value in periods of
peace and prosperity.

When the conflicting voices of partisan spirits are
hushed, and the rancorous jealousies of envious and
malignant disputants are consigned to oblivion, posterity

will gaze upon the pile of strange-looking artillery, and still stranger looking tattered flags, and their mutilated flag-staffs, deposited at the Military Academy in 1849, and read above them, in characters penned by the great soldier whose qualifications and position, as the Commanding General of that army, gave him a right to pronounce an opinion: * * * "As under Providence it is mainly to the Military Academy that the United States became indebted for those brilliant achievements, and other memorable victories in the same war, I have a lively pleasure in tendering the seven trophies [semi-national] to the mother of so many accomplished soldiers and patriots." * * * Posterity may then realize, difficult as it may now seem, that these trophies are monuments to professional soldiers, who had no loftier incentive to action than *duty* to their country and the Institution which nourished them.

The close of the year 1849 found the Military Academy in the full tide of usefulness and prosperity. At no time in its history had the institution stood higher in the estimation of the National Legislature. Its requirements were carefully studied, and its wants fully supplied.

On August 28, the western portion of the New Barracks, commenced in 1845, was first occupied by the cadets, the South Barracks having undergone demolition during the summer encampment. Two years later (August 28, 1851), witnessed the completion and occupation of the whole edifice, and the removal of the North Barracks. The old Mess-Hall was demolished, and the New Hall occupied in the summer of 1852.

Captain Brewerton was succeeded, on September 1,

1852, by Captain and Brevet-Colonel Robert E. Lee, Corps of Engineers, as Superintendent, under whose administration the course of study, by direction of the Secretary of War, was on August 28, 1854, extended so as to embrace a term of five years at the Academy.

This change was made upon the repeated and urgent recommendation of the Boards of Visitors, who had in preceding years reported upon the comprehensive range of subjects taught at the institution, and who had dwelt with much earnestness upon the necessity of an enlargement of the course of English studies, so as to admit of the introduction of Declamation, Military Law, &c., as well as to permit, in several of the departments, field instruction of a practical character.

As the cadets were bound to serve for the period of eight years, unless sooner discharged, this change was wholly within the power of the Secretary of War, who directed the class which entered in June, 1854, to be divided, according to the age of the members, into two equal portions; the youngest portion to remain and complete the curriculum of study, in accordance with the new programme for a five years' course.

The new arrangement went into operation under the most favorable auspices, and for a time bid fair to accomplish all that its ardent advocates had predicted. The amplest facilities were afforded the cadets to acquire practical instruction in the erection of pontoon bridges, field fortifications, duty of sappers and miners, topographical drawing and sketching, and in other departments of study; while the completion of the new Riding-Hall in November, 1855, greatly increased the opportunities for cavalry exercises, and excited additional interest in this department.

Colonel Lee having been promoted to the cavalry arm of the service, and thereby by law incapacitated from exercising superintendence at the Military Academy, he was succeeded on April 1, 1855, by Captain and Brevet-Major JONATHAN G. BARNARD, Corps of Engineers, as Superintendent, whose term of service might have been indefinitely extended with advantage to the institution; but on September 8, 1856, Major Barnard was relieved by the appointment of Major RICHARD DELAFIELD, Corps of Engineers, as Superintendent for the second time.

The erection of the bell and clock-tower on the Academy, the completion of the gas-works for lighting the public buildings on the Post, the restoration of ·the old relic of the Revolution, Fort Clinton, and the enlargement and erection of additional accommodations for the families of the officers and professors, demonstrated the possession still of the energy which had before marked Major Delafield's career.

By the Act of February 16, 1857, Congress enacted that there should be, in addition to the professors authorized by existing laws, a Professor of Spanish, who was placed upon the same footing as the other Professors; and later, in the department thus created, Patrice De Jañon was appointed Professor.

On March 3, 1857, the monthly pay of each cadet was raised from twenty-four to thirty dollars; and on June 12, 1858, Congress further provided that the Superintendent of the Military Academy should be appointed by the President of the United States, with the local rank, the pay, and the allowances, while acting in this capacity, of a Colonel of Engineers.

The same act declared that the Commandant of the Corps of Cadets, while serving as such by appointment of the President, should have the local rank, pay, and allowances of a Lieutenant-Colonel of Engineers, and be charged with the instruction of the cadets in the Artillery, Infantry, and Cavalry branches of the army. By this law the practice, which had found favor heretofore, of appointing officers from these arms of the service respectively, to serve as instructors to the cadets, was virtually ignored.

On October 11, 1858, the course of study, before prescribed for five years, was abruptly changed by the Secretary of War back to four years; and on April 5, 1859, the course was again changed by the same authority from four back to five years. The indecision thus displayed, and the confusion arising from reversing the decisions, at Washington, of the Academic Board, and disregarding their recommendations, were among the lesser evils which pervaded every department of the Government, and were preliminary to still more disastrous management on the part of those who controlled the nation.

On June 21, 1860, Congress organized a Commission, to consist of two senators, two representatives, and two army officers, to examine into the organization, discipline, and course of instruction at the Military Academy, with a view to ascertain what changes, if any, were desirable to enable the Institution to accomplish in the best possible manner the object of its establishment. This Commission, consisting of Jefferson Davis, *Chair-*

man, and Solomon Foot, of the Senate, John Cochrane
and H. Winter Davis, of the House of Representatives,
Major Robert Anderson and Captain A. A. Humphreys,
of the United States Army, with a Recording Secretary,
met at West Point on July 17, and after a session of
more than seven weeks, adjourned to meet at the city
of Washington, November 28, 1860.

On December 13 following, the Commission submitted
to Congress a report* of three hundred and fifty pages of
closely printed matter, in which they recommended an
entire reorganization of the Academy. An Act was
introduced for this purpose, but owing to the excited
state of public affairs, or other causes, no action was
taken upon the subject.

On January 23, 1861, Major Delafield was relieved by
the appointment of Captain and Brevet-Major PETER G.
T. BEAUREGARD, Corps of Engineers, as Superintendent.
Five days after this officer entered upon his duties,
an order from the Secretary of War directed him to
transfer back to Major Delafield the command at West
Point; and on March 1, 1861, the latter was succeeded
by Major ALEXANDER H. BOWMAN, Corps of Engineers,
as Superintendent, who is yet present.

The outbreak of the civil war was the signal for a
number of the cadets who were appointed from the
Southern States, influenced by family ties, tempting offers of position, and the examples in Congress, to tender
their resignations and repair to their homes, in disregard
of the sworn articles previously signed by them to serve
faithfully the Government of the United States.

As many published accounts, more or less incorrect,

* XXXVI. Cong., 2d Session, Mis. Doc. No. 3.

have gone forth relative to the changes which occurred at this time, the following statement has been carefully prepared and may be regarded as authentic :

The total number of Cadets present at the Academy on November 1, 1860, was 278

Of this number, there were appointed from the Southern States 86

Of the number thus appointed, there were discharged, dismissed, or resigned, from causes connected with the civil war 65

Leaving at the Academy to prosecute their studies, from the Southern States 21

These changes failed in the slightest degree to affect the organization of the Institution, or seriously to impair its code of discipline: a return, however, from the five back to the old four years' programme of instruction was a measure which experience dictated, and which the Secretary of War sanctioned in July, 1861. By the Act of Congress dated August 3, same year, the oath of allegiance to be administered to all cadets present, and to those appointed in future, was so amended as to abjure all allegiance, sovereignty, or fealty conceived to be due any State, County, or Country whatsoever, and further required unqualified support to the Constitution and the National Government. The same act secured the Academy from the repetition of an evil against which it had long struggled, and which, if unchecked, would have destroyed its vitality if not its existence.

Section 8th declared that no Cadet, after having been pronounced deficient in conduct or studies, and recommended for discharge, should be returned to the Academy except upon the recommendation of the Academic Board; nor should any cadet be reappointed, or appointed into the army, while his class yet remained at the Academy, except upon a like recommendation. The effect of this legislative enactment has been to produce a marked change, accompanied by the happiest results, in regard to the studious habits of the several classes at the Academy.

The Act of July 2, 1862, prescribing the "Oath of Office," even more comprehensive in its requirements, has been substituted for the one already referred to, and is now administered to all cadets entering the Institution.

Bills for enlarging the number of cadets at the Military Academy, by permitting each senator in Congress to appoint one cadet, as well as the attempt made to fill the vacancies from the portions of seceded States not represented, have been only partially successful.

A brief description of the public buildings, past and present, comes within the design of this work, and may be here appropriately introduced.

The only buildings of Revolutionary origin yet in existence are, the first wooden cottage north of the Hospital, and the first wooden cottage south of the Superintendent's quarters. In 1780–'82, the former stood directly south of the present Chapel, and was afterwards known as "North's," and then as "Gridley's" Tavern. A piazza has been added to it in later years.

As already mentioned, the "Long Barracks" of the Revolution stood near the site of the present Hotel, and was destroyed by fire on December 26, 1827.

THE SOUTH BARRACKS. (Looking Southwest.)
Erected, in 1815; Demolished, in 1849.

This wooden two-storied building fronted south, with a piazza to each story, and in it the cadets were quartered until the completion of the South Barracks, in 1815. The latter, together with the Mess-Hall and the Academy, occupied an east and west line directly in front of the present Cadet Barracks.

THE SOUTH BARRACKS, constructed of stone, stuccoed, consisted of a central building, $128 \times 25 \times 35$ feet, terminated at each end by two wings, each $25 \times 43 \times 35$ feet. The former contained fifty rooms, forty-eight of which were 13×10 feet, and two 20×26 feet; these

THE NORTH BARRACKS. (Looking Northeast.)
Erected, in 1817; Demolished, in 1851.

large central rooms were originally stairways by which
access was had to the North and South piazzas, and
thereby to the rooms without any other connection.
The twelve rooms in the wings were used as offices and
officers' quarters. The building was demolished in the
summer of 1849.

THE NORTH BARRACKS, four stories high, $164 \times 56 \times 45$
feet, was built of stone, and placed at a right angle with
the South Barracks, less than 100 feet distant from the
northeastern corner of the latter. It was completed in
1817, and contained forty rooms 25×19 feet. It was
demolished in July, 1851.

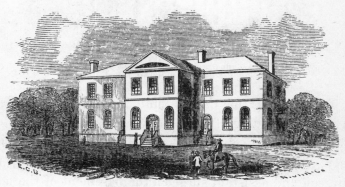

THE ACADEMY. (Looking Southeast.)
Erected, 1815; Destroyed by Fire, Feb. 19th, 1838.

THE ACADEMY, next west of the South Barracks, was
a stone building, two stories high, completed in 1815,
having on its first floor, in the centre, a room used as a
chapel; the Chemical Laboratory adjoined on the west,
and the Engineering Room on the east. The Library
was above the Chapel, the Philosophical Department
above the Laboratory, and the Adjutant's Office above
the Engineering Department. It was destroyed by fire
on February 19th, 1838.

The Mess-Hall, next west of the Academy, was also completed in 1815, two stories high, built of stone, and stuccoed, 144 × 30 feet. The Cadets occupied both the upper and lower floors for mess purposes, the steward residing in the western end. A kitchen was attached in rear, 46 × 25 feet. It was entirely demolished in the summer of 1852.

THE MESS-HALL. (Looking Southwest.)
Erected, 1815; Demolished, 1852.

The Hospital for Cadets, built in 1830, 131 × 40 feet, is a stone building of two stories and a basement. In the centre are twelve wards for the sick, and a dispensary. The wings are occupied as quarters by the surgeon and assistant-surgeon, the basement of the main building furnishing similar accommodations for the attendants.

The Band Barracks, built in 1829, 108 × 52 feet, is a wooden structure, one and a half stories high, containing twenty-two rooms; another building adjacent, 53 × 43 feet, also two stories, contains ten rooms. The Band and their families and the Field Music occupy both buildings.

The Hotel, also built in 1829, is a stone building, stuccoed, 50 × 60 feet, and contains sixty-four rooms.

It was built chiefly from the proceeds of the sale of wood cut from the public lands, and cost about $18,000.

THE WEST POINT HOTEL. (Looking Northeast.)

A wing three stories high, 62×29, of brick, corresponding with the main building, was added in 1850.

THE CHAPEL. (North Front.)

THE CHAPEL, a stone structure* west of the Library,

* 400 feet north of the north face of the Chapel, a red sandstone bench level is planted in the ground.

The surface of this stone is above low-water mark . . .		157 feet.
The northeast angle of Fort Putnam above the stone .		338 feet.
Height of Fort Putnam above low-water mark . . .		495 feet.

83×54 feet, was built in 1836.   It is fitted with pews, &c., for Church service.

THE ACADEMY, fronting east, and situated directly west of the Chapel, was erected in 1838.   It is a stone edifice, with red sandstone pilasters, 275×75 feet, and three stories high.   In the first story, at the south end, is the Chemical Department, consisting of the Laboratory proper, a lecture-room, a room for electrical experiments, and a work-room : these four rooms are each about thirty-six feet square.   The Fencing Department, 75×38 feet, occupies the north end of the first story, while the central portion contains a large gymnasium, and a room for courts-martial, committees, &c.   In the second story, the Cabinet of Minerals and Fossils is over the Chemical Department, and over the Fencing is the Engineering Academy, of the same size as the former, to which are attached two Engineering model-rooms,

THE ACADEMIC BUILDING.

each 46×22 feet.   On the same story are seven recitation-rooms, 24×22 feet.   In the third story, over the Cabinet of Minerals, is the Artillery Model-Room, $75 \times$

38 feet; the Mineralogical Recitation-Room, the Geographical Room, the Mathematical Model-Room; and over the Engineering Academy is the Drawing Academy, of the same size. To the latter are attached the Picture Gallery and Gallery of Sculpture, each 70×22 feet. On this story are likewise three rooms used for recitations, which, with four store-rooms, complete the interior of the building. The clock occupies a tower on the northwest angle of the building.

The original cost of the building was $68,254.

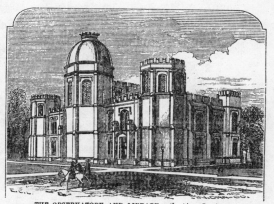

THE OBSERVATORY AND LIBRARY. (Looking Southeast.)

THE OBSERVATORY AND LIBRARY, on the southeast corner of the Plain, was erected in 1841. It is a stone structure, 160 feet front and 78 in depth, castellated and corniced with red sandstone, in the Elizabethan style.

The east wing contains the Library, forty-six feet square and thirty-one feet high; it contains 20,000 volumes. The offices of the Superintendent, Adjutant, Quartermaster, and Treasurer of the Academy occupy the first floor of the west wing; while above them are the

THE NEW CADET BARRACKS.

Lecture Hall and apparatus of the Philosophical Department. The Equatorial Telescope, in a circular dome twenty-seven feet in diameter, surmounts the whole, the transit instrument being in the northeast tower, while the Mural Circle occupies a similar tower in the north-west angle.

The original cost of the building was $50,216.

THE ORDNANCE and ARTILLERY LABORATORY, on the north side of the Plain, was erected in 1840, and consists of three two-story stone buildings, used for fabrication of ammunition, repairing, &c.; all within a stone-enclosed yard, containing, besides, shelter for Field Batteries.

Two stone buildings, 155×23 feet, and 75×23 feet, lower down, formerly used as stables, now serve as a storehouse, and for the Gas-Works.

THE CADETS' BARRACK, on the south side of the Plain, four stories high, was completed in 1851. It constitutes the most imposing structure at the Institution. It is built of stone, with fire-proof rooms, castellated and corniced with red sandstone, in the Elizabethan style. The building is 360×60 feet, with a wing extending in rear of the west tower, 100×60 feet. It contains 176 rooms, of which 136 are Cadets' quarters, 14×22 feet, arranged in eight divisions, without interior communications. The West Tower and the adjacent division are at present used as officers' quarters. The basement contains a profusion of bathing-rooms, the hot-water apparatus for heating the whole building, and quarters for the employés. The large Hall in the centre, over the sally-port, is appropriated to the Dialectic Society.

The original cost of the building was $186,000.

THE MESS-HALL, built of stone, in 1852, stands

18

directly south of the Academy, fronting east, and is 170 feet front by 62 feet in depth. It is one of the structures which command general admiration for their symmetry and beautiful proportions. It comprises a Central Hall, 96 × 46 feet, and 20 feet high, which is the

CADETS' MESS-HALL.   (Looking Southwest.)

mess-room for all the cadets. The north wing affords quarters for the Purveyor, and that on the south is used for mess-rooms for the officers attached to the Academy. A kitchen and bakery in rear, and quarters for the employés in the basement, compose the remainder of the building. Its original cost was $43,187.

The Cavalry Stables, built of brick, in 1854, occupy a plateau southeast of the Library, extending 301 × 38 feet along the bank of the Hudson, with a wing extending west from the south end, 109 × 38 feet. The whole building is built upon the most approved principles, containing stalls for 100 horses, and cost $20,468.

A few yards south of the stables stands the Riding-Hall, 218 × 78 feet, built of stone, in 1855, and spanned by a single curved roof. It is the largest building in the United States for equestrian exercises, and cost $22,000.

THE CAVALRY BARRACKS, 57×41 feet, occupy a position on the northwest slope of the Plain, and are two stories high, built in 1857, of brick, with a stone basement, at a cost of $6,500.

THE ARTILLERY BARRACKS, 46×40 feet, standing beside the former, are also two stories high, of brick, with a stone basement; built in 1858, at an expense of $6,500. Both barracks front east, and each contains ample accommodations, kitchens, &c., for a full company of soldiers.

Farther on to the northwest, near the ceded district line, stand the ENGINEER BARRACKS, fronting north, 100×43 feet, built in 1858, of brick, two stories high, with a stone basement. Besides officers' quarters in the east end, it contains kitchens and accommodations for one hundred men. Its original cost exceeded $10,000.

In front of these barracks, and near the water's edge, stands the building, 154×54 feet, for the army pontoon trains, built of brick.

THE POWDER MAGAZINE, a fire-proof brick building, 100×25 feet, stands directly in rear of the Engineer Barracks, and is one of the oldest buildings on the Post.

Stretching farther away to the northwest, is a row of nine small double wooden cottages, erected in 1837, for the accommodation of the families of the non-commissioned officers, and of laundresses for the cadets.

THE HOSPITAL FOR SOLDIERS, 50×28 feet, near the Cavalry Barracks, is a two-story brick building, with a basement; erectedin 1851, at an expense of $5,530, and contains 4 wards, a dispensary, kitchen, &c., &c.,

Of the brick dwellings situated on the west side of the Plain, the one nearest the Cadets' Barrack was built in 1816; the second, northward, in 1829; the third and fourth, in 1816; the fifth, in 1858; the sixth, seventh, and eighth, in 1821; and the ninth, in 1857.

Of the three double stone dwellings overlooking the north crest of the Plain, the one farthest west was erected in 1821, and the other two in 1826 and 1828.

The buildings and dwellings described, with twenty-two smaller ones of the latter class, the Soldiers' Church, and six guardhouses, storehouses, workshops, &c., constitute all that are now in existence, and compose the Military Post at West Point.*

* The area of the Plain at West Point, bounded by the carriage road which passes by the Superintendent's quarters and around Fort Clinton, is 41½ acres. The distance around the Plain, measured on the carriage road mentioned, is 1 mile 26½ feet.

CHAPTER XV.

Appointment of Cadets.—The Qualifications Necessary.—Admission into the Academy.—Instruction and Examination of the Candidates.—Outfit Procured for the New Cadet.—Classification and System of Military Instruction.—Academic Instruction.—Arrangement into Classes and Sections.—Programme for the Employment of Time.—Thoroughness in Learning and Teaching.—Importance of the Conduct-Roll.—Successful Workings of the System.—Discipline among the Cadets.—Determination of Class-Rank, and its Importance.—Proportion of Graduates to the Number of Cadets Admitted.—Services of the Graduates.

As frequent inquiries are made in regard to the appointment and admission of cadets into the Military Academy, the necessary information is herewith appended.

By provision of law, each Congressional and Territorial district and the District of Columbia is entitled to one cadet and no more.

Appointments from the first two are made on the nomination to the Secretary of War by the Representative in Congress from the district in which he and the applicant are actual residents.

Application for appointment may be made direct to the Secretary of War by the candidate himself, his parent, guardian, or any of his friends; and the name thus presented will be enrolled at the War Department. No preference will be given to applications on account of priority; nor will any application be enrolled, when the candidate is under or over the prescribed age. The precise age must be given; and no relaxation of the qualifications appended will be entertained or permitted. The fixed residence of the applicant, and the number of the Congressional district in which his home is situated, must be set forth in the application. However large the number of applications from any district, it is generally understood that the appointee is selected at the instance of the Representative in Congress. The President of the United States is authorized by law, every year, to appoint ten cadets in addition to the foregoing, selected according to his own will and pleasure, and entirely independent of Congressional districts.

The appointments are usually made public in the months of February or March, from the applications made within the preceding year. No information can be given as to the probable success of an applicant, before the arrival of the period of making the selections. Persons, therefore, making applications, must not expect to receive information on this point.

THE QUALIFICATIONS.

Candidates must be over sixteen and under twenty-one years of age at the time of entrance into the Military Academy; must be at least five feet in height, and free from any deformity, disease, or infirmity, which would render them unfit for the military service, and from any disorder of an infectious or immoral character. They must be able to read and write well, and perform with facility and accuracy the various operations of the four ground rules of Arithmetic, of Reduction, of simple and compound Proportion, and of vulgar and decimal Fractions.

It must be understood that a full compliance with the above conditions will be insisted on :—that is to say— the candidate must write in a fair and legible hand, and without any material mistakes in spelling, such sentences as shall be dictated by the examiners ; and he must answer promptly, and without errors, all their questions in the above-mentioned rules of Arithmetic : —failing in any of these particulars, he will be rejected.

It must be also understood that every candidate will, soon after his arrival at West Point, be subjected to a rigid examination by an experienced Medical Board ; and should there be found to exist in him any causes of disqualification, to such a degree as will immediately, or in all probability may, at no very distant period, impair his efficiency, he will be rejected.

Furnished with his official appointment, each new cadet is required to report in person to the Superintendent of the Military Academy at West Point, between the first and twentieth days of June ; but if sickness or other unavoidable cause prevents this, he may report on the 28th day of August.

No admissions into the Military Academy are allowed, save at these two periods.

After the arrival and necessary enrolment of the new cadet, he is at once inducted into the preliminary drill, daily, of the School of the Soldier, and instructed in all the subjects upon which he is soon to be examined for admission. It is, therefore, an advantage to the new cadet to be punctual in reaching the Academy on the first of June.

The examination of the candidates commences on the twenty-first of June, and is conducted in the presence of the whole Academic Board. The examination is strict, but it is by no means a fearful ordeal, from the few requirements demanded ; and usually the number rejected does not exceed half a dozen.

The new cadet is ranked, from the first day of July, as a member of the lowest, or FOURTH class. From this date his pay of $30 per month, allowed him by the Government, commences. As this sum is small, compared with the expenses of the new uniform and outfit, it is decidedly advantageous for the new cadet to bring with him, and deposit with the Treasurer, to be credited on his account, a sum not exceeding $60 or $80 (dollars). Henceforth all wants and necessaries are supplied the new cadet by the Government, the prices of which are regulated at a trifle above cost, and charged to the account of the cadet, while every month he is credited with $30 (dollars). At the termination of his cadet career a balance is struck, and whatever amount is in his favor is paid over to him. A careful and economical cadet may thus secure a position, his education, the necessary supplies of cadet life, and a sum which seldom exceeds one hundred dollars at the time of his graduation. Very few attain the last sum mentioned.

No payments in full of balances due are made except at the final departure of the cadet, and no moneyed transactions with the cadets are permitted.

For the purposes of *Military* instruction, the cadets, every year after the close of the June examination, leave the barracks, and are encamped in tents upon the Plain during the months of July and August, under all the regulations, discipline, and police of an army in the field. Their organization varies while undergoing instruction in the particular arms of the service, but the permanent organization is that of a Battalion of Infantry, composed of four Companies.

In these companies the four Academic classes are indiscriminately mixed. Each company has its Captain, three Lieutenants, four Sergeants, and four Corporals. The Battalion Staff comprises an Adjutant, SergeantMajor, Quartermaster, and Quartermaster's Sergeant. All the remaining cadets serve in the ranks as soldiers, though required to act as officers at stated times.

The FIRST class furnishes the commissioned officers; the SECOND class, the Sergeants; and the THIRD class, the Corporals.

These appointments are annually made by the Superintendent, and are regarded as honorable distinctions. Each company is further supervised by an officer of the army, detailed for that purpose, and the whole is commanded by an army officer, who is ranked as Commandant of Cadets.

Strict military etiquette is observed towards the cadet officers by the other cadets on duty. The Captains and Lieutenants serve their tours of guard duty, according to the Army Regulations.

The ranking Cadet Captain is Superintendent of the Mess-Hall. He marches the battalion to and from meals, preserves order, and enforces obedience to the mess regulations. For the purposes of meals, the cadets are assigned by companies to tables, at which they are seated by command, and they leave in a body by the same means. Generally, a cadet officer is charged with the preservation of good order at his particular table.

Upon the faithfulness of these officers much of the discipline depends, and the degree of faithfulness is proportioned to the military spirit of the corps.

Their duties are strictly defined, and an undue exercise of authority, or a captious and domineering manner, is restrained by what may be termed the public opinion of the corps. The cadet officers never act as spies. Treacherous information is despised and unknown among them. When not on duty, there is no distinction between them and the other cadets; but on all other occasions the distinction is well understood and properly maintained.

The cadet privates perform in rotation the duties of Sentinels and Guards, night and day, through the encampment; but only at meals, orduring the hours allotted to study in the evening, and on Sundays, when in barracks.

They are drilled daily from the 15th of March until the 1st of November, except on Saturday and Sunday, and several times each day during the encampment, as Artillery or Infantry, the cavalry exercises being continuous nearly the entire year.

All are thus taught practically the use of the rifled musket, the field-piece, mortar, siege and sea-coast guns, small-sword, and the bayonet, as well as the construction of field-works, and the fabrication of all munitions and *matériel* of war.

Throughout the whole year, when the weather permits, guard-mounting at half-past seven A. M., and evening dress parade at sunset, accompanied by the Band, are imposing and pleasing spectacles which break the monotony of cadet life.

For the purpose of *Academic* instruction, the cadets break up the encampment at the end of August and return to barracks, where the remaining nine months of the year are passed in prosecuting their studies in their respective classes. This period is divided into two terms: the first extending from September 1st to January 2d, when the semi-annual examination commences; the second follows the close of the latter, and terminates May 31st.

Instruction is conveyed by the Professors and the principal Instructors, who, with the Superintendent as presiding officer, constitute the Academic Board. To aid this body, as many officers are detailed as assistants from the army, by the Secretary of War, as the wants of the Institution require.

The Academic Board is charged with the general direction of studies, under a programme approved by the Secretary of War, with the selection of text-books, maps, models, and apparatus, and finally decides the merit of each cadet in every branch of study at the several examinations.

In this latter duty, the Assistant Professor of each department, and the immediate teacher of each cadet, are also temporarily members of the Board. The classes of cadets are numerically arranged into the FIRST, SECOND, THIRD, and FOURTH classes, corresponding to the *Senior, Junior, Sophomore,* and *Freshman* classes of other Collegiate Institutions.

The FOURTH class, commencing on the first of September, is arranged in alphabetical order, and thus divided into sections of about twelve cadets in each branch of study. After the lapse of three or four weeks, transfers between the sections occur at the close of each week, and continue until those most distinguished in their studies will be found in the first section; those next in order of scholarship, in the second section; and those who have made least proficiency, will be found in the lowest section.

At all recitations, in every branch of study at the Military Academy, the blackboard is a ruling feature in the performance of each cadet, and by it the thorough understanding of the subject given him is determined, while memory is thereby rendered subservient to the powers of reason.

The progress of each cadet is measured daily by a scale of marks given by each instructor, ranging decimally by tenths, from 0 to 3, the maximum. The aggregate of all these marks, coupled with the performance at the examination, determines the relative merit of each cadet in each study. These marks are weekly submitted by the Professor to the Superintendent, and during the following week exhibited to the cadets, who are thus made acquainted with their daily progress. At the termination of each month a transcript of these marks is forwarded to the Inspector of the Academy, who transmits them to the parents of every cadet.

The result of the semi-annual examination in January determines the relative merit of the whole class, the most distinguished being first, and the least proficient, last.

After the first alphabetical enrolment of the FOURTH class it is not repeated, but its sections in other branches of study about to be commenced are cut off from the relative merit of the class, already determined; this latter method applies to all the other classes.

As some of the cadets stand higher in one branch of study than in others, and as the studies themselves are ranked as presenting greater or less importance than others, arbitrary numbers are assigned to each branch, and the general relative merit is ascertained by determining the proportional proficiency of each cadet, with reference to these numbers, and then combining the latter.

The passage of the January examination terminates the term of probation of the FOURTH class cadet; he then receives his warrant, and is sworn into the service of the United States for eight years. Those who fail, and are pronounced "not proficient" in this class, are recommended to the Secretary of War for discharge; and in all the other classes, at all examinations in January or June, those similarly "not proficient" in these classes, are also recommended for discharge or for a second trial in the succeeding class. By law of Congress, no cadet thus discharged can be returned to the Academy, or be appointed into the army until his classmates are promoted, except upon the recommendation of the Academic Board.

The following detailed programme of the course of instruction, drawn up by the Academic Board, and approved by the Secretary of War, regulates the studies at the Institution until changed by the same authority. The time to be occupied in each branch is determined by the Academic Board, and the daily allowance for class study is not less than nine and not more than ten hours.

" WAR DEPARTMENT, *September* 16, 1861.

"The following is a synopsis of the course of studies and the employment of time at the Military Academy :"

		DEPARTMENT.	EMPLOYMENT OF TIME.
FIRST YEAR.	FOURTH CLASS.	Mathematics.	3 hours daily, September to June.
		English Grammar, including Etymological and Rhetorical Exercises, Composition, Declamation, and Geography of the United States.	4 hours daily, September to June.
		French.	4 hours every other day, January to June.
		Use of Small Arms.	Practical instruction, 1 hour every other day, 23 weeks.
SECOND YEAR.	THIRD CLASS.	Mathematics.	3 hours daily, September to June.
		French.	2 hours daily, September to June.
		Drawing.	2 hours daily, 20 weeks; every other day,17 weeks.
		Cavalry.	2 hours every other day, 16 weeks, practical instruction.
THIRD YEAR.	SECOND CLASS.	Natural and Experimental Philosophy.	3 hours daily September to June.
		Chemistry.	2 hours every other day, September to June.
		Drawing.	2 hours every other day, September to June.
		Infantry Tactics.	2 hours every other day, 6 weeks.
		Artillery Tactics.	2 hours every other day 4 weeks.
		Cavalry.	Practical instruction, every other day, September to June.
FOURTH YEAR.	FIRST CLASS.	Engineering, Civil and Military.	3 hours daily, September to June.
		Practical Engineering.	Practical instruction during a part of the Encampment, and from 1st April to 15th May, 1 hour.
		Ethics, Constitutional, International, and Military Law.	2 hours every other day, September to June.
		Mineralogy and Geology.	2 hours every other day, 17 weeks.
		Ordnance and Gunnery.	2 hours every other day, 14 weeks.
		Spanish.	2 hours every other day, September to June.
		Cavalry Tactics.	2 hours every other day, 5 weeks.
		Cavalry.	Practical instruction, 1 hour every other day, September to June.

The studies pursued at the Academy are for the most part scientific. General literature, the languages, except French and Spanish, and classical studies, form no part of the course.

The curriculum of study, as contrasted with that of our collegiate institutions, affords a marked difference in the small number of studies pursued. In place of the crowded array of branches taught, and the necessary half hourly recitations, to encompass the whole in the brief time allotted, it is the distinctive feature in the programme at the Military Academy to study but few subjects comparatively, and to learn those well.

To the method of instruction, uniting the practice of the school with that of our universities, the success of the Military Academy as a Collegiate Institution is chiefly owing. It is the fault of most colleges that the students individually receive but little attention. Recitations so directed as to produce a perfect understanding and comprehension of the subject taught, are not among the prominent characteristics of American college management. Difficult parts of the course are slighted, and, in many cases, such a superficial knowledge is amassed as to render a diploma an uncertain criterion of the owner's acquirements.

At the Military Academy the pupil does not go through a formal recitation merely; he is subjected to a daily examination, which involves the reputation of his instructor as well as his own in the effort to understand, as well as remember what he studies. Every cadet who passes annually from one class to a higher one, does so only when he has proven to the satisfaction of the Examining Board that he is not only acquainted with, but knows the course of study upon which he has been examined.   It is thus that a diploma granted at the Military Academy, affords a conviction that the owner was possessed of every thing taught at the Institution at the time he became the owner of it.

The conduct-roll is the main-spring to the whole system of discipline at the Military Academy; and yet it has been publicly censured, as based upon principles which permitted no discrimination between acts morally wrong in themselves, and acts which, destitute of immorality, are nevertheless criminal, because prohibited by the Regulations of the Institution.

No such charge, unless designed to be at variance with the facts, could have originated, except under a most thorough misconception of the subject; for the conduct-roll is neither a record of immoralities nor criminalities, both of which are referred to the highest tribunal known to military life.   But it is a record, and a most salutary one, of the *delinquencies* against a system having for its object to instill neatness, order, regularity, and implicit obedience to lawfully constituted authority.

In every calling in life, where power is enforced, and command exercised, these requirements are rendered indispensable.   Experience has taught, that whoever is careless, negligent, or indifferent in the performance of any legitimate and proper duty, is not likely to exact a rigid fulfilment of details from subordinates.

The Code of Regulations is a code of preventions and warnings, not materially unlike those governing other collegiate institutions; but its enforcement affords a marked difference, even to an untutored observer.   It is admitted that the system is rigid, and it is all-important that it should be so; for the destiny of the cadet is not like that of a student in a private college. He is, and is to be, a soldier. Obedience is his first duty; it is the pivot on which his profession and the whole army can alone successfully move. Thoughtlessness, carelessness, and inattention, are not tolerated; for the faithful performance of the most minute duties on the part of a soldier is indispensable to military efficiency.

And in regard to the successful workings of the system, without drawing invidious distinctions between the Military Academy and our most celebrated colleges, one may search in vain for the existence of riots, uprisings, and barrings-out. Looking to the army for its results, the very nature of the system is so impressed upon the character of the cadet, as to promote the exercise of gentlemanly courtesy, forbearance, morality, and Christian feeling. When has the army furnished a scene for duels and brawls? Where is the complaint of the soldier for inhumanity against the subaltern? Where have the volunteers and militia complained of tyranny or superciliousness on the part of the graduates who command them? And yet they have been associated together by strong ties of attachment, when not to murmur was a positive virtue.

Fashioned under the eye of the Military Academy, the habits and destinies of the graduates of the Institution inculcate the truly American doctrine of thorough contempt for all the adventitious advantages of wealth and fortune, and proclaim the innate nobility of individual merit; for here alone the poor boy feels that a man is but a man, and that native talent, with good conduct, is the true and real source of respectability.

19

Discipline among the Cadets is maintained by a system of punishments, not so remarkable for severity as for rigid enforcement. They consist of privation of hours allotted to recreation, *extra* tours of guard, reprimands in public, confinement to room, tent, or prison, and dismissal; the two latter being only inflicted by a court-martial, while the others are decreed by the Superintendent.

For every minor offence against the standing Regulations, violations of special orders, and of what may be called common military law, including unsoldierlike conduct and breaches of military etiquette, the offender is reported to the Commandant of Cadets. An opportunity is afforded for explanation; and if the latter be unsatisfactory, the offence is registered against the Cadet, who receives one or more demerit, according to the magnitude or criminality of the offence.

For the purpose of determining the degree of the delinquencies, all offences which experience has shown that Cadets are liable to commit, are arranged in five classes. The first embraces all the minor infractions of the Code, for each of which one demerit is awarded; the gravity of other offences causes them to be classed in the second, third, fourth, or fifth grade, and a number of demerit is awarded equal to the number of the class in which the offence is enrolled. Any Cadet who receives 100 demerit in six months, ending June 6th and December 6th, is declared deficient in conduct, and discharged from the Academy. But the punishment of those who fail to reach this number does not cease with the entry on the Register. Each number, like a guilty conscience, accompanies them through Cadet-life, and affects their after career in the Army; for the conduct-roll is an element, in connection with proficiency in studies, in determining the relative rank of each member in the different classes.

As the Cadets of the youngest class are less experienced, and more likely to err, one-third of the number of demerit incurred by them is stricken off at the end of each six months, and the remainder stands as a permanent record. But for the FIRST class Cadet, the sum of all the demerit for the last three years is reduced by one-sixth, and the balance affords the basis by which the standing and proficiency of each member of the class, in conduct, is determined. As in the case of studies, an arbitrary number is assigned to conduct, and the relative proficiency of the Cadet is combined with those which determine his final graduating class rank.

Thorough knowledge of the course of study alone, therefore, does not secure the Cadet the highest rank. His general deportment sensibly affects his position, and he is thus urged by its permanent influence to render, during his academic career, that spirit of subordination and implicit obedience to lawfully constituted authority, without which a soldier is an enemy to himself and his country.

A general view of the system of discipline presents many features peculiar to the Military Academy. In whatever situation a Cadet may be placed, he is observed by some superior. If he is on military duty, he is watched from the colonel to the corporal; if at meals, the supervision extends from the Commandant of the Mess-Hall to the carver; if in his room, from the Superintendent to a sentinel; from the Officer of the Day to the orderly; and if at recitation, from the Professor to the section-marcher. Under such close inspection, violations of discipline are made known to some one whose duty it is to make a report of it. Military deportment, being everywhere and at all times required, becomes insensibly a fixed habit, and the effect of this system of discipline appears in the natural emulation it excites.

The desire to stand high is more or less operative on each Cadet in the first half of every class, while the lowest strain every nerve to attain the minimum of merit, that they may not be degraded to the succeeding class, or be separated from the Academy. The Government requires not only those who are willing, but those whose capacity has been proved able to perform its required military duties. As several fail every examination, and disappear from the Institution, every Cadet is impelled to save himself and his friends from disappointment, or to secure such a standing as foreshadows his future position in the army.

The promotion of the class upon graduating is accomplished by dividing it into three sections, accompanied by a recommendation from the Academic Board to the Secretary of War, that the first may be assigned to any corps in the Army that they may elect; the second to any corps except the Corps of Engineers; and the last to the Infantry and Cavalry branches only. The rank of the young officer, in each corps, is made to correspond with that held by him among his classmates upon leaving the Academy.

From an examination of the tables given in the Appendix, showing the number of cadets admitted and graduated, and dividing the years of the existence of the

Military Academy into six decennial periods, it appears, that the proportion of graduates to the number of cadets admitted into the Academy was, for the

First period of ten years, 1802 to 1811 . . 0.606
Second period of ten years, 1812 to 1821 . . 0.289
Third period of ten years, 1822 to 1831 . . 0.377
Fourth period of ten years, 1832 to 1841 . . 0.472
Fifth period of ten years, 1842 to 1851 . . 0.510
Sixth period of ten years, 1852 to 1861 . . 0.523

Such is the organization of the United States Military Academy. In the thoroughness of its course of instruction and discipline, it compares favorably with similar European military academies, and rivals, if it does not excel, the principal scientific institutions of America.

"Proved in all manner of ways by a half-century's trial, the two thousand graduates which the Institution has sent forth have maintained the highest reputation for integrity, zeal, efficiency, and high moral character —without which last attribute there can be no real integrity, zeal, or efficiency.

"As soldiers, they have borne with unflinching fortitude their life of exertion and privation; and, notwithstanding the temptations to which their duties have exposed them, and their isolation (on frontier service) from the restraints of society, they have borne themselves with a propriety which a high moral character only could maintain.

"As disbursing officers of the Government, they have proved faithful, when too many, *not* graduates, have failed.

"As Engineers, they have commanded the entire con-

fidence of the Government and the communities which
they served, and have been the principal agents by
which our fortifications, our magnificent works of internal improvement, our railroads, our canals, our public
buildings, and our lighthouses and harbor works have
been brought into existence.

"In the ranks, too, of our legislators, our jurists, our
agriculturists, our merchants, our ministers of the Gos-
pel, even, they have been found, and have ever acquitted
themselves with honor, and commanded their full share
of respect from their fellow-men."*

* General J. G. Barnard.

CHAPTER XVI.

WEST POINT IN 1863.—SCENERY.—PRINCIPAL OBJECTS OF INTEREST.
—FORT CLINTON.—KOSCIUSZKO'S MONUMENT.—DADE'S MONUMENT.
—NARRATIVE OF THE SURVIVOR OF THE MASSACRE.—CHAIN BAT-
TERY WALK.—LIBRARY AND OBSERVATORY.—CHAPEL.—TROPHIES
ON THE WALLS.—ACADEMIC BUILDING.—MUSEUM.—PICTURE GAL-
LERY.—SCULPTURE GALLERY.—ENGINEERING AND CHEMICAL DE-
PARTMENTS.—CADETS' BARRACK.—MESS-HALL.—HOSPITAL.—RID-
ING-HALL.—SCENERY FROM FORT PUTNAM.—THE CEMETERY.—
MEXICAN TROPHIES.—THE GREAT CHAIN.—THE ENCAMPMENT.—
AUTUMNAL LANDSCAPE AT WEST POINT.

> " The moon looks down on old Cro'nest,
> She mellows the shades on his shaggy breast,
> And seems his huge gray form to throw,
> In a silver cone on the wave below;
> His sides are broken by spots of shade,
> By the walnut bough and the cedar made,
> And through their clustering branches dark,
> Glimmers and dies the fire-fly's spark—
> Like starry twinkles that momently break
> Through the rifts of the gathering tempest's rack."
>
> [THE CULPRIT FAY.]

WEST POINT, situated within three hours' ride by the
railway and steamboat from the great commercial empo-
rium of the United States, and accessible by those
conveyances many times during each day, presents, like
Niagara, attractions to the tourist which excite the most
pleasurable and permanent impressions. The unrivalled
Rhine-like landscape, viewed by the light of an evening
sunset, in the month of June, with the ear charmed by
the delicious strains of the Band at parade, fills the

mind of the traveller with novelty, satisfaction, and contentment.

Thirty years ago, the arrival of a stranger at West Point, to witness the signs of promise and development of one united by the ties of kindred or friendship, was in itself a novelty; but now, the increased facilities for travelling, and the existence of two fashionable hotels, bring, or carry away daily, a hundred votaries of pleasure from this once secluded spot.

To satisfy these, there are no medicinal waters, no cataracts, or surf-bathing; but there are walks, and talks, and drives, and hops, with two hundred chosen of Columbia's youth, whose gallant bearing and courteous attentions are sometimes remembered with a sigh, and sometimes borne along with a matron's affection through the voyage of life.

The visitor at the West Point Hotel may direct his view up the river northward to Newburg, nine miles distant, and note the Shawangunk Mountains in the extreme distance; and if the atmosphere be unusually clear, the Catskill Mountains, while the intervening distance is dotted with steamers and vessels, significant of the wealth of the West and the enterprise of the East.

To the left, and this side of Newburg, is the " Storm King" Mountain, otherwise called *Butter Hill*, behind which nestle the villages of Cornwall and New Windsor; and, nearer yet, the *Crow Nest*, fifteen hundred feet above the waters of the Hudson, with its overhanging cliffs and precipices.   To the right, and opposite to the " Storm King," is *Break Neck* Mountain, tunnelled by the Hudson river railroad; and nearer yet, *Bull Hill*, the villages of Cold Spring and Phillipstown, opposite

the Crow Nest; and directly across the river, Martelaer's Rock, now known as Constitution Island.

The works of the West Point Foundry Association
are partially concealed by the Island on the northeast.
This establishment, presided over and conducted by
Robert P. Parrott, Esq., formerly of the army, and
a graduate of the Military Academy, is one of the
largest of its kind in the United States; and in the
manufacture of ordnance and machinery of all kinds, it
furnishes employment to six or eight hundred employés.
The famous Parrott Guns are supplied from these works,
which, with the fabrication of shot, shells, steamship
machinery, &c., &c., render a visit to the works one of
unrivalled interest and instruction.

RUINS OF FORT CONSTITUTION.

A ferry-boat leaves the landing below the Hotel every
hour, for the Foundry wharf, passing Constitution
Island, upon which the ruins of old Fort Constitution,

near the water's edge, and of the old Block-House, a little distance north of it, are yet distinctly to be seen.

From the West Piazza, upon the northern slope of the Plain, may be seen the Siege-Battery, the Ordnance and Artillery Laboratory, the habitations and Barracks of the soldiers in Camptown, and, farther away to the right, Washington's Valley, overlooked by the Cemetery of the Cadets, situated on the crest of the hill above.

Directly in front, Redoubt Hill rises to an altitude of six hundred feet above the Plain, on the summit of which the ruins of the old " Redoubt No. 4" are discernible ; and to the left, the grim walls of Fort Putnam, on Mount Independence, overlook the row of dwellings occupied by the Superintendent and officers of the Academy on the west side of the Plain.

From the south front the view includes the grassy parapet of old Fort Clinton on the extreme left, the Library and Observatory, with its turrets and dome, further south; the unpretending Chapel, the Academy, and the massive Barracks of the Cadets, above which, enveloped in a growth of cedars, are the ruins of Fort Wyllis; and at the prescribed times, the lines of white tents, the mad charging of the Cavalry Squadron, or the evolutions of a Battery of Horse Artillery, or of an Infantry exercise, diversify the grassy plain spread before the admiring spectator.

Under the permission easily obtained from the Superintendent, the public buildings may be visited, and afford many objects of rare interest. Leaving the Hotel for this purpose, by a path to the left, the tourist enters Fort Clinton, on the northeast angle of which stands a monument, erected to the patriot hero from Poland,

Kosciuszko. A plain panelled base, surmounted by a capped and fluted column, bearing the exile's name only, tells all that marble can say, without encroaching upon

KOSCIUSZKO'S MONUMENT.

the duty of every American mother, in whose heart a love of country is implanted. The mo. .1ent was erected in 1828, by the Corps of Cadets, at an expense of $5,000.

The rushing of the Hudson river railroad trains along the surface of the river, on the east; the tiny steam ferry-boat; Garrison's Station, overlooked by the North and South Redoubts on the hill above; and an uninterrupted view down the river of eight miles, interspersed with steamers, vessels, and barges, will arouse, even in

those habitually indifferent, a lively sensation of the
beauty of the landscape here displayed.

DADE'S MONUMENT.

Leaving the Fort, a few yards to the south, a path
leads down to a little plateau on the river's bank, on
which stands a Cenotaph of more than ordinary beauty
and interest. It is of white Italian marble, bearing a
fluted column upon a square base ; the latter, encircled
with stars, and supported at the four corners with
marble cannon, is surmounted above by an eagle, from
whose beak a wreath of laurel depends, and entwines the
column. The simple inscription, " Dade and his Command," with the names and the date, convey but little
idea of the mournful occasion which called forth this
emblem. It was erected in 1845. The report of Cap-

tain Hitchcock, and the narrative of the last survivor, inform the reader what sacrifices *duty* demanded of those engaged in the war with the Seminole Indians in Florida :

" FORT KING, FLORIDA, *February* 22, 1836.

GENERAL :—Agreeably to your directions, I observed the battle-ground six or seven miles north of the Wythlacoochee river, where Major Dade and his command were destroyed by the Seminole Indians, on the 28th of December last, and have the honor to submit the following report :

" The force under your command, which arrived at this post to-day from Tampa Bay, encamped, on the night of the 19th instant, on the ground occupied by Major Dade on the night of the 17th December. He and his party were destroyed on the 28th of December, about four miles in advance of that position. He was advancing towards this post, and was attacked from the north, so that, on the 20th instant, we came upon the rear of his battle-ground, about 9 o'clock in the morning. Our advanced guard had passed the ground without halting, when the General and his staff came upon one of the most appalling scenes that can be imagined. We first saw some broken and scattered boxes ; then a cart, the two oxen of which were lying dead, as if they had fallen asleep, their yokes still on them : a little to the right, one or two horses were seen. We then came to a small enclosure, made by felling trees in such a manner as to form a triangular breastwork, for defence. Within the triangle, along the north and west faces of it, were about thirty bodies, mere skeletons, although much of the clothing was left upon them. They were lying, almost every one of them, in precisely the position they must have occupied during the fight—their heads next to the logs over which they had delivered their fire, and their bodies stretched, with striking regularity, parallel to each other. They had evidently been shot dead at their posts, and the Indians had not disturbed them, except by taking the scalps of most of them. Passing this little breastwork, we found other bodies along the road and by the side of the road, generally behind trees, which had been resorted to for covers from the enemy's fire. Advancing about two hundred yards further, we found a cluster of bodies in the middle of the road. These were evidently the advanced guard, in the rear of which was the body of Major Dade, and to the right that of Captain Fraser.

" These were all doubtless shot down on the first fire of the Indians, except, perhaps, Captain Fraser, who must, however, have fallen very early in the fight. Those in the road and by the trees fell during the first attack. It was during a cessation of the fire, that the little band still remaining, about thirty in the number, threw up the triangular breastwork, which, from the haste with which it was constructed, was necessarily defective, and could not protect the men in the second attack.

" We had with us many of the personal friends of the officers of Major Dade's command, and it is gratifying to be able to state that every officer was identified by undoubted evidence. They were buried, and the cannon, a six-pounder, that the Indians had thrown into a swamp, was recovered, and placed vertically at the head of the grave, where it is to be hoped it will long remain. The bodies of the non-commissioned officers and privates were buried in two graves, and it was found that every man was accounted for. The command was composed of eight officers, and one hundred and two non-commissioned officers and privates. The bodies of eight officers and ninety-eight men were interred, four men having escaped; three of whom reached Tampa Bay : the fourth was killed the day after the battle.

" It may be proper to observe, that the attack was not made from a hammock, but in a thinly wooded country ; the Indians being concealed by palmetto and grass, which has since been burned.

" The two companies were Captain Fraser's, of the 3d Artillery, and Captain Gardiner's, of the 2d Artillery. The officers were Major Dade, of the 4th Infantry ; Captains Fraser and Gardiner, Second Lieutenant Basinger, Brevet Second Lieutenants R. Henderson, Mudge, and Keais, of the Artillery, and Doctor J. S. Gatlin.

" I have the honor to be,

" With the highest respect,

" Your obedient servant,*

" E. A. HITCHCOCK,

" *Captain 1st Infantry, Acting Inspector-General.*

" Major-General Edmund P. Gaines,

    " Fort King, Florida."

The circumstances attending the escape of Ransom Clarke, the sole survivor of the detachment under Major Dade, massacred by the Indians after a gallant contest, are truly marvellous.

"It appears that the surprise of the corps was complete. About 8 A. M., of December 28th, Major Dade rode

* Savannah Georgian, March 9, 1836.

in front of the column of march, and told his men to 'have a good heart; that their difficulties and dangers were now over; and as soon as they arrived at Fort King they should have three days' rest, and keep Christmas gayly.' The words were scarcely out of his mouth when a discharge took place, and the Major and his horse both fell. This sudden attack naturally disconcerted the troops, but in three minutes they were all as steady as veterans, and the fighting commenced in earnest. It continued, with varied success, until the six-pounder came up, on the discharge of which the Indians retreated. Advantage was taken of this, and a hastily constructed breastwork was thrown up in expectation of another attack, which took place in about an hour, when the enemy came on like devils, yelling and whooping in such a manner that the reports of the rifles were scarcely perceptible. The action lasted from 8 A. M. to 4 in the afternoon. The United States troops amounted to 117, and the Indians are supposed to have been 800 strong, with 100 negroes, who were more savage than the Seminoles. The enemy fired principally from a distance, and only made one charge with tomahawks and clubs, but were repulsed. So long as a man stood, the resistance continued, and the six-pounder was fired quickly and regularly as long as men remained to load it. With respect to the officers, as long as life remained they cheered and encouraged their men, and fell sword in hand. Captain Fraser, second in command, and Lieutenant Mudge, fell at the first fire, when the Major was killed. Clarke was at the extreme right flank, and when he heard the crack of the rifles he looked at the Major for the word of command, but a volley from 800 rifles swept the advance-guard entirely, and not a man remained standing. Lieutenant Henderson had his left arm shattered, and Lieutenant Keys had both arms broken. The latter got one of the men to tie both arms with a handkerchief, and was placed against a tree, where he was tomahawked by the negroes. The troops then took each to his tree, and an irregular firing commenced, till the arrival of the six-pounder, and the temporary retreat of the Indians as above mentioned.

"At the second attack, nothing could equal the coolness and deliberation of the troops; and, as Clarke observes, 'they were as cool as if they were in the woods shooting game.' The weather was very warm, and about 1 o'clock the action began to slacken, upwards of sixty or seventy having fallen, and two officers only then surviving, Captain Gardiner and Lieutenant Basinger. While a man could load a musket, the firing was continued. Captain Gardiner received five or six shots before he fell; the mortal wound was in the breast. When he fell, Basinger said: 'Now, my boys, let us do the best we can—I am the only officer left;' and the firing recommenced. About half-past 2 o'clock he was brought down by a rifle-shot in the thighs, and he was afterwards cruelly massacred by a negro. Clarke received his first wound in the thigh, about 1 o'clock, outside the breastwork, which brought him to the ground. He soon recovered himself, and crawled and limped in. He placed himself along it [the breastwork], and commenced firing in that position; but, in the act of elevating the musket, received a wound between the elbow and right shoulder. He still continued to fire and load, but again received two wounds, one in the head, from buckshot, and a small rifle-ball in the back.   He still kept on till about 4 o'clock, when he received a ball on the right scapula from a negro, who, when he fired, cried out: 'There, damn you!'   This disabled him, and he fell on his face and continued motionless.   The enemy immediately rushed into the breastwork, and took possession of the arms and ammunition, provisions and baggage, which they carried out of the fortification. About fifty or sixty negroes then came up on horseback, and began stripping the dead, and cutting and mutilating all who showed any signs of life.   They seemed to be in a hurry, and after finishing their work of slaughter, they hurried off.   All this time Clarke was lying by the side of Basinger, and they stripped his jacket off, one observing that 'he had a wound in the head, and was not dead.'   Another said: 'Let him lie; he will suffer more than if he were killed outright.'   One of them remarked that 'he had a good pair of boots on, and they would fit him,' whereupon he pulled them off, and they fled precipitately.   This was about 4 o'clock, and Clarke remained as the negroes left him till about nine; when he got up, and looking around in the moonlight, he crawled over the bodies, and feeling one warm, found that it was a private named De Courcy, who was wounded in the side and left arm, but slightly.   Clarke told him that he was thinking of trying to get back to Fort Brook, on Tampa Bay, about sixty-five miles distant.   He agreed to accompany him, and Clarke crawled along on his left hand and knees part of the way, and part of the way he was led by De Courcy. Next day, about noon, they came upon an Indian on

20

horseback, who was loading his rifle. They agreed to separate, in the hope of easier escaping him, and Clarke darted into a hammock of palmettos and brush. The Indian pursued De Courcy, and fired, but missed. He then crossed a road and ran over a hill, which was the last Clarke saw of his hapless comrade. After hearing the report, Clarke, from his retreat, saw the Indian return on horseback, and ride about the hammock, searching all around. At one time he came within ten feet of him, but at length gave up the pursuit, and rode away. Clarke then resumed his painful journey, and on the fourth day after the massacre got into Fort Brook, where he found private Thomas, one of the detachment, who had also escaped; and next morning another, named Sprague, came in; but they are since dead, and Clarke is the only survivor of this gallant and devoted band."*

A few steps south of the Cenotaph, at the foot of a flight of stone steps, is the shelving plateau overhung with foliage called "Kosciuszko's Garden" and said by tradition to have been his favorite resort. The marble fountain, the shrubbery, and the secluded seats, with an occasional bit of ribbon or a glove, suggest that it is yet a resort for some, who, it is to be hoped, are as patriotic, and quite as sincere, as the unfortunate Pole.

From this enchanting retreat a gravelled path, called "Chain Battery Walk," pursues its way northward, past Battery Knox, a relic of the Revolution, along steep precipices and cliffs overhanging the river for three-fourths of a mile, penetrating the site of the old "Lantern Battery," on Gee's Point, and the Chain Bat-

* Charleston (S. C.) Courier, August, 1836.

tery, for the protection of the old Chain of the Revolution; abounding, moreover, in windings, abrupt turnings,
nooks, and secluded places, the path ascends directly
up the north slope of the Plain to the Hotel, while a
branch continues on to the Siege Battery of sea-coast
guns on the north landing.

THE 13-INCH MORTAR AT THE SEA-COAST BATTERY.

Returning to the Library, its beauty, and the portraits
of the distinguished officers therein, command the attention of the spectator. The number of volumes is about
20,000, chiefly upon military and scientific subjects.
Additions are constantly made, from an annual appropriation by Congress of $1,000 for this purpose.

The Chapel contains a beautiful painting over the
chancel, by Professor Weir, and the walls are adorned
by memorial tablets of distinguished American generals,
standards, and guns. The colors on the west side were
taken from the English; and the guns, as early as 1823,
were, with the permission of the heirs* of Major-General

* Official Records, 1842, U. S. M. A.

Greene, deposited at the Military Academy.   They bear the following inscription :

" TAKEN

FROM THE BRITISH ARMY

AND PRESENTED BY ORDER OF

THE UNITED STATES IN CONGRESS ASSEMBLED

TO MAJOR GENERAL GREENE

AS A MONUMENT OF

THEIR HIGH SENSE OF

THE WISDOM, FORTITUDE AND MILITARY TALENTS

WHICH DISTINGUISHED HIS COMMAND

IN THE SOUTHERN DEPARTMENT

AND OF

THE EMINENT SERVICES

WHICH

AMIDST COMPLICATED DANGERS AND DIFFICULTIES

HE PERFORMED FOR

HIS COUNTRY

OCTOBER Y^E 18, 1783."

The standard and guns on the east side are a portion of those taken during the war with Mexico.

Besides the Chemical Laboratory, and the Cabinet of Minerals and Fossils in the Academy, the Ordnance and Artillery Museum, on the third floor, presents much to interest the observer.   Its walls are draped with the colors of the veteran regiments engaged in the war of 1812, and with those which waved defiance at Vera Cruz, Cerro Gordo, Chapultepec, and over the National Palace in the City of Mexico.   There are glazed cases, exhibiting models of the progressive manufacture of every part of the musket, from the beginning unto the completion ; of all the varieties of artillery, shot, shells, cartridges, small and great, fuzes, swords, pistols, and ancient implements of war.

In the centre of the room stands a model of the celebrated Silver Mine of Valenciana, at Guanaxuato, in Mexico, one of the richest in that republic. This model, upwards of six feet high and six feet square, exhibits the shafts and galleries of the mine, with its multitude of miners, horses, and operatives, at their respective callings, on the surface, made of silver amalgam.

It was originally designed as a present for the Pope, and constructed at a cost of $3,000. After the occupation of the City of Mexico by the American Army, in 1847, it was purchased by subscription among the officers for the Military Academy.

The Museum had its origin in 1854, and under the law of 1814, which authorizes the President of the United States to preserve and display trophies of war. Secretary Marcy, under date of December 28, 1848, declared : " Among the considerations which render the Military Academy at West Point an appropriate depository of the trophies of the successful victories of our arms in Mexico, is the admitted fact, that the graduates of that institution contributed in an eminent degree to our unexampled career of success."*

Besides the Geographical room and the Mathematical model-room on this floor, the Picture gallery, at the north end, presents attractions not easily forgotten. This Gallery contains more than two hundred specimens, most of which are pen, pencil, and water-color sketches, executed by the cadets. Their excellence illustrates the rapid progress in the improvement of untrained minds and hands, during the limited period allotted to

* Official Records, 1848, U. S. M. A.

this subject ; being only one or two hours daily during the second and third years of cadet pupilage.

The centre of the Gallery contains a large portrait, by Professor Weir, of an early Superintendent, Colonel Thayer, placed there by officers who were cadets under his administration.

Across the hall is the Gallery of Sculpture, containing casts and models for the cadet pupil, to aid in sketching from life. The east side of the Gallery presents a model of the "Progress of Civilization in America," from the pediment of the Capitol at Washington.

On the second floor beneath this portion of the Academy are the Engineering model-rooms, exhibiting orders of architecture, bridges, buildings, fortifications, attack and defence of fortified places, &c., &c.

A single room in the Cadets' Barrack is a type of the rest. Uniformly with two occupants, every article is arranged according to a prescribed system. The iron bedsteads, iron tables, and the few simple articles of necessity, betray in a marked degree the absence of all luxurious creature comforts, as unworthy of a soldier's home.

The Mess-Hall, south of the Academy, presents an object of interest to those who would inquire further into cadet life. Supplied by a Purveyor, who receives a salary entirely disconnected from the number of cadets, or the quality of their food, he has simply to furnish a plain, substantial soldier's regimen, the cost of which is divided monthly among the whole number of cadets, and paid for from funds which never pass into the Purveyor's hands. The hours for meals are prescribed, their duration is limited, the seats are assigned, and the disorders of College Commons are unknown.

The Hospital, with its two attending Surgeons, two Matrons, and Steward, presents an illustration of neatness throughout the wards which may well excite emulation in the most ambitious housewife.

The Riding-Hall, and its exercises of leaping bars, running at the ring, cutting and firing at mock heads, never fail to attract and fill the Gallery with an interested audience, while the horses and their accommodations are alike worthy of observation.

A failure to visit Fort Putnam would deprive the tourist of witnessing some of the most memorable points of Revolutionary interest. The old Fort, subjected to the tempests and wintry blasts of three-fourths of a century, yet retains its form, enveloped in crumbling walls. These, and the dilapidated casemates, may arrest the attention of only reflective minds, but the view from this point commands the homage of all.

To the enthusiast of the picturesque, to whose worship alone the *Genius Loci* reveals all his treasures, the scenery around West Point presents at all seasons, and through each varying hour of the day, a succession of *tableaux*, unequalled, perhaps, in any other portion of our country,—from the tender beauties of leaf and flower of the opening summer, to the sublime and stern aspect of winter, when the massive forms of Crow Nest and Bull Hill are enveloped in their heavy mantle of snow, and the broad bosom of the Hudson is locked in the tight embrace of the Ice King.

These beauties are best taken in, however, near the close of the day, when, the sun descending towards the crests of the hills on the west, the broad shadows are thrown across the river upon those which skirt the eastern bank, and, slowly flitting from hill-top to hill-top, unveil, at each change of position, some new feature of loveliness concealed by the diffused light of the earlier part of the day.

Among the many objects which diversify this natural picture, as seen from Fort Putnam, on the eastern shore, is the sturdy form of Anthony's Nose, looming up in the distance, six miles below, enveloped in the dreamy mists that follow the setting sun, and apparently an everlasting barrier to the huge volume of water which, in its deep channel, is abruptly turned aside at this point in its onward sweep to the ocean. A little nearer, on the same side, is seen the ever-memorable " Robinson House," half hidden under a mantle of foliage ; and nearer yet, nestling amid a cluster of evergreen trees, the stately mansion of Ex-Governor Hamilton Fish ; while the rocky point through which the Hudson river railroad defiantly speeds its way, marks the spot from which the apostate Arnold fled, in his barge, to the Vulture below.

Garrison's Station is opposite the residence of H. W. Belcher, Esq., and of Upjohn, the architect, above it, upon soil once whitened by Continental tents ; and stretching farther away to the northward, upon lands alike consecrated, is the hospitable home of Honorable Gouverneur Kemble, and that of the poet-General, whose plaintive appeal to the " Woodman" is known and sung in every American home.

Full fifteen miles in view, beneath, the placid waters of the Hudson roll on, at times literally covered with the products of commercial industry, and the Sabbath-like silence is broken only by the rushing of paddle-wheels, or the panting and throbbing locomotive opposite.

One mile and a half to the south, and upon the west bank, the palatial Hotel of COZZENS stands boldly upon the very precipice of the river, like a beacon inviting the weary traveller to repose beneath its ample shelter; and, sweeping northward, the eye scans the picturesque little Church of the Holy Innocents; the ruins of Forts Webb and Wyllis; the Plain of West Point, carpeted with green, over which waves the flowery flag of the nation; and lingers with a sigh upon the cemetery, beneath whose marble piles repose the remains of those whose dying murmurs in Florida, Mexico, Oregon, and on distant frontiers, besought a resting-place here.

CADETS' MONUMENT.

Conspicuous among the many beautiful military monuments, is the one erected by the Corps of Cadets in 1818, to commemorate the premature death of Cadet Lowe, of New York, and of other cadets and officers in the Institution. It is a frustum of a cone in marble, composed of separate blocks, upon which the names are inscribed; the whole surmounted by a field-piece, flags, and other appropriate emblems.

Returning to the Hotel, upon a natural mound at the northwest angle of the Plain is placed a neat Cenotaph, commemorative of the death of Lieutenant-Colonel E. D. Wood, a graduate of the class of 1806, who was killed in the sortie from Fort Erie upon the British siege-works. Its completion, in October, 1818, was accompanied by an impressive military ceremony.

WOOD'S MONUMENT.

Near the flag-staff, arranged around a relic of the

great Chain of the Revolution, is a formidable array of
mortars, siege-guns, and field-pieces, of which fourteen
were taken from the English, and eighty-eight from the

TROPHY GUNS.

Mexicans. The names indicate the fields upon which
they were won. Within the circle formed by the Chain
is the beautiful gun "Le Monarque," presented by Congress to the Marquis de Lafayette; and in the middle
of the south row of guns is the iron 18-pounder which
caused the death of Cadet Lowe, before mentioned.

From this point, the view northward cannot be surpassed in beauty. The Hudson, with the city of Newburg in the distance, the village of Cold Spring and the
West Point Foundry in the foreground, closed in on the
two sides by the Crow Nest and Bull Hill, and showing the misty outline of the Shawangunk Mountains in
the far background, recall to the European traveller,
from its lake-like character, the appearance of the Lake
of Geneva, with Vevay in the distance. Here the eye
may gaze by the hour upon the ever-varying spectacle
of the whole stretch of the river, at times covered by a

fleet of steamboats, bearing along what is in truth freight of an empire; or, turning from this towards the right, embrace a landscape worthy of Church's pencil, in the receding valley-view seen over the furnace vapors of the ever-clanking machinery works of the Foundry.

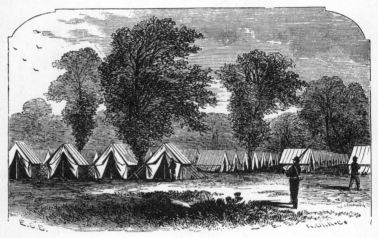

THE ENCAMPMENT.

The "Encampment," commencing at the close of each annual June examination, and continuing until the end of August, is the carnival season at West Point. The period first referred to marks a perceptible change in the deportment of the respective classes, characteristic of the advancement of each cadet from a lower to a higher class. The THIRD CLASS, just released from plebeian servitude by the arrival of a class of new cadets, and numerically stronger than their elder brethren present, exercise a powerful influence in shaping the future career of their younger associates, and in contributing to the pleasures of the gay season.

The new cadet, about to enter upon an honorable competition with classmates of whose attainments and antecedents he is ignorant, finds less to enjoy than those whose familiarity with the duties and details of military life affords courteous attentions and lively entertainment to the numerous throngs of visitors. Many, charged with the idea that stature, and form, and martial bearing are elements of success, soon learn that perseverance, industry, and close application to study are indispensable; and that even these, unaccompanied by such gifts as the power of perception, power of comprehension, power to understand, and power to impart information to others, are qualifications which do not insure success at the Military Academy.

Aroused by the shrill fifes and drums at 5 o'clock in the morning, drummed to their meals, drummed to the performance of various military duties during the day, and drummed to sleep at ten at night, the weary life and hardships of the cadet are not visible at the tri-weekly evening hops, nor during the sentimental rambles amid the sweet strains of the Band upon those nights not thus appropriated. And yet the season is indeed a trying one. It is a season when all the duties of an army in the field prevail. It is a season when hopes and expectations are excited, as well as one in which doubt and uncertainty for the future arise. It is a season whose approach and departure are alike welcomed with satisfaction and pleasure.

The cadets return from Camp to the Barracks at the end of August, when the spectacle of striking the tents is well worthy of the effort of the visitor to be present and witness it.

Though a visit to West Point at all seasons affords pleasure, the months of June, when the foliage is still tender, but fully developed, and October, when it is matured in all its autumnal gorgeousness, are the most pleasant to those to whom rambles among mountain paths are a delight. But those who are not afraid of the keen, bracing air of the late autumn, will be more than repaid when it is clothed in the sear leaf of this period. They will then find a landscape which none of our artists have yet attempted, among the many views they have given of it, and which, if truly rendered, would stand unrivalled.

About the middle of November, when the sun has nearly attained its southern limit, and its last level rays at the close of the day are thrown in a single beam, through the valley between the Crow's Nest and Redoubt Hill, upon the hills on the opposite shore, it frequently occurs that the upper sky is covered by a mottled veil of clouds; while along the lower there is a narrow unclouded belt, which being reached by the sun, the general autumnal sombreness is, as if by a stroke of magic, converted into one broad sheet of bright copper-colored light overhead, whilst the hill-tops are tinged with a golden hue, which, as the sun descends, almost imperceptibly creeps along, as if the broad brush of an artist were slowly moved along the crests, bearing in its path the tint with which it was charged.

This gorgeous scene rapidly dies away, whilst the clouds assume their chameleon tints, gradually fading through all the gradations of purple to a cold inky hue, leaving the spectator in that saddened state of feeling which Lamartine appropriately expresses in his adieux to the close of this delightful season:

"Adieu ! derniers beaux jours. Ce deuil de la nature convient à ma douleur et plaît à mes regards."

APPENDIX.

APPENDIX.

THE aggregate amount of money appropriated by the United States to defray the expenses of the Military Academy, from its establishment, March 16, 1802, to June 30, 1864—

For purchase of the lands; erection and repairs of buildings; construction of roads, wharfs, fences, water and gas works; purchase of library, maps, instruments, philosophical and chemical apparatus, models in engineering and drawing; purchase of minerals; grading ground, &c., &c., &c.

And for pay and subsistence of Officers, Professors, Teachers, and Cadets; fuel and stationery; transportation of *matériel*; stores; postage; expenses of Boards of Visitors; Adjutant and Quartermaster's Clerks; contingent and incidental expenses,—being for a period of sixty-two years,— is as follows:

AMOUNT APPROPRIATED FOR THE MILITARY ACADEMY FROM 1802 TO 1843, INCLUSIVE, AND THEREAFTER ANNUALLY TO DATE.

1802 to 1843	$4,002,901 15
1844, April 12	116,845 50
1845, March 3	138,049 00
1846, August 8	123,976 00
1847, March 2	124,906 00
1848, May 31	143,472 00
1849, February 19	171,294 00
1850, September 16	202,535 30

1851, March 3	$130,528 00
1852, August 6.	130,050 00
1853, March 2	150,253 83
1854, May 10	161,281 00
1855, March 3	146,940 92
1856, April 23	158,894 00
1857, February 16	161,179 00
1858, May 11	182,804 00
1859, January 12	179,588 00
1860, June 1	183,796 00
1861, January 5	184,337 00
1862, February 10	156,211 00
1863, January 23	183,394 00

$7,133,235 70

LIST OF THE SECRETARIES OF WAR, AND THEIR TERM OF SERVICE, FROM THE FOUNDATION OF THE PRESENT GOVERNMENT TO SEPTEMBER 1, 1863.

NAME.	STATE.	TERM OF SERVICE.
1 Henry Knox	Mass.	September 12, 1789, to January 1, 1795.
2 Timothy Pickering	Penn.	January 2, 1795, to December 10, 1796.
3 James McHenry	Md.	January 27, 1796, to June 1, 1800.
4 Samuel Dexter	Mass.	June 1, 1800, to December 31, 1800.
5 Roger Griswold	Conn.	February 3, 1801, to March 4, 1801.
6 Henry Dearborn	Mass.	March 5, 1801, to March 4, 1809.
7 William Eustis	Mass.	March 7, 1809, to January 13, 1813.
8 John Armstrong	N. Y.	January 13, 1818, to September 27, 1814.
9 James Monroe	Va.	September 27, 1814, to February 28, 1815.
10 William H. Crawford	Ga.	March 3, 1815, to October 22, 1816.
11 George Graham	Va.	April 7, 1817, to October 8, 1817.
12 John C. Calhoun	S. C.	October 8, 1817, to March 4, 1825.
13 James Barbour	Va.	March 7, 1825, to May 26, 1828.
14 Peter B. Porter	N. Y.	May 26, 1828, to March 4, 1829.
15 John H. Eaton	Tenn.	March 9, 1829, to August 1, 1831.
16 Lewis Cass	Mich.	August 1, 1831, to October 4, 1836.
17 Benjamin F. Butler	N. Y.	October 4, 1836, ad interim to March 7, 1837.
18 Joel R. Poinsett	S. C.	March 7, 1837, to March 5, 1841.
19 John Bell	Tenn.	March 5, 1841, to October 12, 1841.
20 John C. Spencer	N Y.	October 12, 1841, to March 8, 1843.
21 James M. Porter	Penn.	March 8, 1843, to February 15, 1844.
22 William Wilkins	Penn.	February 15, 1844, to March 5, 1845.
23 William L. Marcy	N. Y.	March 5, 1845, to March 8, 1849.
24 George W. Crawford	Ga.	March 8, 1849, to July 23, 1850.
25 Winfield Scott	U. S. A.	July 23, 1850, ad interim to August 15, 1850.
26 Charles M. Conrad	La.	August 15, 1850, to March 7, 1853.
27 Jefferson Davis	Miss.	March 7, 1853, to March 3, 1857.
28 John B. Floyd	Va.	March 6, 1857, to January 18, 1861.
29 Joseph Holt	Ky.	January 18, 1861, to March 5, 1861.
30 Simon Cameron	Penn.	March 5, 1861, to January 15, 1862.
31 Edwin M. Stanton	Penn.	January, 15, 1862........Present.

A LIST OF THE INSPECTORS, SUPERINTENDENTS, PROFESSORS, TEACHERS, HEADS OF DEPARTMENTS, SURGEONS, AND ADJUTANTS, AND THEIR TERM OF SERVICE AT THE MILITARY ACADEMY, FROM ITS ORIGIN TO THE PRESENT DATE.

☞ Officers whose names are marked with a * are Graduates of the Military Academy.

INSPECTORS OF THE U. S. MILITARY ACADEMY.

NO.	APPOINTMENT AND NAME.	ARMY RANK, WHEN APPOINTED.	TERM OF SERVICE.	
			FROM	TO
	Inspectors.			
1	*JOSEPH G. SWIFT.	Col. Corps of Eng. and Bvt. Brig.-General U. S. A.	Feb. 28, 1815.	Nov. 12, 1818.
2	*WALKER K. ARMISTEAD.	Col. Corps of Eng.	Nov. 12, 1818.	June 1, 1821.
3	ALEXANDER MACOMB.	Col. Corps of Eng. and Bvt. Brig.-General U. S. A.	June 1, 1821.	May 24, 1828.
4	*CHARLES GRATIOT.	Col. Corps of Eng. and Bvt. Brig.-General U. S. A.	May 24 1828.	Dec. 6, 1838.
5	*JOSEPH G. TOTTEN.	Col Corps of Eng.	Dec. 7, 1838.	Present.

SUPERINTENDENTS OF THE U. S. MILITARY ACADEMY, FROM MARCH 16, 1802, TO SEPTEMBER 1, 1863.

NO.	APPOINTMENT AND NAME.	ARMY RANK, WHEN APPOINTED.	TERM OF SERVICE.	
			FROM	TO
	Superintendents.			
1	JONATHAN WILLIAMS.	Maj. Corps of Eng.	April, 1802.	July 31, 1812.
2	*ALDEN PARTRIDGE.	Capt. Corps of Eng.	Jan. 3, 1815.	Nov. 25, 1816.
3	*JOSEPH G. SWIFT.	Col. Corps of Eng. and Bvt. Brig.-General U. S. A.	Nov. 25, 1816.	Jan. 13, 1817.
4	*ALDEN PARTRIDGE.	Capt. Corps of Eng.	Jan. 13, 1817.	July 28, 1817.
5	*SYLVANUS THAYER.	Capt. Corps of Eng. Bvt. Maj. U. S. A.	July 28, 1817.	July 1, 1833.
6	*RENÉ E. DE RUSSY.	Maj. Corps of Eng.	July 1, 1833.	Sept. 1, 1838.
7	*RICHARD DELAFIELD.	Maj. Corps of Eng.	Sept. 1, 1838.	Aug. 15, 1845.
8	*HENRY BREWERTON.	Capt. Corps of Eng.	Aug. 15, 1845.	Sept. 1, 1852.
9	*ROBERT E. LEE.	Capt. Corps of Eng. and Bt. Col. U. S. A.	Sept. 1, 1852.	April 1, 1855.
10	*JONATHAN G. BARNARD.	Capt. Corps of Eng. and Bt. Maj. U. S. A.	April 1, 1855.	Sept. 8, 1856.
11	*RICHARD DELAFIELD.	Maj. Corps of Eng.	Sept. 8, 1856.	Jan. 23, 1861.
12	*PETER G. T. BEAUREGARD.	Capt. Corps of Eng. and Bt. Maj. U. S. A.	Jan. 23, 1861.	Jan. 28, 1861.
13	*RICHARD DELAFIELD.	Maj. Corps of Eng.	Jan. 28, 1861.	March 1, 1861.
14	*ALEXANDER H. BOWMAN.	Maj. Corps of Eng.	March 1, 1861.	Present.

DEPARTMENT OF ORDNANCE AND GUNNERY.

NO.	APPOINTMENT AND NAME.	ARMY RANK, WHEN APPOINTED.	TERM OF SERVICE.	
			FROM	TO
	Instructors.			
1	*JAMES G. BENTON.	Capt. Ordnance.	June 22, 1857.	April 26, 1861.
2	*STEPHEN V. BENÉT.	1st Lt. Ordnance.	May 19, 1861.	Present.

† See note to p. 313.

DEPARTMENT OF NATURAL AND EXPERIMENTAL PHILOSOPHY.

NO.	APPOINTMENT AND NAME.	ARMY RANK, WHEN APPOINTED.	TERM OF SERVICE.	
			FROM	TO
	Professors.			
1	JARED MANSFIELD.	Lt.-Col. Corps of Eng.	Oct. 7, 1812.	Aug. 31, 1828.
2	*EDWARD H. COURTENAY.	2d Lt. Corps of Eng.	Feb. 16, 1829.	Dec. 31, 1834.
3	*WILLIAM H. C. BARTLETT.	2d Lt. Corps of Eng.	April 20, 1836.	Present.
	Acting Professors.			
1	JARED MANSFIELD.	Capt. Corps of Eng.	May 3, 1802.	1803.
2	*EDWARD H. COURTENAY.	2d Lt. Corps of Eng.	Sept. 1, 1828.	Feb. 16, 1829.
3	*WILLIAM H. C. BARTLETT.	2d Lt. Corps of Eng.	Nov. 22, 1834.	April 20, 1836.

DEPARTMENT OF MATHEMATICS.

NO.	APPOINTMENT AND NAME.	ARMY RANK, WHEN APPOINTED.	TERM OF SERVICE.	
			FROM	TO
	Professors.			
1	*ALDEN PARTRIDGE.	Capt. Corps of Eng.	April 13, 1813.	September 1, 1813.
2	ANDREW ELLICOTT.		September 1, 1813.	August 29, 1820.
3	DAVID B. DOUGLASS.	Capt. Corps of Eng.	August 29, 1820.	May 1, 1823.
4	*CHARLES DAVIES.		May 1, 1823.	May 31, 1837.
5	*ALBERT E. CHURCH.	1st Lt. 3d Artillery.	March 13, 1838.	Present.
	Acting Professors.			
1	WM. AMHERST BARRON.	Capt. Corps of Eng.	April 1, 1802.	February 14, 1807.
2	FERDINAND R. HASSLER.		Feb. 14, 1807.	February 14, 1810.
3	*ALBERT E. CHURCH.	1st Lt. 3d Artillery.	June 1, 1837.	March 13, 1838.

DEPARTMENT OF GEOGRAPHY, HISTORY, AND ETHICS.

NO.	APPOINTMENT AND NAME.	ARMY RANK, WHEN APPOINTED.	TERM OF SERVICE.	
			FROM	TO
	Professors.			
1	REV. CAVE JONES.		April 13, 1818.	January 1, 1825.
2	REV. THOMAS PICTON.		July 23, 1818.	December 31, 1827.
3	REV. C. P. MCILVAIN.		January 28, 1825.	
4	REV. THOMAS WARNER.		January 1, 1828.	September 1, 1838.
5	REV. JASPER ADAMS.		September 1, 1838.	November 15, 1840.
6	*REV. M. P. PARKS.		December 5, 1840.	December 31, 1846.
7	REV. WILLIAM T. SPROLE.		March 2, 1847.	August 16, 1856.
8	REV. JOHN W. FRENCH.		August 16, 1856.	Present.
	Acting Professors.			
1	REV. ADAM EMPIE.		August 9, 1813.	April 30, 1817.

DEPARTMENT OF CHEMISTRY, MINERALOGY, AND GEOLOGY.

NO.	APPOINTMENT AND NAME.	ARMY RANK, WHEN APPOINTED.	TERM OF SERVICE.	
			FROM	TO
	Professors.			
1	*JACOB W. BAILEY.	1st Lt. 1st Artillery.	July 8, 1838.	February 26, 1857.
2	*HENRY L. KENDRICK.	{ Capt. 2d Art'y, and Bt. Major U. S. A.	March 3, 1857.	Present.
	Acting Professors.			
1	JAMES CUTBUSH.	Post Surgeon.	September 1, 1820.	December 15, 1823.
2	JAMES G. PERCIVAL.	Asst. Surgeon.	March 4, 1824.	July 6, 1824.
3	JOHN TORREY.	Asst. Surgeon.	August 25, 1824.	August 31, 1828.
4	*WILLIAM F. HOPKINS.	2d Lt. 4th Artillery.	Sept. 1, 1828.	August 31, 1835.
5	*JACOB W. BAILEY.	2d Lt. 1st Artillery.	August 31, 1835.	July 8, 1838.

DEPARTMENT OF DRAWING.

NO.	APPOINTMENT AND NAME.	ARMY RANK, WHEN APPOINTED.	TERM OF SERVICE.	
			FROM	TO
	Professors.			
1	ROBERT W. WEIR.		August 8, 1846.	Present.
	Teachers.			
1	CHRISTIAN E. ZOELLER.		September 1, 1808.	April 30, 1810.
2	CHRISTIAN E. ZOELLER.		July 1, 1812.	January 5, 1819.
3	THOMAS GIMBREDE.		January 5, 1819.	December 25, 1832.
4	CHARLES R. LESLIE.		March 2, 1833.	April 15, 1834.
5	ROBERT W. WEIR.		May 8, 1834.	August 8, 1846.

DEPARTMENT OF FRENCH.

NO.	APPOINTMENT AND NAME.	ARMY RANK, WHEN APPOINTED.	TERM OF SERVICE.	
			FROM	TO
	Professors.			
1	CLAUDIUS BERARD.		August 8, 1846.	May 6, 1848.
2	H. R. AGNEL.		May 16, 1848.	Present.
	First Teachers.			
1	FRANCIS DE MASSON.		March 27, 1804.	March 31, 1812.
2	FLORIMOND DE MASSON.		March 31, 1812.	January 3, 1815.
3	CLAUDIUS BERARD.		January 3, 1815.	August 8, 1846.
	† *Second Teachers.*			
1	JOSEPH DU COMMUN.		March 1, 1818.	August 31, 1831.
2	JULIAN MOLINARD.		September 1, 1831.	September 12, 1839.
3	H. R. AGNEL.		February 4, 1840.	May 16, 1848.

† The Second Teacher of French was discontinued, by order of the Secretary of War, June 29th, 1848.

DEPARTMENT OF SPANISH.

NO.	APPOINTMENT AND NAME.	ARMY RANK, WHEN APPOINTED.	TERM OF SERVICE.	
			FROM	TO
	Professors.			
1	PATRICE DE JANON.		July 1, 1857.	Sept. 16, 1863.

DEPARTMENT OF INFANTRY TACTICS.

NO.	APPOINTMENT AND NAME.	ARMY RANK, WHEN APPOINTED.	TERM OF SERVICE.	
			FROM	TO
	Commandants of Cadets.			
1	JOHN BLISS.	Capt. 6th Infantry.	April 2, 1818.	January 11, 1819.
2	*JOHN R. BELL.	Capt. Lt. Artillery.	February 8, 1819.	March 17, 1820.
3	WILLIAM J. WORTH.	Bvt. Maj. 2d Infantry.	March 17, 1820.	December 2, 1828.
4	*ETHAN A. HITCHCOCK.	Capt. 1st Infantry.	March 18, 1829.	June 24, 1833.
5	JOHN FOWLE.	Maj. 3d Infantry.	July 10, 1833.	March 31, 1838.
6	*CHARLES F. SMITH.	1st Lt. 2d Artillery.	April 1, 1838.	September 1, 1842.
7	*JOHN A. THOMAS.	1st Lt. 3d Artillery.	September 1, 1842.	December 14, 1845.
8	*BRADFORD R. ALDEN.	Capt. 4th Infantry.	December 14, 1845.	November 1, 1852.
9	*ROBERT S. GARNETT.	Capt. 7th Infantry and Bvt. Major U. S. A.	November 1, 1852.	July 31, 1854.
10	*WILLIAM H. T. WALKER.	Major 10th Infantry and Bvt. Lt.-Col. U. S. A.	July 31, 1854.	May 27, 1856.
11	*WILLIAM J. HARDEE.	Maj. 2d Cavalry and Bvt. Lt.-Col. U. S. A.	July 22, 1856.	September 8, 1860.
12	*JOHN F. REYNOLDS.	Capt. 3d Artillery and Bvt. Major U. S. A.	September 8, 1860.	June 25, 1861.
13	*CHRISTOPHER C. AUGUR.	Major 13th Infantry.	August 26, 1861.	December 5, 1861.
14	*KENNER GARRARD.	Capt. 5th Cavalry.	December 5, 1861.	September 25, 1862.
15	*HENRY B. CLITZ.	Major 12th Infantry.	October 23, 1862.	Present.

† DEPARTMENT OF PRACTICAL ENGINEERING.

NO.	APPOINTMENT AND NAME.	ARMY RANK, WHEN APPOINTED.	TERM OF SERVICE.	
			FROM	TO
	Instructors.			
1	*ALEXANDER J. SWIFT.	Capt. Corps of Eng.	June 30, 1841.	September 12, 1846.
2	*FREDERIC A. SMITH.	Capt. Corps of Eng.	September 12, 1846.	March 25, 1848.
3	*GEORGE W. CULLUM.	Capt. Corps of Eng.	March 25, 1848.	March 2d, 1855.
4	*JONATHAN G. BARNARD.	Capt. Corps of Eng. and Bvt. Major U. S. A.	March 2, 1855.	September 8, 1856.
5	*ANDREW J. DONELSON.	1st Lt. Corps Eng.	September 9, 1856.	October 15, 1858.
6	*JAMES C. DUANE.	1st Lt. Corps Eng.	October 15, 1858.	(Detached Jan. 18, 1861.)

† Upon the recommendation of the Chief Engineer, on April 24th, 1844, the Secretary of War directed that " An Officer of the Corps of Engineers shall be assigned to the Military Academy, as Instructor in *practical Military Engineering;* and shall be a member of the Academic Board."

DEPARTMENT OF CIVIL AND MILITARY ENGINEERING.

NO.	APPOINTMENT AND NAME.	ARMY RANK, WHEN APPOINTED.	TERM OF SERVICE.	
			FROM	TO
	Professors.			
1	*ALDEN PARTRIDGE.	Capt. Corps of Eng.	Sept. 1, 1813.	Dec. 31, 1816.
2	CLAUDE CROZET.		March 6, 1817.	April 28, 1823.
3	DAVID B. DOUGLASS.		May 1, 1823.	March 1, 1831.
4	*DENNIS H. MAHAN.	2d Lt. Corps of Eng.	Jan. 1, 1832.	Present.
	Acting Professors.			
1	*DENNIS H. MAHAN.	2d Lt. Corps of Eng.	March 1, 1831.	Jan. 1, 1832.

† DEPARTMENT OF ARTILLERY AND CAVALRY.

NO.	APPOINTMENT AND NAME.	ARMY RANK, WHEN APPOINTED.	TERM OF SERVICE.	
			FROM	TO
	Instructors.			
1	*GEORGE W. GARDINER.	2d Lt.Corps of Artillery.	September 15, 1817.	February 1, 1820.
2	FABIUS WHITING.	Capt. Corps of Artillery.	August 15, 1820.	August 7, 1821.
3	*Z. J. D. KINSLEY.	2d Lt. 3d Artillery.	December 18, 1823.	December 1, 1835.
4	*ROBERT ANDERSON.	1st Lt. 3d Artillery.	December 1, 1835.	November 6, 1837.
5	*MINER KNOWLTON.	1st Lt. 1st Artillery.	November 9, 1837.	July 1, 1844.
6	*E. D. KEYES.	Capt. 3d Artillery.	July 25, 1844.	December 24, 1848.
7	*WILLIAM H. SHOVER.	Bvt. Maj. 3d Artillery.	December 24, 1848.	September 8, 1850.
8	*GEORGE H. THOMAS.	1st Lt. 3d Artillery and Bvt. Major U. S. A.	April 3, 1851.	May 1, 1854.
9	*FITZ JOHN PORTER.	1st Lt. 4th Artillery and Bvt. Major U. S. A.	May 1, 1854.	September 11, 1855.
10	*HENRY F. CLARKE.	1st. Lt. 2d Artillery and Bvt. Captain U. S. A.	September 11, 1855.	August 6, 1856.

SURGEONS.

NO.	APPOINTMENT AND NAME.	ARMY RANK, WHEN APPOINTED.	TERM OF SERVICE.	
			FROM	TO
	Surgeons.			
1	SAMUEL A. WALSH.	Surgeon.	Aug. 9, 1813.	June 22, 1820.
2	JAMES CUTBUSH.	Surgeon.	June 22, 1820.	Nov. 18, 1821.
3	JOSIAH EVERETT.	Surgeon.	Aug. 6, 1822.	Nov. 10, 1826.
4	WALTER V. WHEATON.	Surgeon.	Nov. 10, 1826.	May 1, 1846.
5	CHARLES McDOUGALL.	Surgeon.	Sept. 18, 1846.	June 20, 1848.
6	J. J. B. WRIGHT.	Surgeon.	June 20, 1848.	Dec. 12, 1848.
7	JOHN M. CUYLER.	Surgeon.	Dec. 12, 1848.	April 3, 1855.
8	SAMUEL P. MOORE.	Surgeon.	June 2, 1855.	April 2, 1860.
9	CHARLES McDOUGALL.	Surgeon.	April 2, 1860.	Jan. 23, 1862.
10	JOHN F. HEAD.	Surgeon.	Jan'y 23, 1862.	July 3, 1862.
11	EUGENE H. ABADIE.	Surgeon.	July 3, 1862.	Present.

† On December 5th, 1856, the Academic Board recommended that the portion of the course of Artillery not included in the "Tactics" be taught in a separate Department, under the title of *Ordnance and Gunnery.* The recommendation was approved by the Secretary of War, December 31st, 1856.

ADJUTANTS.

NO.	APPOINTMENT AND NAME.	ARMY RANK, WHEN APPOINTED.	TERM OF SERVICE.	
			FROM	TO
	Adjutants.			
1	*GEORGE W. GARDINER.	2d Lt. Corps Artillery.	Oct, 12, 1816.	Sept. 15, 1817.
2	*JAMES D. GRAHAM.	3d Lt. Corps Artillery.	Oct. 12, 1817.	Feb. 10, 1819.
3	*GEORGE W. GARDINER.	1st Lt. Corps of Art'y.	Feb. 10, 1819.	March 9, 1820.
4	*GEORGE BLANEY.	1st Lt. Corps of Eng.	March 9, 1820.	March 1, 1821.
5	PATRICK H. GALT.	1st Lt. 2d Artillery.	May 20, 1821.	May 13, 1822.
6	*GEORGE BLANEY.	1st Lt. Corps of Eng.	Aug. 12, 1822.	May 25, 1824.
7	*HENRY H. GIRD.	2d Lt. 4th Artillery.	June 9, 1824.	Apr. 20, 1827.
8	*FREDERICK L. GRIFFITH.	1st Lt. 2d Artillery.	May 14, 1827.	Sept. 1, 1831.
9	*CHARLES F. SMITH.	2d Lt. 2d Artillery.	Sept. 1, 1831.	April 1, 1838.
10	*GEORGE G. WAGGAMAN.	1st Lt. 1st Artillery.	Feb. 17, 1839.	July 1, 1841.
11	*JOSEPH HOOKER.	1st Lt. 1st Artillery.	July 1, 1841.	Oct. 3, 1841.
12	*IRVIN McDOWELL.	2d Lt. 1st Artillery.	Nov. 11, 1841.	Oct. 8, 1845.
13	*ISAAC S. K. REEVES.	1st Lt. 1st Artillery.	Oct. 31, 1846.	Sept. 28, 1850.
14	*SETH WILLIAMS.	1st Lt. 1st Art'y, Bt. Capt. U. S. A.	Sept. 28, 1850.	Sept. 1, 1853.
15	*FITZ JOHN PORTER.	1st Lt. 4th Art'y, Bt. Major U. S. A.	Sept. 1, 1853.	May 1, 1854.
16	*JAMES B. FRY.	1st Lt. 1st Artillery.	July 31, 1854.	Aug. 31, 1859.
17	*SAMUEL B. HOLABIRD.	1st Lt. 1st. Infantry.	Sept. 2, 1859.	May 13, 1861.
18	*HERMAN BIGGS.	2d Lt. 1st Infantry.	May 13, 1861.	Oct. 10, 1861.
19	*EDWARD C. BOYNTON.	Capt. 11th Infantry.	Oct. 10, 1861.	Present.

SWORD-MASTERS.

NO.	APPOINTMENT AND NAME.	ARMY RANK, WHEN APPOINTED.	TERM OF SERVICE.	
			FROM	TO
	Sword-Masters.			
1	PIERRE THOMAS.		March 1, 1814.	Dec. 12, 1825.
2	PIERRE TRAINQUE.		Dec. 13, 1825.	June 27, 1826.
3	LOUIS S. SIMON.		Oct. 5, 1826.	Nov. 30, 1831.
4	NICHOLAS A. JUMEL.		Dec. 1, 1831.	Feb. 15, 1837.
5	FERDINAND DUPARE.		Feb. 16, 1837.	July 31, 1840.
6	PATRICE DE JANON.		Jan. 6, 1846.	July 1, 1857.
7	ANTONÉ LORENTZ.		March 30, 1858.	Present.

† RIDING-MASTERS.

NO.	APPOINTMENT AND NAME.	ARMY RANK, WHEN APPOINTED.	TERM OF SERVICE.	
			FROM	TO
	Riding-Masters.			
1	JAMES McAULEY.		June 11, 1839.	Jan. 1, 1842.
2	HENRY R. HERSHBERGER.		Jan. 6, 1842.	Sept. 18, 1848.
3	F. R. O. DE BÉVILLE.		Nov. 1, 1850.	Sept. 9, 1852.

† Since 1852, the exercises in Riding have been conducted by cavalry officers of the army.

The number of Cadets actually admitted into the Military Academy from its origin, with the States and Territories whence appointed, is shown in the following tables.

STATEMENT SHOWING THE NUMBER OF CADETS ACTUALLY ADMITTED INTO THE UNITED STATES MILITARY ACADEMY FROM ITS ORIGIN, MARCH 16TH, 1802, TO OCTOBER 19TH, 1863.

Year of Admission	Maine	New Hampshire	Vermont	Massachusetts	Rhode Island	Connecticut	New York	New Jersey	Pennsylvania	Delaware	Maryland	Virginia	West Virginia	North Carolina	South Carolina	Georgia	Alabama	Mississippi	Louisiana	Ohio	Kentucky	Tennessee	Indiana	Illinois	Missouri	Arkansas	Michigan	Florida	Texas	Iowa	Wisconsin	California	Minnesota	Oregon	New Mexico	Utah	Washington	Nebraska	Kansas	Dakota	Colorado	Nevada	Dist. of Columbia	At Large	Unknown	Total
1802				5		1	1				1	1		1											1																				2	10
1803			8				1		1																																				1	9
1804		2	1	1			1		2		1			1											3																				1	9
1805	1		3	2		2	1																		1																					9
1806	1		3	2		4	2			1	1														1																			4		9
1807			5	2			10								2	1					1	2				1																	1	11		17
1808		2	6				1	2							4	1				2	5	2	2			1																	2		4	42
1809	1			1		4					1			1		1						1	1		1																					10
1810			1				1					2																																		2
1811																																														0

Year of Admission.	Maine.	New Hampshire.	Vermont.	Massachusetts.	Rhode Island.	Connecticut.	New York.	New Jersey.	Pennsylvania.	Delaware.	Maryland.	Virginia.	West Virginia.	North Carolina.	South Carolina.	Georgia.	Alabama.	Mississippi.	Louisiana.	Ohio.	Kentucky.	Tennessee.	Indiana.	Illinois.	Missouri.	Arkansas.	Michigan.	Florida.	Texas.	Iowa.	Wisconsin.	California.	Minnesota.	Oregon.	New Mexico.	Utah.	Washington.	Nebraska.	Kansas.	Dakota.	Colorado.	Nevada.	Dist. of Columbia.	At Large.	Unknown.	Total.
Total.	102	78	104	252	42	102	650	101	424	41	179	879	1	190	159	189	88	51	67	248	196	178	109	81	67	17	88	20	11	14	17	10	6	8	5	3	2	2	8	1	1	1	118	880	26	4,626

NOTE.—Owing to the destruction of the records by fire in 1838, the States in which some of the Cadets resided previous to that event is given; though it is believed they were appointed "At Large." The President of the United States having determined late in August, 1863, to fill all the existing vacancies from the seceded States there were in the FOURTH CLASS, numbering 97, on the 19th of October, 48 thus appointed. 10 Cadets similarly appointed had not, on that date, been examined for admission into the Military Academy.

THE FOLLOWING STATEMENT EXHIBITS THE ACTUAL NUMBER OF CADETS WHO HAVE GRADUATED AT THE MILITARY ACADEMY, FROM ITS ORIGIN TO THE PRESENT DATE, WITH THE STATES AND TERRITORIES WHENCE APPOINTED.

Year of Graduation	Maine	New Hampshire	Vermont	Massachusetts	Rhode Island	Connecticut	New York	New Jersey	Pennsylvania	Delaware	Maryland	Virginia	North Carolina	South Carolina	Georgia	Alabama	Mississippi	Louisiana	Ohio	Indiana	Illinois	Kentucky	Tennessee	Arkansas	Missouri	Michigan	Wisconsin	Dist. of Columbia	Florida	At Large	Iowa	Texas	Utah Territory	Minnesota	Washington Ter.	Oregon	New Mexico Ter.	California	Nebraska Ter.	Aggregate
1802				1			1				1																													2
1803				1			1		1				1																											3
1804			1	1			2																																	3
1805	1		5				1		1	1	1			1																										8
1806		2	4	3		2	3		2		1			1																										15
1807	1	1	6	1		3	1	1	1		1	1	1	1														1												15
1808			3	1			1		1		1	1		1								1						1												7
1809			3	2			4	1	2		4	3		1				1	4	1		1	2		4			5												19
1810				3	1		9	1	1		5	3		2								1	1		1			4												18
1811												1																												1
1812		1	2	2		1	14	2	3	2	2	2	1	1		1	1	1	1				1					1												30
1813			1	5		1	4	1	6	1	5	8	1	3	8	1	1	1	1	1		1	1					5												40
1814			1	4			4		4		2	3	1	1				1	1	1		1	1					4												19
1815			1	4		1	6	2	5		5	2		1	1				2			2	1					1												23
1816		1	1	2			16	1	4		2	6	1	3			1		1		1	2	1					1												29
1817	1		1	4		1	6	2	5	2	9	6		1	1	1	1	1	2	1	1	2	1					2												30
1818			3	2			6	1	4		3	6		2	1	1		1		1		2	1					1												24
1819			3	4			5	2	5		3	2		2					8			2	1					2												40
1820		1		2		5	6	2	4	2	3	2	1	1	1	1	1	1	2		1	2	1					1												35
1821		2	2	4		8	9		5		3	2		3								2						3												31
1822	1	1	1	2			6	1	4		3	8	3	2		1	1	1		2		2	1					1												37
1823		1	2	4			9		1		3	4		2	2	1	1	1	8	1	1	4	1	1	4															41
1824	3	3	2	4			2	3	4		2	1	3	2	1	1	1		2	2	1		2			1		1												38
1825				4			6		4	1	2	2	2	2		1		1	4	1		2	2			1		1												38
1826	2	2	2	5		5	2	1	4		2	2	3	2	2	1		1	1		1	4	2		1			1												46
1827	2	1	1	1	2	8	7	1	4	1	4	2	2	1		1			7	1	1	4	2		1			1	1											42
1828																																								
1829																																								
1830																												8												

CADETS WHO HAVE GRADUATED AT THE MILITARY ACADEMY.

Year of Graduation	Maine	N. Hampshire	Vermont	Massachusetts	Rhode Island	Connecticut	New York	New Jersey	Pennsylvania	Delaware	Maryland	Virginia	North Carolina	South Carolina	Georgia	Alabama	Mississippi	Louisiana	Ohio	Indiana	Illinois	Kentucky	Tennessee	Arkansas	Missouri	Michigan	Wisconsin	Dist. Columbia	Florida	At Large	Iowa	Texas	Utah Territory	Minnesota	Washingt'n Ter	Oregon	N. Mexico Ter.	California	Nebraska Ter.	Aggregate
1831																																								38
1832																																								45
1833																																								43
1834																																								36
1835																																								56
1836																																								49
1837																																								50
1838																																								45
1839																																								31
1840																																								42
1841																																								52
1842																																								56
1843																																								39
1844																																								25
1845																																								41
1846																																								59
1847																																								38
1848																																								38
1849																																								44
1850																																								48
1851																																								52
1852																																								46
1853																																								34
1854																																								48
1855																																								39
1856																																								27
1857																																								22
1858																																								41
1859																																								30
1860																																								28
1861																																								28
1862																																								25
Total	54	47		75 181		20	55 829		51 197		18	79 142	63	59	44	26	14	15	118	48	80	68	56	5	24	17	7	50		6 189	6	8	1	2	2	1	1	1	1	2020

STATEMENT EXHIBITING THE CONDITION IN LIFE OF THE PARENTS OF THE CADETS OF THE U. S. MILITARY ACADEMY AT WEST POINT, NEW YORK, FOR THE LAST TWENTY-TWO YEARS, FROM 1842 TO 1863, INCLUSIVE.

	1842	1843	1844	1845	1846	1847	1848	1849	1850	1851	1852	1853	1854	1855	1856	1857	1858	1859	1860	1861	1862	1863
Fathers are or were farmers or planters	59	61	61	68	72	67	69	75	70	68	67	58	66	62	60	52	48	57	65	29	38	88
Fathers are or were mechanics	14	12	15	22	22	25	22	21	16	14	14	13	12	17	26	22	15	30	12	13	8	12
Fathers are or were judges or lawyers	27	25	30	35	32	30	29	21	34	33	35	35	36	36	25	29	32	32	26	23	35	39
Fathers are or were merchants	18	15	23	37	29	29	31	38	36	38	35	35	39	40	25	26	41	32	36	23	24	29
Fathers are or were boarding-house or hotel keepers	5	2	8	8	7	6	4	2	2	2	3	3	5	8	9	1	4	10	3	4	4	5
Fathers are or were physicians	12	15	15	13	11	19	21	21	18	14	13	18	5	8	9	17	16	10	8	10	18	18
Fathers are or were in the army, navy, or marine corps	12	16	13	13	11	18	17	17	18	22	24	27	28	22	20	20	26	29	18	18	25	88
Fathers are or were clergymen	14	6	6	6	8	8	3	4	4	4	6	5	6	6	5	6	5	6	7	7	8	11
Fathers are or were in the civil employment of the General or State government	4	15	16	9	5	2	8	7	7	8	10	11	14	13	13	7	31	29	18	8	11	14
Miscellaneous: as, bank officers, editors, professors, masters of vessels, &c.	15	11	15	23	35	36	41	24	32	39	30	26	14	25	18	13	12	6	37	44	39	42
Occupation not stated, or no occupation	48	34	23	17	1	2	2	8	7	11	13	7	10	19	15	20	25	39	22	18	18	19
Total	221	212	224	236	241	232	242	240	244	239	247	232	237	289	223	221	251	266	279	202	218	260
Of these numbers, there are without fathers living	26	57	44	48	42	41	34	48	40	45	36	35	29	33	33	24	46	33	42	25	25	36
Without fathers or mothers living	22	16	18	15	21	20	18	16	26	17	19	17	15	9	6	7	7	8	10	11	9	7
Total orphans	48	73	62	63	63	61	52	64	66	62	55	52	44	42	39	31	53	41	52	36	34	42
Of these numbers the parents are stated to be in moderate circumstances	182	156	150	164	192	182	198	203	215	207	218	205	206	215	196	195	216	218	289	184	199	232
Of these numbers the parents are stated to be in reduced circumstances		26	26	36	35	38	40	29	25	16	9	8	8	7	8	8	8	7	6	2	5	5
Of these numbers the parents are stated to be in indigent circumstances		6	8	8	8	8	4	4	2	2		1	1	1	1	1	1	1	7	2	1	1
Of these numbers the parents are stated to be in independent circumstances	6	6	8	8	6	4	5	4	2	2		1	1	1	1	1	1		6	2	1	5
Of these numbers the parents are stated to be in unknown circumstances	39	18	19	16										16			26	41	34	16	12	17
Total	221	212	224	236	241	232	242	240	244	239	247	232	237	289	223	221	251	266	279	202	218	260

NOTE.—Of the 97 Cadets admitted, to October 19th, 1863, as given in the table on page 321, 46 were appointed from the U. S. Volunteers engaged in the War, who held the following rank: 1 *Captain*, 5 *First Lieutenants*, 3 *Second Lieutenants*, 10 *Non-commissioned Officers*, 20 *Privates*, 1 *Musician*, and 6 *Clerks*, from military departments.

LIST OF CADETS ATTACHED TO THE ARMY REGISTER ANNUALLY, IN CONFORMITY WITH A REGULATION FOR THE GOVERNMENT OF THE MILITARY ACADEMY, REQUIRING THE NAMES OF THE MOST DISTINGUISHED CADETS, NOT EXCEEDING FIVE IN EACH CLASS, TO BE REPORTED FOR THIS PURPOSE, AT EACH ANNUAL EXAMINATION.

	FIRST CLASS.	STATE.	SECOND CLASS.	STATE.	THIRD CLASS.	STATE.	FOURTH CLASS.	STATE.
1818.	1 Richard Delafield	N. Y.	1 Wilson M. C. Fairfax	Va.	1 Henry Brewerton	N. Y.	1 Stephen Tuttle	N. J.
	2 Andrew Talcott	Conn.	2 William A. Eliason	D. C.	2 Robert S. Brooke	Va.	2 Andrew J. Donelson	Tenn.
	3 Samuel S. Smith	Del.	3 Aaron K. Woolley	Pa.	3 William H. Bell	N. C.	3 Alvin Edson	Vt.
	4 Horace Webster	Vt.	4 Frederick A. Underhill	N. Y.	4 Thomas E. Sudler	Md.	4 Joshua Baker	La.
	5 Samuel Ringgold	Md.	5 Edward D. Mansfield	N. Y.	5 John L'Engle	N. C.	5 John C. Holland	S. C.
1819.	1 William A. Eliason	D. C.	1 Henry Brewerton	N. Y.	1 Edw. C. Ross	Pa.	1 Edw. H. Courtenay	Md.
	2 Frederick Underhill	N. Y.	2 Stephen Tuttle	N. J.	2 William W. Wells	Ind.	2 Jonathan Prescott	Mass.
	3 Cornelius Ogden	Ohio.	3 Thos. E. Sudler	Md.	3 John C. Holland	S. C.	3 Thomas R. Ingalls	N. Y.
	4 Edw. D. Mansfield	N. Y.	4 Joshua Baker	La.	4 Clark Burdine	Geo.	4 William Wall	Ohio.
	5 John R. Bowes	Mass.	5 Andrew J. Donelson	Tenn.	5 David Wallace	Ohio.	5 Nicholas P. Trist	La.
1820.	1 Stephen Tuttle	N. J.	1 Clark Burdine	Geo.	1 George Dutton	Ct.	1 William T Washington	D. C.
	2 Andrew J. Donelson	Tenn.	2 Charles Dimmock	Mass.	2 Nicholas P. Trist	La.	2 Alfred Mordecai	N. C.
	3 Thomas E. Sudler	Md.	3 William W. Wells	Ind.	3 Thomas R. Ingalls	N. Y.	3 Frederick Guyon	Miss.
	4 William H. Bell	N. C.	4 Edw. H. Courtenay	Md.	4 John H. Latrobe	Md.	4 Reuben Holmes	Ct.
	5 William C. DeHart	N. Y.	5 John C. Holland	S. C.	5 William Wall	Ohio.	5 John McCartney	Pa.
1821.	1 Edward H. Courtenay	Md.	1 John H. Latrobe	Md.	1 Wm. T. Washington	D. C.	1 Dennis H. Mahan	Va.
	2 Clark Burdine	Geo.	2 George Dutton	Conn.	2 Alfred Mordecai	N. C.	2 John K. Findlay	Pa.
	3 Jonathan Prescott	Mass.	3 Joseph K. F Mansfield	Conn.	3 Reuben Holmes	Conn.	3 Robert G. Wirt	D. C.
	4 William W. Wells	Ind.	4 Nicholas P. Trist	La.	4 George S. Green	R. I.	4 Samuel McCoskry	Pa.
	5 Charles Dimmock	Mass.	5 William Wall	Ohio.	5 Stephen Lee	S. C.	5 Robert P. Parrott	N. H.

22

LIST OF CADETS ATTACHED TO THE ARMY REGISTER ANNUALLY—CONTINUED.

	FIRST CLASS.	STATE.	SECOND CLASS.	STATE.	THIRD CLASS.	STATE.	FOURTH CLASS.	STATE.
1822.	1 George Dutton	Conn.	1 Alfred Mordecai	N. C.	1 Dennis H. Mahan	Va.	1 Alexander D. Bache	Pa.
	2 Joseph K. F. Mansfield	Conn.	2 Reuben Holmes	Conn.	2 Robert P. Parrott	N. H.	2 Horace Smith	N. Y.
	3 Charles G. Smith	Conn.	3 George C. Richards	N. Y.	3 John K. Findlay	Pa.	3 Matthew R. T. Harrison	Geo.
	4 Thomas R. Ingalls	N. Y.	4 George S. Green	R. I.	4 John W. A. Smith	Me.	4 Peter McMartin	N. Y.
	5 Horace Bliss	N. H.	5 Samuel U. Southerland	N. C.	5 Napoleon B. Bennett	Pa.	5 Thompson S. Brown	N. Y.
1823.	1 Alfred Mordecai	N. C.	1 Dennis H. Mahan	Va.	1 Alexander D. Bache	Pa.	1 William H. C. Bartlett	Mo.
	2 George S. Green	R. I.	2 John W. A. Smith	Me.	2 Peter McMartin	N. Y.	2 William Bryant	Va.
	3 George C. Richards	N. Y.	3 Robert P. Parrott	N. H.	3 Horace Smith	N. Y.	3 Charles G. Ridgely	Del.
	4 Reuben Holmes	Conn.	4 Napoleon B. Bennett	Pa.	4 Thompson S. Brown	N. Y.	4 George Woodbridge	Mass.
	5 Samuel U. Southerland	N. C.	5 R. Edward Hazzard	S. C.	5 Raphael C. Smead	N. Y.	5 Daniel S. Herring	Va.
1824.	1 Dennis H. Mahan	Va.	1 Alexander D. Bache	Pa.	1 William H. C. Bartlett	Mo.	1 Pierce B. Anderson	Tenn.
	2 John W. A. Smith	Me.	2 Thompson S. Brown	N. Y.	2 William Bryant	Va.	2 William Maynadier	D. C.
	3 Robert P. Parrott	N. H.	3 Alexander H. Bowman	Pa.	3 Thomas S. Twiss	Vt.	3 Ebenezer S. Sibley	Mich.
	4 R. Edward Hazzard	S. C.	4 Stephen V. R. Ryan	N. Y.	4 Charles G. Ridgely	Del.	4 Lucien J. Bibb	Ky.
	5 John K. Findlay	Pa.	5 Peter McMartin	N. Y.	5 Daniel S. Herring	Va.	5 Alexander S. Hooe	Va.
1825.	1 Alexander D. Bache	Pa.	1 William H. C. Bartlett	Mo.	1 William Maynadier	D. C.	1 Hugh W. Mercer	Va.
	2 Peter McMartin	N. Y.	2 Thomas S. Twiss	Vt.	2 Lucien J. Bibb	Ky.	2 Wm. P. N. Fitzgerald	N. Y.
	3 Alexander H. Bowman	Pa.	3 William Bryant	Va.	3 Ebenezer S. Sibley	Mich.	3 Albert E. Church	Conn.
	4 Thompson S. Brown	N. Y.	4 Thomas J. Cram	N. H.	4 Pierce B. Anderson	Tenn.	4 Walter B. Guion	Miss.
	5 Daniel S. Donelson	Tenn.	5 Charles G. Ridgely	Del.	5 John Childe	Mass.	5 David M. Farrelly	Pa.
1826.	1 William H. C. Bartlett	Mo.	1 James A. J. Bradford	Ky.	1 Wm. P. N. Fitzgerald	N. Y.	1 Charles Mason	N. Y.
	2 Thomas S. Twiss	Vt.	2 Ebenezer S. Sibley	Mich.	2 Hugh W. Mercer	Ky.	2 William H. Harford	Geo.
	3 William Bryant	Va.	3 William Maynadier	D. C.	3 Albert E. Church	Conn.	3 Robert E. Lee	Va.
	4 Thomas J. Cram	N. H.	4 John Childe	Mass.	4 Walter B. Guion	Miss.	4 William Boylan	N. C.
	5 Charles G. Ridgely	Del.	5 Edwin Schenck	N. Y.	5 Richard C. Tilghman	Md.	5 James Barnes	Mass.

LIST OF CADETS ATTACHED TO THE ARMY REGISTER ANNUALLY—Continued.

	FIRST CLASS.	STATE.	SECOND CLASS.	STATE.	THIRD CLASS.	STATE.	FOURTH CLASS.	STATE.
1827.	1 Ebenezer S. Sibley	Mich.	1 Albert E. Church	Conn.	1 Charles Mason	Conn.	1 Alexander J. Swift	N.Y.
	2 John Childe	Mass.	2 Hugh W. Mercer	Va.	2 Robert E. Lee	Va.	2 William E. Basinger	Geo.
	3 William Maynadier	D.C.	3 Robert E. Temple	Vt.	3 Cath. P. Buckingham	Vt.	3 Walter S. Chandler	D.C.
	4 James A. J. Bradford	Ky.	4 Charles O. Collins	N.Y.	4 William H. Harford	N.Y.	4 Thomas J. Lee	D.C.
	5 Lucien J. Bibb	Ky.	5 Richard C. Tilghman	Md.	5 James Barnes	Md.	5 Francis Vinton	R.I.
1828.	1 Albert E. Church	Conn.	1 Charles Mason	N.Y.	1 Alexander J. Swift	N.Y.	1 Roswell Park	N.Y.
	2 Richard C. Tilghman	Md.	2 Robert E. Lee	Va.	2 Walter S. Chandler	D.C.	2 Henry Clay	Ky.
	3 Hugh W. Mercer	Va.	3 Cath. P. Buckingham	Ohio.	3 William N. Pendleton	Va.	3 William A. Norton	N.Y.
	4 Robert E. Temple	Vt.	4 William H. Harford	Geo.	4 William E. Basinger	Geo.	4 Richard H. Peyton	Va.
	5 Charles O. Collins	N.Y.	5 James Barnes	Mass.	5 Francis Vinton	R.I.	5 George H. Talcott	N.Y.
1829.	1 Charles Mason	N.Y.	1 Alexander J. Swift	N.Y.	1 Roswell Park	N.Y.	1 Benjamin S. Ewell	Va.
	2 Robert E. Lee	Va.	2 Walter S. Chandler	D.C.	2 Henry Clay	Ky.	2 Robert P. Smith	Miss.
	3 William H. Harford	Geo.	3 William N. Pendleton	Va.	3 William A. Norton	N.Y.	3 Jacob W. Bailey	R.I.
	4 Joseph A. Smith	Pa.	4 Francis Vinton	R.I.	4 James Allen	N.C.	4 George W. Ward	Mass.
	5 James Barnes	Mass.	5 George W. Lawson	Tenn.	5 Richard H. Peyton	Va.	5 Joseph C. Vance	Ohio.
1830.	1 Alexander J. Swift	N.Y.	1 Roswell Park	N.Y.	1 Robert P. Smith	Miss.	1 Frederick A. Smith	Mass.
	2 William E. Basinger	Geo.	2 James Allen	N.C.	2 Benjamin S. Ewell	Va.	2 John H. Allen	N.Y.
	3 Walter S. Chandler	D.C.	3 Henry Clay	Ky.	3 George W. Ward	Mass.	3 Francis H. Smith	Va.
	4 Francis Vinton	R.I.	4 Richard H. Peyton	Va.	4 Jacob W. Bailey	R.I.	4 David B. Harris	Va.
	5 William N. Pendleton	Va.	5 William A. Norton	N.Y.	5 Lewis Howell	Pa.	5 William H. Sidell	N.Y.
1831.	1 Roswell Park	N.Y.	1 Robert P. Smith	Miss.	1 Frederick A. Smith	Mass.	1 William Smith	N.Y.
	2 Henry Clay	Ky.	2 George W. Ward	Mass.	2 William H. Sidell	N.Y.	2 Harris Loughborough	Ky.
	3 James Allen	N.C.	3 Jacob W. Bailey	R.I.	3 Jonathan G. Barnard	Mass.	3 John F. Lee	Va.
	4 Henry E. Prentiss	Me.	4 Benjamin S. Ewell	Va.	4 Roswell W. Lee	Mass.	4 John Sanders	Fla.
	5 Albert M. Lea	Tenn.	5 George W. Cass	Ohio.	5 Rufus King	N.Y.	5 Curran Pope	Ky.

LIST OF CADETS ATTACHED TO THE ARMY REGISTER ANNUALLY—Continued.

	FIRST CLASS.	STATE.	SECOND CLASS.	STATE.	THIRD CLASS.	STATE.	FOURTH CLASS.	STATE.
1832.	1 George W. Ward	Mass.	1 Jonathan G. Barnard	Mass.	1 William Smith	N. Y.	1 George M. Legate	N. Y.
	2 Robert P. Smith	Miss.	2 Frederick A. Smith	Mass.	2 Harris Loughborough	Ky.	2 Thomas T. Gantt	Va.
	3 Benjamin S. Ewell	Va.	3 William H. Sidell	N. Y.	3 John Sanders	Fla.	3 Charles H. Bigelow	Mass.
	4 George W. Cass	Ohio.	4 George W. Cullum	Pa.	4 John F. Lee	Va.	4 Charles J. Whiting	Me.
	5 Jacob W. Bailey	R. I.	5 Rufus King	N. Y.	5 James Duncan	N. Y.	5 Montgomery Blair	Ky.
1833.	1 Frederick A. Smith	Mass.	1 William Smith	N. Y.	1 Charles H. Bigelow	Mass.	1 James L. Mason	Large.
	2 Jonathan G. Barnard	Mass.	2 John Sanders	Fla.	2 Charles J. Whiting	Me.	2 Danville Leadbetter	Me.
	3 George W. Cullum	Pa.	3 Robert T. P. Allen	Md.	3 George M. Legate	N. Y.	3 Alexander Hamilton	N. Y.
	4 Rufus King	N. Y.	4 Harris Loughborough	Ky.	4 John H. Martindale	N. Y.	4 Barnabas Conkling	N. Y.
	5 Francis H. Smith	Va.	5 William T. Stockton	Pa.	5 Thomas T. Gantt	Va.	5 Joseph R. Anderson	Va.
1834.	1 William Smith*	N. Y.	1 Charles J. Whiting	Me.	1 James L. Mason	Large.	1 John W. Gunnison	N. H.
	2 John Sanders	Fla.	2 John H. Martindale	N. Y.	2 Danville Leadbetter	Me.	2 Henry W. Benham	Conn.
	3 Harris Loughborough	Ky.	3 George W. Morell	N. Y.	3 Montgomery C. Meigs	Pa.	3 Edwin W. Morgan	Pa.
	4 Thomas A. Morris	Ind.	4 Charles H. Bigelow	Mass.	4 Alexander Hamilton	N. Y.	4 Alexander B. Dyer	Mo.
	5 Robert T. P. Allen	Md.	5 George M. Legate	N. Y.	5 Barnabas Conkling	N. Y.	5 John Bratt	N. Y.
1835.	1 George W. Morell	N. Y.	1 Montgomery C. Meigs	Pa.	1 Edwin W. Morgan	Pa.	1 William H. Wright	N. C.
	2 Charles H. Bigelow	Mass.	2 Alexander Hamilton	N. Y.	2 Henry W. Benham	Conn.	2 Alex. H. Dearborn	N. Y.
	3 John H. Martindale	N. Y.	3 George L. Welcker	Tenn.	3 Alexander B. Dyer	Mo.	3 Stephen H. Campbell	Vt.
	4 Charles J. Whiting	Me.	4 James L. Mason	Large.	4 John W. Gunnison	N. H.	4 P. G. T. Beauregard	La.
	5 George M. Legate	N. Y.	5 Fisher A. Lewis	Va.	5 John Bratt	N. Y.	5 John T. Metcalfe	Miss.
1836.	1 George L. Welcker	Tenn.	1 Henry W. Benham	Conn.	1 William H. Wright	N. C.	1 Isaac I Stevens	Mass.
	2 James L. Mason	Large.	2 Edwin W. Morgan	Pa.	2 P. G. T. Beauregard	La.	2 Henry J. Biddle	Pa.
	3 Danville Leadbetter	Me.	3 John W. Gunnison	N. H.	3 Alex. H. Dearborn	N. Y.	3 Robert Q. Butler	Va.
	4 Joseph R. Anderson	Va.	4 John Bratt	N. Y.	4 Stephen H. Campbell	Vt.	4 Henry W. Halleck	N. Y.
	5 Montgomery C. Meigs	Pa.	5 William W. Chapman	Mass.	5 James H. Trapier	S. C.	5 Jeremy F. Gilmer	N. C.

* After his graduation changed his name to William D. Fraser.

LIST OF CADETS ATTACHED TO THE ARMY REGISTER ANNUALLY—Continued.

Year	First Class	State	Second Class	State	Third Class	State	Fourth Class	State
1837	1 Henry W. Benham	Conn.	1 William H. Wright	N. C.	1 Isaac I. Stevens	Mass.	1 Paul O. Hebert	La.
	2 John W. Gunnison	N. H.	2 P. G. T. Beauregard	La.	2 Henry J. Biddle	Pa.	2 William P. Jones	Large.
	3 Edwin W. Morgan	Pa.	3 Alex. H. Dearborn	N. Y.	3 Robert Q. Butler	Va.	3 Bryant P. Tilden, jr.	Mass.
	4 John Bratt	N. Y.	4 James H. Trapier	S. C.	4 Jeremy F. Gilmer	N. C.	4 William H. Churchill	Large.
	5 Braxton Bragg	N. C.	5 John T. Metcalfe	Miss.	5 Henry W. Halleck	N. Y.	5 Stewart Van Vliet	N. Y.
1838	1 William H. Wright	N. C.	1 Isaac I Stevens	Mass.	1 Paul O. Hebert	La.	1 Zealous B. Tower	Mass.
	2 P. G. T. Beauregard	La.	2 Robert Q. Butler	Va.	2 William P. Jones	Large.	2 Thomas J. Rodman	Ind.
	3 James H. Trapier	S. C.	3 Henry W. Halleck	N. Y.	3 Charles P. Kingsbury	N. C.	3 Henry Wilson	Pa.
	4 Stephen H Campbell	Vt.	4 Jeremy F. Gilmer	N. C.	4 John McNutt	Ohio.	4 Josiah Gorgas	N. Y.
	5 Jeremiah M. Scarritt	Ill.	5 Henry L. Smith	Me.	5 Sylvanus Wilcox	N. Y.	5 Smith Stansbury	Md.
1839	1 Isaac I. Stevens	Mass.	1 Paul O. Hebert	La.	1 Zealous B. Tower	Mass.	1 Henry L. Eustis	Mass.
	2 Robert Q. Butler	Va.	2 William P. Jones	Large.	2 Horatio G. Wright	Conn.	2 John D. Kurtz	D. C.
	3 Henry W. Halleck	N. Y.	3 John McNutt	Ohio.	3 Masillon Harrison	Large.	3 George W. Rains	Ala.
	4 Jeremy F. Gilmer	N. C.	4 Charles P. Kingsbury	N. C.	4 Smith Stansbury	Md.	4 William S. Rosecrans	Ohio.
	5 Henry L. Smith	Me.	5 William Gilham	Ind.	5 Josiah Gorgas	N. Y.	5 Richard W. Johnston	Va.
1840	1 Paul O. Hebert	La.	1 Zealous B. Tower	Mass.	1 John Newton	Va.	1 William B Franklin	Pa.
	2 Charles P. Kingsbury	N. C.	2 Horatio G. Wright	Conn.	2 Henry L. Eustis	Mass.	2 Thomas J. Brereton	Large.
	3 John McNutt	Ohio.	3 Masillon Harrison	Large.	3 George W. Rains	Ala.	3 William F. Raynolds	Ohio.
	4 William P. Jones	Large.	4 Josiah Gorgas	N. Y.	4 John D. Kurtz	D. C.	4 Joseph J. Reynolds	Ind.
	5 William Gilham	Ind.	5 Smith Stansbury	Md.	5 William S. Rosecrans	Ohio.	5 James A. Hardie	Large.
1841	1 Zealous B. Tower	Mass.	1 Henry L. Eustis	Mass.	1 Thomas J. Brereton	Large.	1 William G. Peck	Conn.
	2 Horatio G. Wright	Conn.	2 John Newton	Va.	2 George Deshon	Conn.	2 Joseph H. Whittlesey	N. Y.
	3 Masillon Harrison	Large.	3 John D. Kurtz	D. C.	3 William B. Franklin	Pa.	3 Asher R. Eddy	R. I.
	4 Smith Stansbury	Md.	4 George W. Rains	Ala.	4 William F. Raynolds	Ohio.	4 Samuel Gill	Ky.
	5 Amiel W. Whipple	Mass.	5 William S. Rosecrans	Ohio.	5 Roswell S. Ripley	N. Y.	5 Henry B. Schroeder	Md.

LIST OF CADETS ATTACHED TO THE ARMY REGISTER ANNUALLY—CONTINUED.

1842.

#	FIRST CLASS.	STATE.	SECOND CLASS.	STATE.	THIRD CLASS.	STATE.	FOURTH CLASS.	STATE.
1	Henry L. Eustis	Mass.	Thomas J. Brereton	Large.	William G. Peck	Conn.	Louis Hébert	La.
2	John Newton	Va.	William B. Franklin	Pa.	Samuel Gill	Ky.	Wm. H. C. Whiting	Large.
3	George W. Rains	Ala.	George Deshon	Conn.	Joseph H. Whittlesey	N. Y.	Henry Coppée	Ga.
4	John D. Kurtz	D. C.	William F. Raynolds	Ohio.	Daniel M. Frost	N. Y.	Edward B. Hunt	N. Y.
5	William S. Rosecrans	Ohio.	Roswell S. Ripley	N. Y.	Asher R. Eddy	R. I.	William F. Smith	Vt.

1843.

#	FIRST CLASS.	STATE.	SECOND CLASS.	STATE.	THIRD CLASS.	STATE.	FOURTH CLASS.	STATE.
1	William B. Franklin	Pa.	William G. Peck	Conn.	Wm. H. C. Whiting	Large.	Charles S. Stewart	N. J.
2	George Deshon	Conn.	Joseph H. Whittlesey	N. Y.	Louis Hébert	La.	Charles E. Blunt	Large.
3	Thomas J. Brereton	Large.	Francis J. Thomas	Md.	Edward B. Hunt	N. Y.	George B. McClellan	Pa.
4	John H. Grelaud	Pa.	Samuel Gill	Ky.	William F. Smith	Vt.	Francis T. Bryan	N. C.
5	William F. Raynolds	Ohio.	Daniel M. Frost	N. Y.	Henry Coppée	Ga.	Jesse L. Reno	Pa.

1844.

#	FIRST CLASS.	STATE.	SECOND CLASS.	STATE.	THIRD CLASS.	STATE.	FOURTH CLASS.	STATE.
1	William G. Peck	Conn.	Wm. H. C. Whiting	Large.	Charles S. Stewart	N. J.	Julian McAllister	Large.
2	Joseph H. Whittlesey	N. Y.	Louis Hébert	La.	Charles E. Blunt	Large.	John C. Symmes	Ohio.
3	Samuel Gill	Ky.	Edward B. Hunt	N. Y.	George B. McClellan	Pa.	Daniel T. Van Buren	N. Y.
4	Daniel M. Frost	N. Y.	William F. Smith	Vt.	John G. Foster	N. H.	Daniel Beltzhoover	Miss.
5	Asher R. Eddy	R. I.	Josiah H. Carlisle	Me.	Francis T. Bryan	N. C.	John Hamilton	Ind.

1845.

#	FIRST CLASS.	STATE.	SECOND CLASS.	STATE.	THIRD CLASS.	STATE.	FOURTH CLASS.	STATE.
1	Wm. H. C. Whiting	Large.	Charles S. Stewart	N. J.	John C. Symmes	Ohio.	William P. Trowbridge	Mich.
2	Edward B. Hunt	N. Y.	Charles E. Blunt	Large.	John Hamilton	Ind.	Andrew J. Donelson	Tenn.
3	Louis Hébert	La.	John G. Foster	N. H.	Julian McAllister	Large.	Nathaniel Michler, jr.	Pa.
4	William F. Smith	Vt.	George B. McClellan	Pa.	Daniel T. Van Buren	N. Y.	James Holmes	N. C.
5	Thomas J. Wood	Ky.	George H. Derby	Mass.	Joseph J. Woods	Ohio.	Walter H. Stevens	N. Y.

1846.

#	FIRST CLASS.	STATE.	SECOND CLASS.	STATE.	THIRD CLASS.	STATE.	FOURTH CLASS.	STATE.
1	Charles S. Stewart	N. J.	John C. Symmes	Ohio.	Wm. P. Trowbridge	Mich.	John G. Parke	Pa.
2	George B. McClellan	Pa.	John Hamilton	Ind.	Walter H. Stevens	N. Y.	David C. Bolles	Ohio.
3	Charles E. Blunt	Large.	Samuel Chalfin	Ill.	Andrew J. Donelson	Tenn.	Quincy A. Gillmore	Ohio.
4	John G. Foster	N. H.	Daniel T. Van Buren	N. Y.	Nathaniel Michler, jr.	Pa.	Stephen V. Benét	Fla.
5	Edm. L. F. Hardcastle	Md.	Julian McAllister	Large.	Robert S. Williamson	N. J.	Edward R. Platt	Vt.

LIST OF CADETS ATTACHED TO THE ARMY REGISTER ANNUALLY—CONTINUED.

Year		FIRST CLASS.	STATE.	SECOND CLASS.	STATE.	THIRD CLASS.	STATE.	FOURTH CLASS.	STATE.
1847.	1	John C. Symmes	Ohio.	Wm. P. Trowbridge	Mich.	John G. Parke	Pa.	Frederic E. Prime	N. Y.
	2	John Hamilton	Ind.	James C. Duane	N. Y	Quincy A. Gillmore	Ohio.	Lucius M. Walker	Large.
	3	Joseph J. Woods	Ohio.	Robert S. Williamson	N. J.	Stephen V. Benét	Fla.	Powell T. Wyman	Mass.
	4	Julian McAllister	Large.	Walter H. Stevens	N. Y.	David C. Bolles	Ohio.	Silas Crispin	Pa.
	5	George W. Hazzard	Ind.	Andrew J. Donelson	Tenn.	Thomas J. Haines	N. H.	Joseph H. Wheelock	Mass.
1848.	1	William P. Trowbridge	Mich.	Quincy A. Gillmore	Ohio.	Frederic E. Prime	N. Y.	George L. Andrews	Mass.
	2	Andrew J. Donelson	Tenn.	John G. Parke	Pa.	Gouverneur K. Warren	N. Y.	George T. Balch	Ohio.
	3	James C. Duane	Pa.	Stephen V. Benét	Fla.	Silas Crispin	Pa.	James St. C. Morton	Pa.
	4	Walter H. Stevens	N. Y.	Johnson K. Duncan	Ohio.	Powell T. Wyman	Mass.	Alexander Piper	Pa.
	5	Robert S. Williamson	N. J.	Thomas J. Haines	N. H.	Cuvier Grover	Me.	William T. Welcker	Tenn.
1849.	1	Quincy A. Gillmore	Ohio.	Gouverneur K. Warren	N. Y.	George L. Andrews	Mass.	George H. Mendell	Pa.
	2	John G. Parke	Pa.	Silas Crispin	Pa.	James St. C. Morton	Pa.	George B. Anderson	N. C.
	3	Stephen V. Benét	Fla.	Frederic E. Prime	N. Y.	James Thompson	N. Y.	Joseph C. Ives	Conn.
	4	Thomas J. Haines	N. H.	Achilles Bowen	Tenn.	Alexander Piper	Pa.	Newton F. Alexander	Tenn.
	5	Johnson K. Duncan	Ohio.	Cuvier Grover	Me.	George T. Balch	Ohio.	Thomas L. Casey	Large.
1850.	1	Frederic E. Prime	N. Y.	George L. Andrews	Mass.	Thomas L. Casey	Large.	William P. Craighill	Va.
	2	Gouverneur K. Warren	N. Y.	James St. C. Morton	Pa.	George W. Rose	N. Y.	James B. McPherson	Ohio.
	3	Silas Crispin	Pa.	George T. Balch	Ohio.	Newton F. Alexander	Tenn.	Joshua W. Sill	Ohio.
	4	Cuvier Grover	Me.	William T. Welcker	Tenn.	Joseph C. Ives	Conn.	Francis J. Shunk	Large.
	5	Powell T. Wyman	Mass.	James Thompson	N. Y.	Jerome N. Bonaparte, jr.	Md.	Walworth Jenkins	Large.
1851.	1	George L. Andrews	Mass.	Thomas L. Casey	Large.	James B. McPherson	Ohio.	Oliver O. Howard	Me.
	2	James St. C. Morton	Pa.	Newton F. Alexander	Tenn.	William R. Boggs	Ga.	G. W. Custis Lee	Large.
	3	George T. Balch	Ohio.	Henry W. Slocum	N. Y.	William S. Smith	Ohio.	Henry L. Abbot	Mass.
	4	William T. Welcker	Tenn.	George W. Rose	N. Y.	William P. Craighill	Va.	Thomas H. Ruger	Wis.
	5	Alexander Piper	Pa.	Joseph C. Ives	Conn.	Francis J. Shunk	Large.	Thomas J. Treadwell	N. H.

LIST OF CADETS ATTACHED TO THE ARMY REGISTER ANNUALLY—Continued.

1852.

FIRST CLASS.	STATE.	SECOND CLASS.	STATE.	THIRD CLASS.	STATE.	FOURTH CLASS.	STATE.
1 Thomas L. Casey	Large.	1 James B. McPherson	Ohio.	1 G. W. Custis Lee	Large.	1 Cyrus B. Comstock	Mass.
2 Newton F. Alexander	Tenn.	2 William R. Boggs	Ga.	2 Thomas H. Ruger	Wis.	2 George H. Elliot	Mass.
3 George H. Mendell	Pa.	3 William P. Craighill	Va.	3 John Pegram	Va.	3 Alexander S. Webb	N.Y.
4 George W. Rose	N.Y.	4 Joshua W. Sill	Ohio.	4 Henry L. Abbot	Mass.	4 John V D. Du Bois	N.Y.
5 Joseph C. Ives	Conn.	5 William S. Smith	Ohio.	5 Thomas J. Treadwell	N.H.	5 John R. Church	Ga.

1853.

FIRST CLASS.	STATE.	SECOND CLASS.	STATE.	THIRD CLASS.	STATE.	FOURTH CLASS.	STATE.
1 James B. JcPherson	Ohio.	1 G. W. Custis Lee	Large.	1 Cyrus B. Comstock	Mass.	1 George W. Snyder	N.Y.
2 William P. Craighill	Va.	2 Henry L. Abbot	Mass.	2 George H. Elliot	Mass.	2 David C. Houston	N.Y.
3 Joshua W. Sill	Ohio.	3 Oliver O. Howard	Me.	3 Godfrey Weitzel	Ohio.	3 Miles D. McAlester	Mich.
4 William R. Boggs	Ga.	4 Thomas H. Ruger	Wis.	4 Alexander S. Webb	N.Y.	4 Charles C. Lee	N.C.
5 Francis J. Shunk	Large.	5 John Pegram	Va.	5 Francis L. Vinton	Large.	5 William E. Webster	Conn.

1854.

FIRST CLASS.	STATE.	SECOND CLASS.	STATE.	THIRD CLASS.	STATE.	FOURTH CLASS.	STATE.
1 G. W. Custis Lee	Large.	1 Cyrus B. Comstock	Mass.	1 David C. Houston	N.Y.	1 John C. Palfrey	Mass.
2 Henry L. Abbot	Mass.	2 Cornelius Van Camp	Pa.	2 Miles D. McAlester	Mich.	2 George C. Strong	Mass.
3 Thomas H. Ruger	Wis.	3 Godfrey Weitzel	Ohio.	3 George W. Snyder	N.Y.	3 Richard K. Meade, jr.	Va.
4 Oliver O. Howard	Me.	4 Junius B. Wheeler	N.C.	4 Charles C. Lee	N.C.	4 E. Porter Alexander	Ga.
5 Thomas J. Treadwell	N.H.	5 Ebenezer Gay	N.H.	5 A. Parker Porter	Pa.	5 J. L. Kirby Smith	Large.

1855.

FIRST CLASS.	STATE.	SECOND CLASS.	STATE.	THIRD CLASS.	STATE.	FOURTH CLASS.	STATE.	FIFTH CLASS.	STATE.
1 Cyrus B. Comstock	Mass.	1 David C. Houston	N.Y.	1 John C. Palfrey	Mass.	1 James H. Hallonquist	S.C.	1 William E. Merrill	Large.
2 Godfrey Weitzel	Ohio.	2 George W. Snyder	N.Y.	2 Richard K. Meade, jr.	N.Y.	2 William C. Paine	Mass.	2 Chauncey B. Reese	N.Y.
3 Cornelius Van Camp	Pa.	3 Miles D. McAlester	Mich.	3 E. Porter Alexander	Ga.	3 John S. Saunders	Large.	3 William Wonderly	Md.
4 George H. Elliot	Mass.	4 Charles C. Lee	N.C.	4 J. L. Kirby Smith	Large.	4 Samuel McKee	Utah.	4 Samuel H. Lockett	Ala.
5 Junius B. Wheeler	N.C.	5 Orlando M. Poe	Ohio.	5 George C. Strong	Mass.	5 Moses J. White	Miss.	5 Orlando G Wagner	Pa.

1856.

FIRST CLASS.	STATE.	SECOND CLASS.	STATE.	THIRD CLASS.	STATE.	FOURTH CLASS.	STATE.	FIFTH CLASS.	STATE.
1 George W. Snyder	N.Y.	1 John C. Palfrey	Mass.	1 William C. Palfrey	Mass.	1 William E. Merrill	Mass.	1 Nicolas Bowen	N.Y.
2 David C. Houston	N.Y.	2 Richard K. Meade, jr.	Va.	2 James H. Hallonquist	S.C.	2 Chauncey B. Reese	N.Y.	2 Horace Porter	Pa.
3 Miles D. McAlester	Mich.	3 George C. Strong	Mass.	3 William H. Echols	Ala.	3 Samuel H. Lockett	Ala.	3 Walter McFarland	N.Y.
4 Charles C. Lee	N.C.	4 E. Porter Alexander	Ga.	4 William H. Bell	Pa.	4 Robert F. Beckham	Va.	4 Benj. F. Sloan, jr.	S.C.
5 Henry V. De Hart	Large.	5 Henry M. Robert	Ohio.	5 Moses J. White	Miss.	5 Orlando G. Wagner	Pa.	5 Jas. M Whittemore, jr	Mass.

LIST OF CADETS ATTACHED TO THE ARMY REGISTER ANNUALLY—Continued.

	FIRST CLASS.	STATE.	SECOND CLASS.	STATE.	THIRD CLASS.	STATE.	FOURTH CLASS.	STATE.	FIFTH CLASS.	STATE.
1857.	1 John C. Palfrey	Mass.	1 William C. Paine	Mass.	1 William E. Merrill	N.Y.	1 Walter McFarland	Large.	1 Charles E. Cross	Mass.
	2 Richard K. Meade, jr.	Va.	2 Moses J. White	Miss.	2 Samuel H. Lockett	N.Y.	2 Nicolas Bowen	Ala.	2 Adelbert Ames	Me.
	3 E. Porter Alexander	Ga.	3 Joseph Dixon	Tenn.	3 Charles R. Collins	N.Y.	3 Horace Porter	Pa.	3 Henry W. Kingsbury	N.Y.
	4 Henry M. Robert	Ohio.	4 William H. Echols	Ala.	4 Orlando G. Wagner	Ill.	4 John A. Tardy, jr.	Pa.	4 Samuel N. Benjamin	N.Y.
	5 George C. Strong	Mass.	5 Richard H. Brewer	Md.	5 Chauncey B. Reese	Pa.	5 Jas. M. Whittemore,jr.	N.Y.	5 Henry A. Du Pont	Large.
1858.	1 William C. Paine	Mass.	1 William E. Merrill	Mass.	1 Walter McFarland	Large.	1 Henry A. Du Pont	Large.	1 Arthur H. Dutton	Conn.
	2 Moses J. White	Miss.	2 Samuel H. Lockett	Miss.	2 John A. Tardy, jr.	Ala.	2 Henry W. Kingsbury	N.Y.	2 Francis U. Farquhar	Pa.
	3 Joseph Dixon	Tenn.	3 Charles R. Collins	Tenn.	3 Horace Porter	Pa.	3 Charles E. Cross	Mass.	3 Patrick H. O'Rorke	N.Y.
	4 William H. Echols	Ala.	4 Orlando G. Wagner	Ala.	4 Nicolas Bowen	Pa.	4 Llewellyn G. Hoxton	Large.	4 Charles C. Parsons	Ohio.
	5 John S. Saunders	Large.	5 Chauncey B. Reese	Large.	5 Benj. F. Sloan, jr.	N.Y.	5 Orville E. Babcock	Vt.	5 Richard M. Hill	Large.
1859.	1 William E. Merrill	Mass.	1 John A. Tardy, jr	N.Y.	1 Charles E. Cross	Mass.	1 Arthur H. Dutton	Conn.	1 George Burroughs	Mass.
	2 Samuel H. Lockett	Ala.	2 Walter McFarland	N.Y.	2 Henry A. Du Pont	Large.	2 Francis U. Farquhar.	Pa.	2 Henry S. Wetmore	Ohio.
	3 Charles R. Collins	Pa.	3 Nicolas Bowen	N.Y.	3 Orville E. Babcock	Vt.	3 Clarence Derrick	Large.	3 William A. Marye	Cal.
	4 Chauncey B. Reese	N.Y.	4 Cornelius Hook, jr	Ill.	4 Henry W. Kingsbury.	N.Y.	4 Patrick H. O'Rorke	N.Y.	4 Jasper Myers	Ind.
	5 Orlando G. Wagner	Pa.	5 Horace Porter	Pa.	5 Llewellyn G. Hoxton.	Large.	5 Alfred Mordecai	Large.	5 Ranald S. Mackenzie.	Large.
1860.	1 Walter McFarland	N.Y.	1 Henry A. Du Pont	Large.	1 Patrick H. O'Rorke.	N.Y.	1 Geo. L. Gillespie, jr.	Tenn.	1 Thomas Rowland	Large.
	2 John A. Tardy, jr.	N.Y.	2 Henry W. Kingsbury.	N.Y.	2 Arthur H. Dutton	Conn.	2 Ranald S. Mackenzie	Large.	2 James D. Rabb	Ky.
	3 Horace Porter	N.Y.	3 Orville E. Babcock	Vt.	3 Francis U. Farquhar.	Pa.	3 William A. Marye	Cal.	3 William J. Twining	Ind.
	4 Nicolas Bowen	N.Y.	4 Adelbert Ames	Me.	4 Clarence Derrick	Large.	4 Henry S. Wetmore	Ohio.	4 John R. Meigs	Large.
	5 Theodore Edson	Mass.	5 Emery Upton	N.Y.	5 Daniel W. Flagler	N.Y.	5 Charles R. Suter	Large.	5 Peter S. Michie	Ohio.

	FIRST CLASS—MAY.	STATE.	FIRST CLASS—JUNE.	STATE.	SECOND CLASS—MAY.	STATE.	THIRD CLASS.	STATE.	FOURTH CLASS.	STATE.	FIFTH CLASS.	STATE.
1861.	1 Henry A. Du Pont	Large.	1 Patrick H. O'Rorke	N.Y.	1 Patrick H. O'Rorke	Large.	1 Charles R. Suter	N.Y.	1 Peter S. Michie	Large.	1 Garrett J. Lydecker	N.Y.
	2 Charles E. Cross	Mass.	2 Francis U. Farquhar	Pa.	2 Richard M. Hill	Pa.	2 George Burroughs	Large.	2 James D. Rabb	Mass.	2 Alexander Mackenzie	Ill.
	3 Orville E. Babcock	Vt.	3 Arthur H. Dutton	Conn.	3 Arthur H. Dutton	Conn.	3 George L. Gillespie,jr.	Tenn.	3 John R. Meigs	Large.	3 Arthur H. Burnham	Mass.
	4 Henry W. Kingsbury	N.Y.	4 Clarence Derrick	Large.	4 Francis U. Farquhar	Large.	4 Jared A. Smith	Me.	4 Hurlbut G. Townsend	N.Y.	4 James W. Cuyler	Large.
	5 Adelbert Ames	Me.	5 Daniel W. Flagler	N.Y.	5 Clarence Derrick	Me.	5 John A. Kress	Ind.	5 William J. Twining	Ind.	5 William A. Jones	Ill.

LIST OF CADETS ATTACHED TO THE ARMY REGISTER ANNUALLY—Continued.

	FIRST CLASS.	STATE.	SECOND CLASS.	STATE.	THIRD CLASS.	STATE.	FOURTH CLASS.	STATE.
1862.	1 Ranald S. Mackenzie	Large.	1 John R. Meigs	Large.	1 Garrett J. Lydecker	N. Y.	1 Charles W. Raymond	N. Y.
	2 George L. Gillespie, jr.	Tenn.	2 Peter S. Michie	Ohio.	2 Arthur H. Burnham	Mass.	2 Alfred K. Hamilton	N. H.
	3 George Burroughs	Mass.	3 James D. Rabb	Ky.	3 Alexander Mackenzie	Ill.	3 Micah R. Brown	Mass.
	4 Charles R. Suter	Large.	4 Hurlbut G. Townsend	N. Y.	4 Oswald H. Ernst	Ohio.	4 Alexander M. Miller	Large.
	5 Jared A. Smith	Me.	5 William J. Twining	Ind.	5 Amos Stickney	N. Y.	5 Lewis C. Overman	Large.
1863.	1 John R. Meigs	Large.	1 Arthur H. Burnham	Mass.	1 Charles W. Raymond	N. Y.	1 James Mercur	Pa.
	2 Peter S. Michie	Ohio.	2 Amos Stickney	N. Y.	2 Alexander M. Miller	Large.	2 Benjamin D. Greene	Me.
	3 James D. Rabb	Ky.	3 Garrett J. Lydecker	N. Y.	3 Thomas H. Handbury	Pa.	3 George M. Wheeler	Col. T.
	4 Wm. J. Twining	Ind.	4 Oswald H. Ernst	Ohio.	4 Lewis C. Overman	Large	4 Charles E. L. B. Davis	Conn.
	5 William R. King	N. Y.	5 James W. Cuyler	Large.	5 William H. Chase	Pa.	5 Henry M. Adams	Mass.

MILITARY ACADEMY BAND.

THE Band at the Military Academy, and its professional reputation, date from 1818; its origin and progress, therefore, may be here appropriately introduced The company of "Bombardiers, Sappers, and Miners," raised under the Act of April 29, 1812, had been for many years stationed at West Point. Under the Act of March 2d, 1821, this company was disbanded* on May 31st, following, by the order of the Superintendent; "but the Military Band and martial music belonging to the company, having been enlisted for the service of the Academy, are to be retained." By this order fifteen musicians became attached to, and have ever since been

* Captain Fanning's Company "A," of the Second Artillery, was then ordered to West Point, and there remained until November, 1827, at which time it was relieved by Captain Whiting's Company "F," Fourth Artillery.

On April 28th. 1829, and August 17th following, orders were issued from the Adjutant-General's Office, at Washington, transferring this company to New York, and authorizing the Superintendent of the Military Academy to enlist a number of musicians, artificers, and privates, equal to the full strength of a company of Artillery, who were to be mustered as a detachment from the army, at the Military Academy. The Superintendent was further authorized to appoint a full complement of non-commissioned officers, and to designate an officer among those on duty at the Academy, to command the whole.—[Official Records U. S. M. A.]

enrolled as, the "musicians attached to the companies of cadets."

Section 3 of the Act of April 29th, 1812, provides that the cadets "shall be arranged into companies of non-commissioned officers and privates, according to the directions of the Commandant of Engineers, and be officered from the said corps for the purposes of military instruction ; and that there shall be added to each company of cadets four musicians." As the number of companies into which the corps of cadets was to be divided is not specified by law, the number of musicians was previous to 1821, not determined. By an arrangement made between the Paymaster-General and the Superintendent, a company of Infantry or of Artillery was, selected as the basis of an organization; and on September 9, 1821, twenty musicians, with the pay and emoluments of musicians in the army, were, by authority of the first named officer, attached to the Corps of Cadets.

As the cadets are organized for battalion exercises and instruction into eight companies, at which time the musicians are present, thirty-two musicians are now regarded as the limit, and constitute at present the strength of the Band. Whether this organization be lawful or not, it has been acquiesced in for many years. The musicians are enlisted and paid as soldiers; there being an extra or additional pay, not exceeding five dollars per month, paid those who are skilful, from a fund derived by a monthly tax of twenty-five cents on each cadet.

The Field Music, six drummers and six fifers, are furnished under the authority of the Adjutant-General of the army, bearing date in 1841, also in October, 1847.

The position of "Teacher of Music" is provided by law, the compensation being regulated by the Secretary of War. The names of those who have held this appointment are herewith given:

RICHARD WILLIS, June 16, 1817, to February, 1830. Died.

ALEXANDER KYLE, July 1st, 1830, to December, 1833.

JOSEPH LUCCHESI, March 5, 1834, to November 1, 1840. [Principal Musician.]

JAMES K. KENDALL, November 1, 1840, to February 2, 1843. Resigned.

AUGUSTUS APELLES, March 14, 1843. Present.

The early uniform of the Band, prescribed by the Superintendent, October 20, 1822, was of white cassimere, the collar, sleeves, and skirts being faced with red, with pantaloons of the same white material, bearing a red stripe. The army dress cap, sword, and an upright white feather, with a red top, completed the costume. It was changed in May, 1850, to assimilate with the uniform then adopted throughout the army.

ABSTRACTS OF ALL THE ACTS OF CONGRESS,

UNDER THE PRESENT GOVERNMENT, PROVIDING FOR THE APPOINTMENT OF CADETS IN THE ARMY, AND FOR THE ESTABLISHMENT AND ORGANIZATION OF THE UNITED STATES MILITARY ACADEMY.

CHAPTER XXIV.—ACT OF MAY 9, 1794.—*Organizes a Corps of Artillerists and Engineers.*

SEC. 3.—Provides for four Companies, &c., each Company to have two Cadets, with the pay, clothing, and rations of a Sergeant.*

SEC. 5.—That it shall be the duty of the Secretary of War to provide, at the public expense, under such regulations as shall be directed by the President of the United States, the necessary books, instruments, and apparatus, for the use and benefit of the said Corps.

CHAPTER XXXIII.—ACT OF APRIL 27, 1798.—*Provides for an additional Regiment of Artillerists and Engineers.*

SEC. 1.—Provides for three battalions, each to contain four Companies, and to include two Cadets, with the pay, clothing, and rations of a Sergeant.

SEC. 3.—That the Secretary of War shall provide, at the public expense, under the direction of the President of the United States, all necessary books, instruments, and apparatus, for the use and benefit of the said regiment.

CHAPTER LXXVI.—ACT OF JULY 16, 1798.—*To augment the Army of the United States, and for other purposes.*†

SEC. 6.—Provides, That the monthly pay of Cadets shall be ten dollars, and two rations per day.

SEC. 7.—That the President of the United States be, and he hereby is authorized to appoint a number, not exceeding four, teachers of the arts and sciences necessary for the instruction of the Artillerists and Engineers,

* Chapter LXXVI., Act July 16, 1798, Sec. 6; Chapter XLVIII., Act March 3, 1799, Sec. 3; and Chapter IX., Act March 16, 1802, Secs. 4, 5, and 26—fixing the pay and rations of Cadets.

† Repealed by Act of March 16, 1802, Chapter IX.

who shall be entitled to the monthly pay of fifty dollars, and two rations per day.

CHAPTER XLVIII.—ACT OF MARCH 3, 1799.—*For the better organizing of the Troops of the United States, and for other purposes.**

SEC. 1.—That the troops heretofore authorized, and which hereafter may be authorized to be raised, shall be composed and organized as follows, to wit: A Regiment of Infantry, * * * * * * A Regiment of Cavalry, * * * * * * A Regiment of Artillery, * * * * * * And the Infantry and Cavalry Regiments shall each have ten Cadets, and the Regiment of Artillery shall have thirty-two.

SEC. 3.—The pay of a Cadet of Cavalry shall be ten dollars per month, two rations per day, or an equivalent in money, and six dollars per month for forage when not furnished. All other Cadets ten dollars per month, and two rations per day, or an equivalent in money.

CHAPTER IX.—ACT OF MARCH 16, 1802.—*Fixing the Military Peace Establishment of the United States.*†

SEC. 2.—That the regiment of Artillerists shall consist of * * * * *, and twenty Companies; each Company shall have two Cadets.

SEC. 4.—Fixes the monthly pay of a Cadet at ten dollars.

SEC. 5.—Allows a Cadet two rations, or money in lieu thereof, at the option of the Cadet.

---

* Repealed and supplied by Act of March 16, 1802, Chapter IX.
† See Act of April 29, 1812, Chapter LXXII.

SEC. 26.—That the President of the United States is hereby authorized and empowered, when he shall deem it expedient, to organize and establish a Corps of Engineers, to consist of one Engineer, with the pay, rank, and emoluments of a major; two Assistant Engineers, with the pay, rank, and emoluments of captains; two other Assistant Engineers, with the pay, rank, and emoluments of first lieutenants; two other Assistant Engineers, with the pay, rank, and emoluments of second lieutenants; and ten Cadets, with the pay of sixteen dollars per month, and two rations per day: and the President of the United States is, in like manner, authorized, when he shall deem it proper, to make such promotions in the said Corps, with a view to particular merit, and without regard to rank, so as not to exceed one Colonel, one Lieutenant-Colonel, two Majors, four Captains, four First Lieutenants, four Second Lieutenants, and so as that the number of the whole Corps shall, at no time, exceed twenty officers and Cadets.

SEC. 27.—That the said Corps, when so organized, shall be stationed at West Point, in the State of New York, and shall constitute a Military Academy; and the Engineers, Assistant Engineers, and Cadets of the said Corps, shall be subject, at all times, to do duty in such places, and on such service as the President of the United States shall direct.

SEC. 28.—That the principal Engineer, and in his absence the next in rank, shall have the superintendence of the said Military Academy, under the direction of the President of the United States; and the Secretary of War is hereby authorized, at the public expense,

* * * to procure the necessary books, implements, and apparatus for the use and benefit of the said Institution.

CHAPTER XIII.—ACT OF FEBRUARY 28, 1803.—*In addition to an Act entitled " An Act fixing the Military Peace Establishment of the United States."*

SEC. 2.—Authorizes the President of the United States to appoint one teacher of the French language, and one teacher of Drawing,* to be attached to the Corps of Engineers, whose compensation shall not exceed the pay and emolument of a captain in the line of the army.

SEC. 3.—Authorizes the Commanding Officer of the Corps of Engineers to enlist one artificer and eighteen men, to aid in making practical experiments, and for other purposes.

CHAPTER XLIII.—ACT OF APRIL 12, 1808.—*To raise for a limited time an additional Military Force.*

Provides for raising five regiments of Infantry, one regiment of Riflemen, one regiment of Light Artillery, and one regiment of Light Dragoons.

SEC. 2.—Provides, That the said regiments of Infantry, Riflemen, and Artillery, shall consist of ten companies each, and the regiment of Light Dragoons of eight troops ; and each company to have two Cadets.

CHAPTER XIV.—ACT OF JANUARY 11, 1812.—*To raise an additional Military Force.*

That there be immediately raised ten regiments of

The Teachers of Drawing and French made Professors, Chap. 96. Act of Aug. 8, 1846. Sec. 3.

23

Infantry, two regiments of Artillery, and one regiment of Light Dragoons. * * *

Sec. 2.—Provides that each regiment of Artillery shall have forty Cadets, and the regiment of Cavalry shall have twenty-four Cadets.

Chapter LXXII.—Act of April 29, 1812.—*Making further provision for the Corps of Engineers.**

That there be added to the Corps of Engineers, two captains, two first lieutenants, with the usual pay and emoluments, according to their grades, respectively, and one paymaster, to be taken from the subalterns of Engineers, with the pay and emoluments of a regimental paymaster; and that there be attached to the said Corps, either from the troops now in service, or by new enlistments, as the President of the United States may direct, four sergeants, four corporals, one teacher of music, four musicians, nineteen artificers, and sixty-two men; which non-commissioned officers, musicians, artificers, and men, together with the artificers and men already belonging to the Corps of Engineers, shall be formed into a company, to be styled a Company of Bombardiers, Sappers, and Miners, and be officered from the Corps of Engineers, according as the commanding officer of that Corps may, with the approbation of the President of the United States, direct. And the said non-commissioned officers, musicians, artificers, and men, shall be allowed the same pay and emoluments as are allowed to the non-commissioned officers, musicians, artificers, and men in the regiment of Artillerists.

---

* See Act of March 16, 1802, Chap. 9; and Act of July 5, 1838, Chap. 162.

SEC. 2.—That the Military Academy shall consist of the Corps of Engineers, and the following professors, in addition to the Teachers of the French language and Drawing, already provided,* viz.: one Professor of Natural and Experimental Philosophy, with the pay and emoluments of lieutenant-colonel, if not an officer of the Corps, and if taken from the Corps, then so much in addition to his pay and emoluments as shall equal those of a lieutenant-colonel; one Professor of Mathematics, with the pay and emoluments of a major, if not an officer of the Corps, and if taken from the Corps, then so much in addition to his pay and emoluments as shall equal those of a major; one Professor of the Art of Engineering, in all its branches, with the pay and emoluments of a major, if not an officer of the Corps, and if taken from the Corps, then so much in addition to his pay and emoluments as shall equal those of a major. Each of the foregoing Professors to have an Assistant Professor, which Assistant Professor shall be taken from the most prominent characters of the officers or cadets, and receive the pay and emoluments of captains, and no other pay or emoluments while performing these duties: Provided, that nothing herein contained shall entitle the Academical Staff, as such, to any command in the army separate from the Academy.

SEC. 3.—That the cadets heretofore appointed in the service of the United States, whether of Artillery, Cavalry, Riflemen, or Infantry, or that may in future be appointed as hereinafter provided, shall at no time exceed two hundred and fifty: that they may be attached

---

* Act of Feb. 28, 1803; Chap. 13, Sec. 2

at the discretion of the President of the United States, as students to the Military Academy, and be subject to the established regulations thereof; that they shall be arranged into companies of non-commissioned officers and privates, according to the directions of the Commandant of Engineers, and be officered from the said Corps, for the purposes of military instruction; that there shall be added to each company of cadets four musicians: and the said Corps shall be trained and taught all the duties of a private, non-commissioned officer, and officer, be encamped at least three months of each year, and taught all the duties incident to a regular camp; that the candidates for cadets be not under the age of fourteen nor above the age of twenty-one years; that each cadet, previously to his appointment by the President of the United States, shall be well versed in reading, writing, and arithmetic, and that he shall sign articles, with the consent of his parent or guardian, by which he shall engage to serve five years, unless sooner discharged; and all such cadets shall be entitled to and receive the pay and emoluments now allowed by law to cadets in the Corps of Engineers.

SEC. 4.—That when any cadet shall receive a regular degree from the Academical Staff, after going through all the classes, he shall be considered as among the candidates for a commission in any Corps, according to the duties he may be judged competent to perform; and in case there shall not at the time be a vacancy in such Corps, he may be attached to it at the discretion of the President of the United States, by brevet of the lowest grade, as a supernumerary officer, with the usual pay and emoluments of such grade, until a vacancy shall happen: Provided, That there shall not be more than one supernumerary officer to any one company at the same time.

SEC. 5.—That $25,000 be appropriated for erecting buildings, and for providing an apparatus, a library, and all necessary implements, and for such contingent expenses as may be necessary and proper, in the judgment of the President of the United States, for such an institution.

SEC. 6.—That so much of the twenty-sixth section of the Act entitled "An Act fixing the Military Peace Establishment, passed the sixteenth day of March, 1802," as confines the selection of the Commander of the Corps of Engineers to the said corps, be, and the same is hereby repealed.

CHAPTER LXXIX.—ACT OF MARCH 3, 1815.—*Fixing the Military Peace Establishment of the United States.**

SEC. 1.—That the Military Peace Establishment of the United States shall consist of such proportions of Artillery, Infantry, and Riflemen, not exceeding, in the whole, ten thousand men, as the President of the United States shall judge proper, and that the Corps of Engineers, as at present established, be retained.

CHAPTER LXI.—ACT OF APRIL 14, 1818.—*Regulating the Staff of the Army.*

SEC. 2.— * * * * [Provides] One Chaplain to be stationed at the Military Academy at West Point, who shall also be Professor of Geography, History, and

* This act, and such intervening acts as relate to organization, are superseded by the provisions of March 2, 1821, Chap. 13.

Ethics, with the pay and emoluments allowed the Professor of Mathematics.

CHAPTER XIII.—ACT OF MARCH 2, 1821.—*To reduce and fix the Military Peace Establishment of the United States.*

SEC. 3.—That the Corps of Engineers (Bombardiers excepted), and the Topographical Engineers, and their Assistants, shall be retained in the service, as at present organized.*

CHAPTER CLXII.—ACT OF JULY 5, 1838.—*To increase the present Military Establishment of the United States, and for other purposes.*

SEC. 2.—That the President of the United States be, and he is hereby authorized to add to the Corps of Engineers,† whenever he may deem it expedient to increase the same, one lieutenant-colonel, two majors, six captains, six first and six second lieutenants; and that the pay and emoluments of the said Corps shall be the same as those allowed to the officers of the regiment of Dragoons.

SEC. 3.—That so much of the Act‡ passed the twenty-ninth day of April, one thousand eight hundred and twelve, entitled "An Act making further provision for the Corps of Engineers," as provides that one paymaster shall be taken from the subalterns of the Corps of Engineers, be, and the same is hereby repealed; and that the

* Act of March 16, 1802, Chap. 9, Secs. 26 and 27.

† Added, one company of engineer soldiers, by Act of May 15, 1846, Chap. 21; by Act of August 3,1861, Chap. 42, Secs. 3 and 4, three first and three second lieutenants, and three companies of soldiers; and by Act of August 6, 1861, Chap. 57, two lieutenant-colonels and four majors.

‡ Chap. 72, Sec. 1.

paymaster so authorized and provided be attached to the pay department, and be in every respect, placed on the footing of other paymasters of the Army.

SEC. 19.—That an additional* Professor be appointed to instruct in the studies of Chemistry, Mineralogy, and Geology, with the pay and emoluments now allowed to the Professor of Mathematics; and that the Secretary of War may assign to the said Professor an Assistant, to be taken from the officers of the line or Cadets; which Assistant Professor will receive the pay and emoluments allowed to other Assistant Professors.

SEC. 28.—That the term for which Cadets hereafter admitted into the Military Academy at West Point shall engage to serve, be, and the same is hereby, increased to †eight years, unless sooner discharged.

CHAPTER L.—ACT OF JULY 20, 1840.—*To provide for the support of the Military Academy for the year eighteen hundred and forty.*

SEC. 2.—That the Commander of the Corps of Cadets at the Military Academy shall be either the instructor of infantry tactics, of cavalry and artillery tactics, or of practical engineering, and that his pay and emoluments shall in no case be less than the compensation allowed by law to the Professor of Mathematics; and that the pay and emoluments of the Instructors in these branches shall in no case be less than is allowed by law to the Assistant Professor of Mathematics.

---

* Act of April 29, 1812, Chap. 72, for Professors and Assistants, and pay of.
† Five years, by Act of April 29, 1812, Chap. 72, Sec. 3.

SEC. 3.—That the Assistant Professor of Ethics shall be allowed the same compensation as is now allowed by law to the other Assistant Professors in the institution.

CHAPTER CLXXXVI.—ACT OF AUGUST 23, 1842.—*Respecting the Organization of the Army, and for other purposes.*

SEC. 6.—That the rations authorized to be allowed to a Brigadier while Commander-in-Chief, and to each officer while commanding a separate post, by the Act of March third, seventeen hundred and ninety-seven, and to the commanding officers of each separate post, by the Act of March sixteen, eighteen hundred and two, shall hereafter be allowed to the following officers and no others : to the Major-General commanding the Army, and to every officer commanding in chief a separate army, actually in the field; to the Generals commanding the Eastern and Western geographical divisions; to the Colonels or other officers commanding military geographical departments; *to the Commandant of each permanent or fixed post, garrisoned with troops, including the Superintendent of the Military Academy at West Point, who is regarded as the Commandant of that post.**

CHAPTER LII.—ACT OF MARCH 1, 1843.—*Making Appropriations for the support of the Army and of the Military Academy, &c., &c., for the fiscal year ending the thirtieth day of June, one thousand eight hundred and forty-four.*

SEC. 2.— * * * * Provided, That hereafter, in all cases of appointments of Cadets to the West Point

* The *italicized* repealed by Act of Aug. 3, 1861, Chap. 42, Sec. 19.

Academy, the individual selected shall be an actual resident of the Congressional district of the State or Territory, or District of Columbia, from which the appointment purports to be made : And provided further, That the number of Cadets by appointments hereafter to be made, shall be limited to the number of the representatives and delegates in Congress, and one for the District of Columbia, and that each Congressional and Territorial district and District of Columbia shall be entitled to have one Cadet at the said Academy: Provided, That nothing in this section shall prevent the appointment of an additional number of Cadets not exceeding ten to be appointed at large, without being confined to a selection by Congressional districts.* *
* * * Provided, That hereafter there shall not be a board of visitors appointed to visit the West Point Academy, unless otherwise ordered by Congress.†

CHAPTER XLVII.—ACT OF MARCH 3, 1845.—*Making Appropriations for the support of the Military Academy, for the year ending the thirtieth of June, eighteen hundred and forty-six.*

SEC. 2.—That from and after the thirtieth June, eighteen hundred and forty-five, the pay of a Cadet shall be twenty-four dollars per month, in lieu of the present pay and emoluments.‡

* See Act of August 3, 1861, Chap. 42, Sec. 8, for conditions of re-admission after discharge, &c.

† Re-established by Act of Aug. 8, 1846, Chap. 96, Sec. 2.

‡ $16 a month and two rations per day, Chap. 9, Act of March 16, 1802, Sec. 26; increased to $30 per month, Chap. 119, Act of March 3, 1857.

CHAPTER XXI.—ACT OF MAY 15, 1846.—*For the Organization of a Company of Sappers, Miners, and Pontoniers.*

SEC. 4.—That the said engineer company shall be attached to and compose a part of the Corps* of Engineers, and be officered by officers of that corps, as at present organized; they shall be instructed in and perform all the duties of sappers, miners, and pontoniers, and shall aid in giving practical instructions in these branches at the Military Academy, &c.

CHAPTER XCVI.—ACT OF AUGUST 8, 1846.—*Making Appropriations for the support of the Military Academy, for the year ending on the thirtieth of June, eighteen hundred and forty-seven.*

SEC. 2.—That the President be authorized to appoint a board of visitors, to attend the annual examination of the Military Academy, whose duty it shall be to report to the Secretary of War, for the information of Congress, at the commencement of the next succeeding session, the actual state of the discipline, instruction, police administration, fiscal affairs, and other concerns, of the Institution: Provided, That the whole number of visitors each year shall not exceed the half of the number of States in the Union; and that they shall be selected, alternately, from every second State, each member being a *bonâ fide* resident citizen of the State from which he shall be appointed; that not less than six members shall be taken from among officers actually serving in the militia; and that a second member shall not be taken

* Three more companies added to the Corps by Act of Aug. 3, 1861, Chap. 42, Sec. 4.

from any Congressional district, until every other district in the State shall have supplied a member : Provided, further, That no compensation shall be made to said members beyond the payment of their expenses for board and lodging while at the Military Academy, and an allowance, not to exceed eight cents per mile, for travelling by the shortest mail route from their respective homes to the Academy, and back to their homes.

SEC. 3.—That the Teacher of Drawing, and the first Teacher of French, at the Military Academy, shall hereafter be, respectively, Professor of Drawing, and Professor of the French Language.*

CHAPTER LII.—ACT OF FEBRUARY 19, 1849.—*Making Appropriations for the support of the Military Academy, for the year ending the thirtieth of June, one thousand eight hundred and fifty.*

SEC. 1.—* * * All Professors shall be entitled to the same amount of forage which is allowed to officers of the rank to which their rank is assimilated.

CHAPTER LIV.—ACT OF SEPTEMBER 16, 1850.—*Making Appropriations for the support of the Military Academy, for the year ending the thirtieth of June, one thousand eight hundred and fifty-one.*

SEC. 1.— * * * Provided, That hereafter, in lieu of the pay proper, ordinary rations, forage, and servants, heretofore received under the provisions of the Act of April twelfth [twenty-ninth], eighteen hundred and †twelve, the Professors of Engineers, Philosophy, Math-

* Office created Feb. 28, 1803, Chap. 13, Sec. 2. See Chap. 22, Act of March 3, 1851.

† Chap. 72; and see Chap. 22, March 3, 1851, which is a substitute for this Section. The compensation of all Professors is now made $2,240 per annum.

ematics, Ethics, and Chemistry, shall be entitled to receive two thousand dollars each per annum; and the Professors of Drawing and French, fifteen hundred dollars each per annum.

Chapter LXXVIII.—Act of September 28, 1850.— *Making Appropriations for the support of the Army, for the year ending the thirtieth of June, one thousand eight hundred and fifty-one.*

Sec. 1.—* * * Provided, That the pay and emoluments of the Superintendent of the United States Military Academy shall in no case be less than the pay and emoluments of the Professor of Natural and Experimental Philosophy.*

Chapter XXII.—Act of March 3, 1851.—*Making Appropriations for the support of the Military Academy, for the year ending the thirtieth of June, one thousand eight hundred and fifty-two.*

Sec. 1.—* * * Provided, That hereafter, in lieu of the pay proper, ordinary rations, forage, and servants, heretofore received under the provisions of the Act of April twelfth [twenty-ninth], eighteen hundred and †twelve, the Professors of Engineers, Philosophy, Mathematics, Ethics, and Chemistry, shall be entitled to receive two thousand dollars‡ each, per annum, and the Professors of Drawing and French,§ fifteen hundred dol-

---

* $2,000 per annum.

† Chap. 72.

‡ All Professors now receive $2,240 per annum.

§ Established Feb. 28, 1803, Chap. 13, Sec. 2, and made Professors by Act of Aug. 8, 1846, Chap. 96, Sec. 3.

lars each* per annum : And that the Adjutant of the Military Academy shall hereafter be entitled to receive the same pay and allowances as an Adjutant of a regiment of dragoons.

CHAPTER LXXXI.—ACT OF AUGUST 6, 1852.—*Making Appropriations for the support of the Military Academy, for the year ending the thirtieth of June, one thousand eight hundred and fifty-three, and for other purposes.*

SEC. 2.—That hereafter the Assistant Professors of French and Drawing† shall receive the pay and emoluments allowed to other Assistant Professors.

CHAPTER LIV.—ACT OF MAY 10, 1854.—*Making Appropriations for the support of the Military Academy, for the year ending the thirtieth of June, one thousand eight hundred and fifty-five.*

SEC. 2.—That the compensation of Master of the Sword be twelve hundred dollars per annum.‡

CHAPTER CCVIII.—ACT OF MARCH 3, 1855.—*Making Appropriations for the support of the Military Academy, for the year ending the thirtieth of June, one thousand eight hundred and fifty-six.*

SEC. 2.—That hereafter the yearly allowance of the Professor of French and Spanish, and of the Professor of Drawing, shall be the same as is now allowed§ to the other professors.

---

* Same salary as the other Professors ; by Act of March 3, 1855, Chap. 208, Sec. 2.

† Pay and emoluments of Captains of Cavalry.

‡ $800 before, and now $1,500, by Act of Feb. 16, 1857, Chap. 45, Sec. 3.

§ $2,000 by Act of March 3, 1851, Chap. 22 ; now $2,240 per annum.

354   HISTORY OF WEST POINT.

CHAPTER XIX.—ACT OF APRIL 23, 1856.—*Making Appropriations for the support of the Military Academy, for the year ending the thirtieth of June, eighteen hundred and fifty-seven.*

SEC. 2.—That the amounts disbursed, or that may be disbursed, out of moneys appropriated for the support of the Military Academy by the Acts of May tenth, eighteen hundred and fifty-four, and March third, eighteen hundred and fifty-five, in payment of additional compensation to the librarian, assistant librarian, and certain enlisted men at that post, be passed to the credit of the disbursing officer: Provided, That the additional pay to said librarian, and assistant librarian, shall not exceed the sum of one hundred and twenty dollars each per annum; and to the non-commissioned officer in charge of mechanics and other labor at the post, the soldier acting as clerk in the Adjutant's office, and the four enlisted men in the philosophical and chemical departments, and lithographic office, not exceeding the sum of fifty dollars each per annum: and that a like measure of compensation be hereby authorized to be allowed hereafter for said services respectively.

SEC. 3.—That the Secretary of the Senate furnish annually the library of the Military Academy at West Point, with a copy of all documents published by the Senate.

CHAPTER XLV.—ACT OF FEB. 16, 1857.—*Making Appropriations for the support of the Military Academy, for the year ending the thirtieth of June, eighteen hundred and fifty-eight.*

SEC. 2.—That there shall be appointed at the Military Academy, in addition to the Professors authorized by the existing laws, a Professor of Spanish, at a salary of two thousand dollars* per annum.

SEC. 3.—That the compensation of the Master of the Sword be fifteen hundred dollars† per annum, with fuel and quarters.

CHAPTER CXIX.—ACT OF MARCH 3, 1857.—*To increase the pay of the Cadets at the West Point Academy.*

That the pay of the Cadets at the Military Academy at West Point shall hereafter be thirty dollars‡ per month.

SEC. 2.—That this act shall take effect from and after the passage thereof.

CHAPTER CLVI.—ACT OF JUNE 12, 1858.—*Making Appropriations for the support of the Army, for the year ending the thirtieth June, eighteen hundred and fifty-nine.*

SEC. 1.—* * * * Provided, That the Superintendent of the Military Academy, while serving as such by appointment of the President, shall have the local rank, the pay, and allowances of a Colonel of Engineers;§ that the Commandant of the Corps of Cadets at the Military Academy, while serving as such by appointment of the President, shall have the local rank, the pay, and allowances of a Lieutenant-Colonel of Engineers,‖ and, besides his other duties, shall be charged

---

* Now $2,240 per annum.

† Formerly $800, and by Act of May 10, 1854, Chap. 54, Sec. 2, $1,200.

‡ By Chap. 9, Act of March 16, 1802, Sec. 26, it was $16 per month, and two rations per day; by Chap. 47, Act of March 3, 1845, Sec. 2, it was fixed to $24 per month.

§ $235 per month. ‖ $211 per month.

with the duty of instructor in the tactics of the three arms at said Academy; and that the senior assistant instructor in each of the arms of service, viz.: of Artillery, Cavalry, and Infantry, shall severally receive the pay and allowances of the Assistant Professor of Mathematics.*

CHAPTER CLXIII.—ACT OF JUNE 21, 1860.—*Making Appropriations for the support of the Army, for the year ending thirtieth June, one thousand eight hundred and sixty-one.*

SEC. 8.—That upon the passage of this act, or as soon thereafter as practicable, a Commission shall be appointed in the manner hereinafter designated, to consist of two Senators, two members of the House of Representatives, and two officers of the army, which Commission shall examine into the organization, system of discipline, and course of instruction of the United States Military Academy, with a view to ascertain what modification or changes, if any, are desirable, in order that the Academy shall best accomplish the object of its establishment. That the said Commission shall report† the result of its examination to the President of the Senate and Speaker of the House of Representatives. That the Commissioners from the Senate shall be appointed by the President of the Senate, those from the House of Representatives by the Speaker of the House, and those from the Army by the President of the United States.

[SEC. 9.—$15,000 appropriated to defray the expenses of the Commission.]

---

* $137.50 per month. † See pages 247, 248.

CHAPTER XLII.—ACT OF AUGUST 3, 1861.—*Providing for the better Organization of the Military Establishment.*

SEC. 3.—That there shall be added to the Corps of Engineers* three first and three second lieutenants, to be promoted thereto in accordance with the existing laws and regulations. * * * And there shall be added to the Ordnance Department of the United States Army, * * * six second lieutenants * * * [which shall be selected] from the graduates of the United States Military Academy, by transfers from the Engineers, Topographical Engineers, or the Artillery.

SEC. 4.—That there shall be added to the corps of Engineers three companies of engineer soldiers, to be commanded by appropriate officers of said corps, to have the same pay and rations, clothing, and other allowances, and be entitled to the same benefits, in every respect, as the company created by the act for the organization of a company of sappers and miners and pontoniers, approved May sixteen (15), eighteen hundred and forty-six.† The said three companies shall be subject to the rules and articles of war; shall be recruited in the same manner and with the same limitation; shall be instructed in and perform the same duties, and be liable to serve in the same way, and shall have their vehicles, pontoons, tools, implements, arms, and other supplies regulated in the same manner as the existing engineer company; and each of the four companies of engineer soldiers shall hereafter be composed of ten sergeants, ten corporals, two musicians, sixty-four privates of the first class, or artificers, and sixty-four privates of the second class, in all one hundred and fifty men each.

Sec. 8.—That no Cadet who has been or shall hereafter be reported as deficient, either in conduct or studies, and recommended to be discharged from the Academy, shall be returned or reappointed, or appointed to any place in the Army before his class shall have left the Academy and received their commissions, unless upon the recommendation of the Academic Board of the Academy: Provided, That all Cadets now in the service, or hereafter entering the Military Academy at West Point, shall be called on to take and subscribe the following oath: "I, A. B., do solemnly swear that I will support the Constitution of the United States, and bear true allegiance to the National Government; that I will maintain and defend the sovereignty of the United States paramount to any and all allegiance, sovereignty, or fealty I may owe to any State, county, or country whatsoever; and that I will at all times obey the legal orders of my superior officers, and the rules and articles governing the armies of the United States." And any Cadet or candidate for admission who shall refuse to take this oath shall be dismissed from the service.

Sec. 19.—That so much of the sixth section of the Act of August 23, 1842,* as allows additional or double rations to the commandant of each permanent or fixed post garrisoned with troops, be, and the same is hereby repealed.

---

* Chap. 186, which included the Superintendent of the Military Academy at West Point as the Commandant of that post.

CHAPTER LVII.—ACT OF AUGUST 6, 1861.—*To promote the efficiency of the Engineer and Topographical Engineer Corps, and for other purposes.*

SEC. 1.—That there shall be added to each of the Corps of Engineers and Topographical Engineers, by regular promotion of their present officers, two lieutenant-colonels, and four majors.*

CHAPTER LVIII.—ACT OF AUGUST 6, 1861.—*To authorize an increase in the Corps of Engineers and Topographical Engineers.*

[The Act preceding this one has five sections, and the latter has three sections, which are in the same words as sections 1, 2, and 4 of the preceding one.]

Under the Act of July 2, 1862, the following oath for the Cadets was substituted for that heretofore taken by the cadets.

CHAPTER CXXVIII.—ACT OF JULY 2, 1862.—*To prescribe an Oath of Office, and for other purposes.*

That hereafter every person elected or appointed to any office of honor or profit under the Government of the United States, either in the civil, military, or naval departments of the public service, excepting the President of the United States, shall, before entering upon the duties of such office, and before being entitled to any of the salary or other emoluments thereof, take and subscribe the following oath or affirmation: "I, A. B., do solemnly swear (or affirm) that I have never voluntarily borne arms against the United States

* See Chap. 162, July 5, 1838, Sec. 2.

since I have been a citizen thereof; that I have voluntarily given no aid, countenance, counsel, or encouragement to persons engaged in armed hostility thereto; that I have neither sought nor accepted, nor attempted to exercise, the functions of any office whatever under any authority or pretended authority in hostility to the United States; that I have not yielded a voluntary support to any pretended government, authority, power, or constitution within the United States, hostile or inimical thereto. And I do further swear (or affirm) that, to the best of my knowledge and ability, I will support and defend the Constitution of the United States against all enemies, foreign and domestic; that I will bear true faith and allegiance to the same ; that I take this obligation freely, without any mental reservation or purpose of evasion, and that I will well and faithfully discharge the duties of the office on which I am about to enter, so help me God ;" which said oath, so taken and signed, shall be preserved among the files of the Court, House of Congress, or Department to which the said office may appertain. And any person who shall falsely take the said oath shall be guilty of perjury, and on conviction, in addition to the penalties now prescribed for that offence, shall be deprived of his office, and rendered incapable forever after of holding any office or place under the United States.

CHAPTER   .—ACT OF MARCH 3, 1863.—*To promote the efficiency of the Corps of Engineers, and of the Ordnance Department, and for other purposes.*

That the Corps of Topographical Engineers, as a distinct branch of the army, is hereby abolished, and from and after the passage of this Act is merged into the Corps of Engineers, which shall have the following organization, viz: one Chief Engineer, with the rank, pay, and emoluments of a brigadier-general; four colonels; ten lieutenant-colonels; twenty majors; thirty captains; thirty first lieutenants, and ten second lieutenants.

SEC. 2.—That the general officer provided by the first section of this Act, shall be selected from the Corps of Engineers as therein established; and that officers of all lower grades shall take rank according to their respective dates of commission in the existing Corps of Engineers, or Corps of Topographical Engineers.

SEC. 3.—That no officer of the Corps of Engineers below the rank of a field officer shall hereafter be promoted to a higher grade before having passed a satisfactory examination before a board of three engineers senior to him in rank; and should the officer fail at said examination, shall be suspended from promotion from (for) one year, when he shall be re-examined, and upon a second failure shall be dropped by the President from the army.

SEC. 12.—That the increase of rank of officers, and in the number of officers provided for in this Act, shall continue only during the existence of the present rebellion; and thereafter the several officers promoted under this Act shall have the respective rank they would have had if this Act had not passed, and the number shall be reduced by the President to the number authorized by law prior to the passage of this Act.

MILITARY EDUCATION IN EUROPE.

The general nature and extent of the military education most suitable to the officers of our Army, arising from the peculiar condition of our country and its military system, have been already indicated. With this in view, it may be well to examine the systems of military education in Europe, and to compare them with our own. The following account of the military schools of Europe is taken almost wholly from the report of the British Commissioners appointed to consider the best mode of reorganizing the English system of training officers for the scientific corps :

"Among the European systems of military education, that of France is pre-eminent. The stimulating principle of competition extends throughout the whole system ; it exists in the appointment of the student, in his progress through the preliminary schools, in his transfer to the higher schools, in his promotion to the army, and in his advancement in his subsequent career.

" The French army is officered partly from the military schools, and partly by promotion from the ranks. The proportions established by law, are one-third of the commissions from the military schools, one-third from the ranks of the army, and the remaining third at the discretion of the Emperor.

" In practice, two-thirds of the officers of engineers and artillery are taken from the Polytechnic School, and one-third from the ranks. All the officers of the Staff Corps are taken from the School of the Staff. One-third of the officers of infantry and cavalry are taken from St. Cyr, and two-thirds are promoted from the ranks. Promotion in the army is partly by seniority and partly by selection, to the rank of major. Above the rank of major promotion is entirely by selection.

" Admission to the military schools of France can only be gained through a public competitive examination by those who have received the degree of Bachelor of Science from the Lycées, or public schools, and from the orphan school of La Flèche.

" A powerful influence has thus been exercised upon the character of education in France. The importance of certain studies has been gradually reduced; while those of a scientific character, entering more directly into the pursuits of life, have been constantly elevated.

" The two great elementary military schools are the School of St. Cyr and the Polytechnic School. These, as well as the other military schools, are under the charge of the Minister of War, with whom the authorities of the schools are in direct communication. Commissions in the infantry, cavalry, and marines, can only be obtained by service in the ranks of the army, or by passing successfully through the School of St. Cyr, admittance to which is gained by the competitive examination already referred to.

"Entire or partial support is given by the government

to those presenting evidence of the necessity of such aid, while those who are able, pay for their education. Students from the orphan school of La Flèche, where the sons of officers wounded or killed in the service receive a gratuitous education, are maintained in the same manner."

THE SPECIAL MILITARY SCHOOL OF ST. CYR.

The School of St. Cyr was established in 1803.

" The course of study lasts two years; the usual number of cadets in time of peace is five, or, at the utmost, six hundred; the admission is by competitive examination, open to all youths, French by birth or by naturalization, who, on the 1st of January preceding their candidature, were not less than sixteen and not more than twenty years old. To this examination are also admitted soldiers in the ranks between twenty and twenty-five years of age, who, at the date of its commencement, have been actually in service in their regiments for two years.

" A board of examiners passes through France once every year, and examines all who present themselves having the prescribed qualifications. All the candidates must have taken the usual degree which terminates the task at the Lycées.

" A list of such candidates as are found eligible for admission to St. Cyr is submitted to the Minister of War.

" Those who succeed in the examination and are admitted, take an engagement to serve seven years, either in the cavalry or infantry, and are thus under the obligation—if they are judged incompetent, at the close of their two years' stay at the school, to receive a commission—to enter and serve as common soldiers. The two years of their stay at the school counts as a part of their service.

"Twenty-seven, or sometimes a greater number, are annually, at the close of their second year of study, placed in competition with twenty-five candidates from the second lieutenants belonging to the army, if so many are forthcoming, for admission to the Staff School at Paris.

"Young men intended for the cavalry are instructed in infantry and artillery movements and drill, just as those intended for the infantry are taught riding, and receive instruction in cavalry as well as artillery drill and movements.

"It is during the second year of their stay they receive most instruction in the arms of the service to which they are not destined, and this, it is said, is a most important part of their instruction. 'It is this that made it practicable, for example, in the Crimea, to find among the old *élèves* of St. Cyr, officers fit for the artillery, the engineers, the staff; and for general officers, of course, it is of the greatest advantage to have known from actual study something of every branch.'

"One lesson weekly is given in drawing, in order to render the students expert in landscape and military drawing, with the pencil, pen, and brush.

"Mathematics is not taught in either yearly course at St. Cyr.

"The students execute certain works, such as the

making of fascines, gabions, saucissons; repair of revetments of batteries; platforms; setting the profiles, defilement, and construction of a field-work; different kinds of sap; plan and establishment of a camp for a battalion of infantry, &c.

" They are practically taught artillery drill, with field and siege guns; practice with artillery; repair of siege batteries; bridges of boats or rafts.

" Ten lectures allowed for the course of military legislation have for their object the explanation of the principles, practice, and regulations relating to military laws, and their connection with the civil laws that affect military men.

" Twelve lectures are given on what is called military administration, relating to the interior economy of a company, and to the various matters appertaining to the soldier's messing, mode of payment, necessaries, equipment, lodging, &c.

" In the practical exercises, the students make an attack or defence of a work, or of a system of field-works, during their course of fortification; or of a house, farm, village, in the immediate vicinity of the school; or make the passage of a river.

" The examinations at the end of the first year take place under the superintendence of the director and assistant director of studies.

" The pupil's position is determined, as at the Polytechnic, partly by the marks gained at the examination, partly by those he has obtained during his previous studies.

"Any student, whose credit is less than the minimum allowed for any branch of study, is retained during the vacation and re-examined before the recommencement of the course. If still deficient, he is reported to the Minister of War for expulsion, unless there is an especial ground for excuse, such as sickness. Irregularity of conduct is also made a ground for exclusion from the school, and a system of demerit marks is established. The demerit of a student has an influence upon his class standing.

" The classification in the order of merit depends upon the total amount of the sum of the numerical marks or credit obtained by each student in every branch of study or instruction.

" A list of the names of those students who are found qualified for the rank of second lieutenant, is sent to the Minister of War; and a second list is also sent, containing the names of those students that have, when subjected to a second or revised examination, been pronounced by the jury, before whom they were re-examined, as qualified.

" Those whose names appear in the first list are permitted to choose, according to their position in the order of merit, the staff corps or infantry, according to the number required for the first-named service, and to name the regiments of infantry in which they desire to serve.

" Those intended for the cavalry, are placed at the disposal of the officer commanding the regiment which they wish to enter.

" Those whose names appear in the second list are not permitted to choose their corps, but are placed by the Minister at War in such corps as may have vacancies in it, or where he may think proper.

"The students who are selected to enter the staff corps, after competing successfully with the second lieutenants of the army, proceed as second lieutenants to the Staff School at Paris.

"Those students who fail, pass into the army as privates, according to the terms of the engagement made on entering the school."

THE POLYTECHNIC SCHOOL.

The other elementary military school, the Polytechnic, is mainly a preparatory school for those branches of the French army which are termed scientific, as three-fourths of its pupils enter the artillery, the engineers, and the staff. It also exclusively supplies some important departments of the civil service. Its scientific teaching is unsurpassed, perhaps unequalled. It was founded during the French Revolution, in 1794. A few years before its creation, all schools, military as well as civil, had been suppressed. The ill effects of this destruction of all means of education were first perceived in the army and in the public works. The result was the establishment of the Polytechnic School, for the preliminary education of engineers and artillerists. Its benefits were extended to the civil service.

Upon quitting the Polytechnic, the student enters the School of Application especially devoted to the particular service to which he is assigned.

"Admission to the school is, and has been since its first commencement, in 1794, obtained by competition in a general examination, held yearly, and open to all. Every French youth between the ages of sixteen and twenty (or, if in the army, up to the age of twenty-five) may offer himself as a candidate.

"A board of examiners passes through France once every year, and examines all who present themselves, that" possess the requisites of age, &c.

"A list of such of the candidates as are found eligible for admittance to the Polytechnic is drawn up from the proceedings of the board, and submitted to the Minister at War. The candidates admitted are invariably taken in the order of merit.

" All the successful candidates whose parents are unable to maintain them at the school, in whole or in part, are supported by the State to the extent necessary.

" The course of study is completed in two years. On its successful termination, which is preceded by a final examination, the students are distributed into the different services, the choice being offered them in the order of their merit, as laid down in the classified list drawn up after the examination. Students who have been admitted into the school from the army, are obliged to re-enter the army.

"All others, as has been said, have the right of choosing, according to their position on the list, the service which they prefer,—so far, that is, as the number of vacancies in that service will allow; or they may, if they please, decline to enter the public service at all.

"Such is a general outline of the plan and object of the school. Besides its military staff, it employs no less than thirty-nine professors and teachers; it has four boards of management; and ten scientific men, unconnected with the school, and among the most distinguished in France, conduct its examinations. The magnitude of this establishment for teaching may be estimated by the fact, that the number of pupils rarely exceeds three hundred and fifty, and is often much less.

"The entrance examination is held yearly, in August. The most important conditions for admission to it are always inserted in the '*Moniteur*' early in the year.

"A list, in the order of merit, of those found qualified for admission, is submitted to the Minister at War, by whom the appointments are made.

"Any student whose mean credit in any branch falls below the minimum allowed for that branch, or whose general mean credit falls below the minimum allowed, is excluded from the school, unless he has been prevented from pursuing his studies by illness.

"During the second year the general examinations include the chief subjects of both years. A general list of all the students is made out, arranged in the order of merit. Formerly, conduct was permitted to exercise some influence on their position, but that is no longer the case. As already stated, the successful graduate has the right to choose the branch of the public service in which to enter, provided there is a vacancy, in the order of his position on the list."

THE SCHOOL OF APPLICATION FOR THE ARTILLERY AND ENGI-
NEERING AT METZ.

"The School of Application, at Metz, is the completion of the Polytechnic scientific training for most of its
military pupils. They are sub-lieutenants on admission," averaging twenty-one years of age, "and they
pursue during two years a course which is partly practical, but in which theory still holds a prominent place.

"The studies of artillery and engineer officers are
conducted entirely in common for the first, and for two-
thirds of the second year; but during the remaining
third they diverge widely. Yet, even at Metz, the instruction of officers for the special arms is not held to
be completed. They join their regiments upon leaving,
and are employed in practical exercises with troops
till they obtain the rank of second captain in their
respective arms; then the training of artillery officers,
apart from their men, is, in a certain sense, resumed;
they are sent to the arsenals, foundries, and manufactories of arms.

There are usually 140 or 150 students, consisting of
two classes of about equal numbers. The system of
instruction, of examinations, and of credits, is generally
the same as at the Polytechnic. A riding-school is
attached to the establishment, and drill exercises and
riding are practised daily. Much greater liberty is
allowed the students than at the Polytechnic. They
are sent upon surveying expeditions, and to measure
and sketch machines in manufactories. These expeditions never occupy more than ten days at a time. Field
fortifications and siege-works are actually laid out upon

the ground, and portions of the work in full relief are executed. The practical training is not extended, being merely sufficient to enable the *élèves* to commence their duties as officers understandingly.

" The studies at Metz consist of topography and geodesy, including military drawing and surveying, under special circumstances; field fortifications, military art and legislation, permanent fortification, and the attack and defence of fortified places, accompanied by a sham siege;" "architecture, as applicable to military buildings and fortifications; the theory and practice of construction, and artillery." " The instruction is given principally (as at the Polytechnic), by means of a series of lectures.

" The examination which takes place prior to their leaving the School of Application, is entirely conducted by a board of six officers, under the presidency of a general officer, alternately of the Artillery or Engineers ; the remaining members of the board consisting of a general officer of each corps and three field-officers of these corps, the last three being specially charged with the duty of examining.

" The final classification in the order of merit, in each arm of the service, is arranged after a comparison of the total of marks obtained by each student.

" It is this final classification which determines their seniority in the respective services.

" On quitting the School of Application, at Metz, the sub-lieutenants of Artillery and Engineers, respectively, join the regiments to which they are then definitely assigned as second lieutenants, and continue to be employed in doing duty, and in receiving practical instruction with them, until they are promoted to the rank of second captain.

" The lieutenants of the Artillery are employed on all duties that will tend to make them efficient artillery officers, and fully acquainted with all details connected with the drill, practice, and manœuvres of Artillery, and also with the interior economy and discipline of a regiment of Artillery."

THE SCHOOL OF APPLICATION FOR THE STAFF.

The French staff is the centre from which issue, and to which are addressed, all orders and military correspondence.

" The only means of entering the Staff Corps, is through the Staff School of Application. Of the fifty student officers, which the School of Application usually contains, twenty-five leave annually to enter the Staff Corps, and are replaced by an equal number.

" Entrance into the School of Application for the Staff Corps may be considered the reward of proficiency at St. Cyr, the twenty-two best pupils of which, together with three from the Polytechnic, constitute the ordinary yearly admission to this school. Strictly speaking, indeed, the twenty-seven best pupils from St. Cyr compete for the entrance to the Staff School with an equal number of sub-lieutenants, who may obtain permission from their commanding officer to appear as candidates.

" The course of teaching lasts for two years, no less than eighteen professors being employed, and the principal studies being topography, military art, and fortifi-

25

cation. The pupils are carefully ranged in the order of merit at their different examinations, and enter the Staff Corps according to the places they finally obtain. Immediately on leaving the school they are made lieutenants, and are then sent to the Infantry to do duty for two years; and at the expiration of this time are attached, for an equal period, to the Cavalry. They may finally be sent, but are not necessarily so, for a year to the Artillery or Engineers.

"Both the studies and examinations at the Staff School hold an intermediate place between those of the Polytechnic and St. Cyr, being less abstract than the former, and higher and more difficult than the latter.

" There are two examinations each year, conducted by a board, consisting of the general commandant or the director of studies, the professor of the course examined in, and two officers appointed by the Council of Instruction.

"Credits are given as in the other schools, and a list of the students is made out in the order of merit.

" Prior to admission into the Staff Corps, the students are obliged to pass an examination before the consulting committee of the Staff Corps.

" Every student officer who, in this examination for leaving, has not obtained the half of the maximum number of numerical credits, is considered to be inadmissible to the Staff Corps."

This review of the French military schools will probably serve to give an idea of the character of the education considered necessary for an officer of the French army, and the length of time required to accomplish it.

The mode of gaining admission into their military

schools is entirely different from ours. The qualifications for admission to the West Point Academy are merely reading, writing, and arithmetic. The students of St. Cyr and the Polytechnic enter those schools with an amount of knowledge and acquirement, the equivalent of which is scarcely attained at the end of the first year at West Point.

The study of mathematics at West Point is carried to about the same extent as at the Polytechnic; and the same remark may be applied to the study of mechanics and physics. In military literature, military history, and military geography and statistics, which constitute nearly half the course at St. Cyr, West Point does not equal St. Cyr; in the study of military art, in physics, fortifications, and artillery, it much exceeds it.

In field and permanent fortifications, construction, machinery, artillery, and the military art, the course at West Point is less extended than at Metz. In astronomy, the course is at least equal to that of the School of the Staff; while in field fortification, military art and administration, it is considerably less. In geodesy and topography but very little, except the drawing of the latter, is taught; but the instruction is sufficient for the wants of an officer of any corps, although topographical drawing in the field is but little practised; and the application of drawing in fortification is not so extensive as at Metz.

At West Point there is much less practical application in the field, of field fortification, siege-works, batteries, and surveying, than at Metz or the School of the Staff. It can scarcely be said there is any in geodesy, topography, and reconnoissance.

In tactics, manœuvres, riding, and infantry, cavalry, and artillery exercises, the cadets at West Point are certainly not less proficient than the students of St. Cyr, the School of the Staff, and the School of Metz. Two foreign languages are taught at West Point; one in the French schools. Instruction in the English language, ethics, and law, extends over two years at West Point. French literature forms part of the course in the two years at the Polytechnic, and military literature part of the course in the first year at St. Cyr; but there is no literary course at either Metz or the School of the Staff.

In many respects the United States Military Academy resembles the Polytechnic School. It receives alike the sons of the rich and poor, the sons of the distinguished and of the unknown. Its standard of scientific instruction is as high. It has the same powerful stimulus to exertion in the high reward it offers to successful effort, and in the penalty which it exacts for neglect or incompetency. It has exercised a powerful influence upon the public schools and colleges of the country; has introduced among them new branches of study in mathematics; and has raised the character of their scientific teaching.

MILITARY EDUCATION IN ENGLAND.

COMMISSIONS in the British Infantry and Cavalry are obtained by purchase, except in the case of the few graduates from the military academy at Sandhurst.

Commissions in the Artillery and Engineers are obtained by graduation at the military academy at Woolwich.

"An education entitling a student to a commission in the infantry or cavalry is given at Sandhurst. Pupils are received at that college between the ages of thirteen and fifteen; they enter on the nomination of the governor; their instruction lasts either for two or four years, according as they are proficient in study or not; and, at the end of this period, if found qualified, they receive a commission without purchase. The usual number of cadets appears to be one hundred and eighty, for whom there are sixteen professors.

"We may add to this list of English military schools, the East India Company's Military College, at Addiscombe, which gives a professional education of two years to pupils of all arms in common, that the admittance is by nomination, and a pass entrance examination, not by competition; and that, on leaving the school, the pupils are chosen by the authorities of the Company for the different services, according to their place in the final examination. The general order of choice is one for the engineers, two for the artillery, three for the infantry.

" It should be added, that both Sandhurst and Woolwich are practically self-supporting; a fact by no means
contemplated on the foundation of either, and which has
been the result of a gradual withdrawal of parliamentary
grants, combined with a large accession of what may
be termed highly paying pupils, i. e., the sons of civilians."

THE ROYAL MILITARY ACADEMY AT WOOLWICH.

The subjects of examination for admission have not
always remained the same, but have been changed from
time to time.   Those required at the beginning of 1855
were : English, mathematics, Latin, French, German,
geography, history, drawing, and printing with the
pen.

The entrance examinaitons were conducted by the
professors and masters belonging to the academy.

At the expiration of one year after the admission into
the academy, the cadets were reported upon by a board
of officers ; and such of them as had not passed satisfactory periodical examinations in mathematics and fortification in the class-rooms, were examined before this
board by the professors of mathematics and fortification.   This examination was called the probationary
examination.   The board were required to state their
opinion, whether the progress and conduct of each cadet
brought before them had been such as to entitle him
to remain at the institution, or to assign the cause or
grounds on which they recommended any cadet to be
removed.

" The regulations limited the duration of the residence for the course of theoretical study to four years, at the close of which, those cadets who were found unqualified for commissions were required to leave the academy; but such cadets as qualified themselves at an earlier period have been permitted to obtain their commissions when they had done so.

" The public examinations of the cadets proposed to be advanced to the practical class, or to be promoted from the practical class to commissions in the artillery and engineers, generally take place at the same time, before a board of superior officers."

There is some reason to believe that the results of the education at the Royal Military Academy have hitherto somewhat failed of that success which might have been hoped for, both as regards artillery and engineer officers.

The causes of the want of success in the teaching of the Academy are stated to have been: the juvenile age of admission; the admission of cadets that did not possess the qualifications required by regulations, the regulations having been disregarded to meet the views of influential complainants; the want of proper severity in the probationary examinations; the irregularity of the duration of the stay at Woolwich, some remaining two, others four years, to complete the same course of study; and, lastly, permitting cadets who were expelled from the academy for misconduct to return.

THE ROYAL ENGINEERS ESTABLISHMENT AT CHATHAM.

" We have already mentioned the deficiencies in the scientific education of the young engineer officer which are stated to exist when he joins at Chatham; and it will be seen that the only instruction he afterwards receives, either in the purely military or civil branch of his profession, which is given immediately he obtains his commission, is not in any way calculated to enable him to supply these deficiencies, however desirous he may be of doing so.

" The course of instruction, which usually occupies about fifteen months, is comprehended under the heads of—

" 1. Field duty.

" 2. Scientific instruction.

" 1. ˙Under the first head are comprised some of those duties which are required of the military engineer in the field, such as sapping, mining, batteries of position, intrenchment; formation of military bridges for the passage of rivers by artillery, cavalry, and infantry; the formation of stockades, and their destruction by gunpowder; subaqueous explosions, escalading, telegraphing, the use of the voltaic battery, and the diving-bell.

" 2. Under the second head, the officer, whilst employed upon the above duties, is also expected to devote a portion of his time to reading the best professional authors on military engineering; and, as a proof of his diligence, he is required, from time to time, to produce translations of the best examples of sieges, defences, extracts of mining operations, &c., accompanied with neatly drawn plans illustrative of the operations detailed; after which he is required to prepare projects, founded on the above elementary course of study.   To these are added a course of practical architecture, with a series of lectures on civil engineering, including the details of erecting and working a steam-engine, which is practically explained on a small engine belonging to the establishment, the whole of the working parts of which are taken to pieces and put together again by the officer.

" A small laboratory affords the means of practising such operations in analytic l chemistry as are required of the Engineers; and it also enables an officer to satisfy himself from actual investigation of the properties of the various building materials with which he may be working.   Surveying, with military reconnoitring and practical astronomy, complete the course of study as detailed under the second head.

" On quitting Chatham, the young officer is ordered to some foreign colony, or to some out-station in England, Ireland, or Scotland, where his duties are much more nearly allied to those of a civil than those of a military engineer."

Although the condition of military education in England does not present itself as a model for our imitation, nor as a standard of comparison, yet it affords a valuable lesson.   Our own Military Academy is open to evil influences of a similar kind to those which, at one time at least, so seriously impaired the value of the English schools, by setting aside the regulations for admission, the standard of graduation, and the discipline of the Academy.

THE PRUSSIAN SYSTEM OF MILITARY EDUCATION.

" Competition enters in a slight degree only into the system of military education in Prussia; the object being to secure a good average of general and professional education. The Infantry and Cavalry are officered chiefly by the appointment of aspirants or ensigns by the colonels of regiments. They must be between seventeen and eighteen years of age, and must pass an examination in their own language, in Latin, elementary mathematics, history, geography, French, and elementary drawing. After serving six months in the army, the ensigns must pass nine months in a division school, studying the theory of arms, tactics, the rules and regulations of the army, field and permanent fortifications, and surveying and plan-drawing. Upon passing an examination in these subjects, and receiving the assent of the officers of the regiment to his appointment in it, he is commissioned."

CADET SCHOOLS.

" There are five cadet schools, four junior and one senior, which are chiefly designed for the education of the sons of officers of the army. Their organization and discipline are military; the instruction is not, with the single exception of the last year, at the senior school.

" The age of entrance at the junior is from ten to eleven; the term of stay, four or five years. At the senior the age of entrance is from fifteen to sixteen; the term of stay, three years. The mathematical and scientific studies of the Senior Cadet School are not carried so far as those of the Gymnasiums of Prussia, schools which prepare youths for the University, and in which the course of studies is about the same as in colleges of this country.

" There are upwards of 420 cadets in the Senior Cadet School, and about 100 in each class. At the end of two years, only sixty of these one hundred are advanced to the highest class; the remaining forty (the lower part of the class) being sent to the army to earn their commissions, in the manner of other aspirants. Of the sixty that graduate, but one-half (the upper part of the class) are commissioned as second lieutenants, the lower half receiving merely the appointments of ensigns. The latter, however, are promoted to the first vacancies without further examination."

SCHOOL OF ARTILLERISTS AND ENGINEERS.

There is an Artillery and Engineer School, to which the colonels in those arms appoint aspirants, as in the Infantry and Cavalry. They must pass the same kind of examination as the Infantry aspirants,—except in mathematics, in which the examination is more severe, —and must serve nine months with troops. Then they join the Artillery and Engineer School, and at the end of a year, during which their studies are similar to those of the last year at the Senior Cadet School, upon passing the required examination, they receive a provisional appointment as sub-lieutenants.

"During the last two years, the instruction is in mathematics, mechanics, and physics, the art of war, military and civil engineering, artillery, tactics, geodesy, topography, the French language, general and special drawing, and the veterinary art. The studies are carried on during nine months of each of the three years, during which there are practical applications in the field; but these are chiefly made during the three months when the theoretical studies are suspended. At that time, also, the students visit the fortresses, armories, foundries, and other public establishments and manufactories of machinery. Cadets who have completed the whole term at the senior school may enter the artillery and engineer school as sub-lieutenants, to pass through the studies of the last two years.

"Upon graduating, the sub-lieutenants are commissioned as lieutenants."

Thus it appears that, in Prussia, the requisites for admission to the Engineer or Artillery service are three years of instruction in higher mathematics, mechanics, and physics, and in professional subjects, superadded to the course of instruction usually given at the colleges of the United States.

THE STAFF SCHOOL AT BERLIN.

"Appointment to the staff of the Prussian army is, with rare exceptions, only to be obtained through the Staff or War School. There is no commission in the Staff Corps of less rank than that of a captaincy. Any officer of the army, of three years' standing, may be examined for admission to the Staff School. The examination is made before commissioners at Berlin. There are usually sixty or seventy candidates, but of these only forty can be selected.

" The term of study is three years. There are three classes, of forty students each.

" Each year's course of study lasts eight months. The method of instruction is by lectures, the taking of notes, and the preparation of essays and memoirs.

"There is no practical instruction during the study term ; but at the end of the first year, the officers are sent for three weeks to make surveys; at the end of the third year, to reconnoitre the frontiers, fortresses, &c.

" During three months of each year they are sent to do military duty with arms of service or corps not their own.

"There is a system of marks or credits, and yearly examinations.

" Of the forty who pass through the Staff School each year, eight or ten only are sent to the topographical department of the staff. There they serve two or three years, when two are selected from the number and appointed captains in the staff. The remainder return to their regiments or corps, sometimes receiving appointments in the division schools."

AUSTRIAN SYSTEM OF MILITARY EDUCATION.

THIS has been entirely remodelled since the wars of 1848 and 1849.

" There are schools of various orders for non-commissioned officers, containing nearly 6,000 pupils, chiefly the children of soldiers. The schools of the lowest order are entered at seven years of age. The boy reaches the highest school at about fifteen. There are twenty schools of the highest order. From each of those connected with the Engineers, Artillery, &c., six or ten of the best pupils are transferred to the engineer or artillery academies, through which they may gain a commission.

" For the education of officers there are four cadet houses, each containing 200 pupils, who enter at eleven and leave at fifteen years of age. Of the 200 that annually leave these houses, 100 enter the infantry and cavalry academy at Wiener-Neustadt; fifty enter the artillery academy, and fifty enter the engineer academy. The infantry and cavalry academy contains 400 students; the other two, each 200.

" Only one in twenty or one in thirty of the officers of the Austrian Infantry and Cavalry enter from the academy of Wiener-Neustadt. This academy receives most of its pupils from the cadet schools. Those appointed to it who have not passed through those schools are examined in German, writing, natural history, geography, geometry, algebra, and plane trigonometry. The age of admission is from fifteen to sixteen years. The course of study lasts four years, during which they are taught four languages—French, Italian, Bohemian, and Hungarian—and receive a fair scientific and military education. The mode of teaching is a mixture of lessons and lectures. There is a system of credits, examinations, and merit-rolls. The discipline is represented to be strict. In this, as in the other two military academies, the student who is habitually neglectful is sent to one of the non-commissioned officer schools. Choice of arms and of regiments is offered in the order of merit."

THE ARTILLERY ACADEMY.

"Formerly, the officers of artillery were taken chiefly from the ranks. Young men of promise in the regimental schools were sent to a special school, where the chief study was mathematics, returned to their regiments, and in time were promoted to the rank of second lieutenant. Mixed with them at the school were a certain number of imperial cadets, who possessed privileges in regard to promotion. The present artillery academy is one of very recent establishment. Forty of the two hundred pupils come from the highest order of non-commissioned officer schools. The course of study prescribed for the four years during which they remain at the academy comprises a good scientific and professional education. The method of instruction is by lessons and recitations, and by lectures. There is a system of credits, examinations, and merit-rolls. Upon the satisfactory completion of the course of study they receive commissions as second lieutenants. After serving two years with their regiments, it is intended that selection by examination shall be made from them of the most promising officers, who are to pass through a two years' course of higher instruction, in common with officers of engineers."

THE ENGINEER ACADEMY.

" The Engineer Academy is an old establishment. In the number of students, course and method of instruction, system of credits, term of stay, examinations, and promotions, it is the same, with the exception of the professional studies, as the Artillery School. In this school, as in all the others in Austria, great improvements have been recently made. The studies are now high, the examinations strict, and the discipline good."

THE HIGHER SCHOOL FOR ENGINEERS AND ARTILLERISTS.

" Is to be composed of twenty officers from each corps, who have served two years with their regiments, and successfully competed for admission at an examination.

" The course is to last two years, and to consist chiefly of applied mechanics, practical physics, construction of ordnance, and the art of war (which forms no part of the course at the Artillery or Engineer School), the use of artillery in the field, and in attack and defence. Promotion from the rank of second to that of first lieutenant will depend upon the examination at the close of the course of study."

THE SCHOOL OF THE STAFF.

" Admission to the staff of the Austrian army was always gained by a competitive examination.

" The general staff consists of:—

" Twelve colonels.

" Twelve lieutenant-colonels.

" Twenty-four majors.

" Eighty captains.

" Within the last six years the School of the Staff has been regularly established. It consists of thirty pupils, taken from all arms of the service, fifteen entering each year. The candidate must have served two years with his regiment, and be over twenty-one and under twenty-six years of age. The competition for entrance is very active. The course is two years.

" During four months of each year, they do duty with troops of a different arm from that to which they belong. One month of the first year is devoted to surveying, and one month of the second to reconnoissance. Immediately after the final examination the students receive appointments in the Staff Corps, if there are vacancies, in the order of merit. If there are no vacancies, the student returns to his regiment until a vacancy occurs. If he is a second lieutenant, he is promoted to the rank of first lieutenant; if a first lieutenant, after three years' service, he is made a captain."

MILITARY EDUCATION IN RUSSIA.

" BUT little information respecting the military schools of Russia has been collected.

" 1. There are twenty-two military colleges for the guards and line, containing more than seven thousand cadets.

" 2. One page corps, of one hundred and sixty scholars.

" 3. One school of ensigns for the guards, with two hundred students.

" 4. One artillery school, with one hundred and twenty students.

" 5. One engineer school, with one hundred and twenty or one hundred and thirty students. Making an aggregate of over eight thousand military students.

" There is, besides, an imperial staff school, into which

twenty or twenty-five officers, possessing certain qualifications, enter each year, after an examination. The term of instruction is two years.

" Upon graduation, the most distinguished scholar of each class is promoted at once to the staff as captain; the next two receive rewards of extra pay and medals. At the end of a year, after leaving the school, all the graduates are attached to the staff, but are not at once promoted in it."

THE END.

GENERAL INDEX.

A.

C.

D.

I.

J.

K.

L.

GENERAL INDEX. 401

M.

PAGE

S.

T.

U.

V.